MASDEVALLIAS

MASDEVALLIAS

❖ ❖ ❖

GEMS OF THE ORCHID WORLD

Mary E. Gerritsen
&
Ron Parsons

*Featuring the photography
of Ron Parsons*

TIMBER PRESS

Published in 2005 by

Timber Press, Inc.
The Haseltine Building
133 S.W. Second Avenue Suite 450
Portland, Oregon 97204-3527
U.S.A.

www.timberpress.com
For contact information for editorial, marketing,
sales, and distribution in the United Kingdom, see
www.timberpress.com/uk

Executive Editor: Neal Maillet
Consulting Editor: Eric Christenson
Project Editor: Franni Bertolino Farrell
Copy Editor: Lisa Theobald
Designer: Susan Applegate

Printed in Singapore

Library of Congress Cataloging-in-Publication Data

Gerritsen, Mary E.
   Masdevallias: gems of the orchid world / Mary E.
Gerritsen and Ron Parsons; featuring the photography of
Ron Parsons.
      p. cm.
   Includes bibliographical references and index.
   ISBN 0-88192-737-6 (hardback)
   1. Masdevallia. I. Parsons, Ron. II. Title.
   SB409.8.M38G47 2005
   635.9′344—DC22   2005001450

A catalog record for this book is also available from the
British Library.

CONTENTS

❖❖❖

5

FOREWORD

❖ ❖ ❖

The genus *Masdevallia* is one of the most unique and diverse in the orchid family. With their striking colors, unusual shapes, and varied sizes, masdevallias provide an endless variety within one genus. Their distribution throughout a wide range of climatic regions in Central and South America adds to the complexity of this genus.

Masdevallias: Gems of the Orchid World is a wonderful treatise on the genus for both the novice and experienced *Masdevallia* grower. It provides a fascinating historical perspective of the first collected species, balanced by the present-day proliferation of hybrids, all complemented by exquisite photography.

Mary Gerritsen and Ron Parsons combine their talents in this thorough presentation of the more notable and significant species along with some of the lesser known varieties. Ron's photography captures the beauty and unique qualities of the *Masdevallia* species and hybrids. The geographic details of each species's native locale give the reader vital information on cultural needs.

Very few orchid books provide such thorough background information and color photographs for each species to create an ideal reference source for masdevallias. For anyone interested in the genus, *Masdevallias: Gems of the Orchid World* is an enjoyable journey and an invaluable tool.

TOM PERLITE
Golden Gate Orchids
San Francisco

ACKNOWLEDGMENTS

❖ ❖ ❖

This book could not have been written without the enthusiastic assistance and advice of many of my colleagues, friends, and family. First, thanks to Anna Chai, whose magnificent *Masdevallia* specimen plants first excited me about the genus and its possibilities. However, without Ron Parsons's wonderful orchid photography and incredible knowledge about orchid species, this book would never have become a reality. I am grateful to Anna Chai (Belmont, California), Ivan Komoda (Komoda Orchids, Hawaii), John Leathers (Berkeley, California), Terry Menifee (Loma Crest Botanicals, Point Loma, California), Dan Newman (Hanging Gardens, San Francisco), Dennis Olivas (D and D Orchids, Richmond, California), Tom Perlite (Golden Gate Orchids, San Francisco), and Gerardus Staal (Peninsula Hybrids, Palo Alto, California) for their advice about *Masdevallia* culture, propagation, and hybridization. To Tom Perlite, John Leathers, Terry Menifee, Gerardus Staal, Dan Newman, and Anna Chai, thank you for allowing me to visit your extensive *Masdevallia* (and related pleurothallids) collections. To Gerardus Staal, special thanks for all of your help and discussions about the science behind *Masdevallia* hybridization and for sharing your rich knowledge about the culture, hybrids, and history of this genus. And thanks also for lending me your backcopies of the Pleurothallid Alliance newsletters! To Bob Hamilton (Berkeley, California), my thanks for the in-depth conversations about tetraploids and how to generate them. I wish to express my sincere gratitude to Rudolf Jenny (Berne, Switzerland) and his incredible Orchid library (BibliOrchidea at http://www.bibliorchidea.net/), which he so kindly allowed me to access. Thank you to Rudolf also for your stories and information about *Masdevallia* and the history of the genus and the people who were and are part of that history. No history of masdevallias would be complete without a visit to the herbarium at the Naturhistorisches Museum in Vienna, and special thanks go to Dr. Ernst Vitek for spending time with me there, helping me find the herbarium specimens and notes of the early orchid hunters, and explaining various aspects of the *Masdevallia* specimens we examined during my stay. I am also grateful to Steve Manning (Tarpoley, U.K.) for some helpful historical discussions and information. I am grateful to David Banks (Australia) and Olaf Gruss (Germany) for their assistance with *Masdevallia* sources. Thank you to Walter Teague and John Leathers for providing us with several slides of *Masdevallia* habitats in Ecuador and Bolivia. Most importantly, I thank Dr. Carlyle Luer (Sarasota, Florida) for his helpful discussions and suggestions during the preparation of this book. Moreover, thank you to Dr. Luer for all of your extensive research, "detective work," and taxonomic efforts that provided much of the framework for this book. To my husband, Tom, and my daughter, Maddie, thank you for your support and interest in this project.

MARY E. GERRITSEN, PH.D.

I have many photos published mostly in other peoples' books, but I have always wanted to do my own. When Mary Gerritsen suggested doing this work on a favorite genus of both of ours, I was at first hesitant. Watching Mary and her relentless research and efforts has been a real inspiration, so my first thanks must go to her for getting me going on something I had only been dreaming about.

Next will have to be my list of friends and acquaintances who allowed me to photograph their beautiful flowers for this book. I could list hundreds of people, but the following list for brevity's sake will be thanks to people and collections where I photographed masdevallias. So thank you to George Marcopoulos, Jim Henrich, and Clare Cangiolosi of the San Francisco Conservatory of Flowers; Steve Beckendorf; Sherry Bridygham; Deborah Buck; Judy Carney; Anna Chai; Pui Chin; Brad Cotten; Paul Delagram; Celine Dion; Don Dragoni (deceased); Ron Ehlers and Jim Hamilton (Petite Plaisance, Valley Ford, California); Dick Emory; Howard Gunn; Clyde Hall; Cordelia Head, Marguerite Webb, and Lucinda Winn (J & L Orchids, Easton, Connecticut); Valerie Henderson; Ernie Katler; Alek Koomanoff; Chris Knudsen; John Leathers; Pamela Leaver; Jean Lee; Bernice Lindner; Jay Moxley; Dan Newman (Hanging Gardens, San Francisco); Jeff Parker (Tropical Orchid Farm, Haiku, Hawaii); Kathy Parker; Tom Perlite (Golden Gate Orchids, San Francisco); Andy Phillips (Andy's Orchids, Encinitas, California); Will Rhodehamel (Hoosier Orchid Company, Indianapolis); Jonathan Riley; Kay Rinaman (deceased); Bartley Schwartz (deceased); Mike Serpa; Lillian Severin (deceased); Gerardus Staal (Peninsula Hybrids, Palo Alto, California); Alicia Stiles; Walter Teague; and Marni Turkel (Stony Point Ceramics, Santa Rosa, California). Thanks for your time, kindness, and generosity. I would also like to thank David P. Banks for help, advice, and guidance. I have to give a special thanks, though, to John Leathers and Tom Perlite for allowing me continuous access to their *Masdevallia* collections, particularly over the last year to photograph the hybrids.

Last, thanks to my family and my friends (many of whom are listed above), who I love, for your support.

RON PARSONS

CHAPTER 1

❖ ❖ ❖

Introduction

"We have here a charming genus of little plants—gems of the first water, and one might say, seeing that they are most of them so chastely beautiful, and comparatively rare—a fact that detracts nothing from their value." So penned the "Orchid King," Professor Heinrich Gustav Reichenbach, as he described this genus in *The Gardeners' Chronicle and Agricultural Gazette*, published 4 November 1871. Plants of this genus have been highly popular among orchid hobbyists for more than 100 years, due in no small part to the colorful, eye-catching blooms with intriguing shapes and markings. Today, the genus *Masdevallia* comprises more than 400 species whose origins range from southern Mexico to southern Brazil and parts of Bolivia. *Masdevallia*, however, are not native to the West Indies. Most of the species are found in the cool cloud forests and alpine areas of the Andes, with some found growing near the snowline. A smaller number of species come from warmer lowland areas.

Masdevallia is a large genus in the family Orchidaceae. The flowers of most orchids are characterized by six segments: three outer segments called *sepals* (although some orchids have lateral sepals united in what is called a *synsepal*) and three inner segments called *petals*, with one petal being modified into what is called the *labellum* or *lip*. The stamens and the styles are fused, forming a usually elongated structure called the *column*. At the extreme end of the column, both male and female parts are found (except for certain dioecious species, such as *Catasetum* and *Cycnoches*, which produce sexual flowers). The column is a unique orchid feature. Only one other plant family has a column, the Asclepidaceae (the milkweed family), although the column of this family is quite different in structure. Another peculiarity of orchids is that the pollen is clumped together into discrete pollinia (in even numbers, such as two, four, or eight) that are adapted to transfer by pollinating vectors (mostly insects, but hummingbirds and bats have also been implicated). Pollinia are usually oval and hard as grains of rice, and they are often accompanied by appendages (stipe and viscidium) that aid in attaching them to pollinators.

What distinguishes the genus *Masdevallia* from other orchids? The most prominent feature of *Masdevallia* is the large sepals that are fused at their base to form a sepaline tube. This tube often hides the diminutive petals and small lips such that at first glance, the flowers appear to have only three sepals and no petals at all. The more precise botanical description, defined by orchid scholar Dr. Carlyle A. Luer (1986), requires a more detailed understanding of the anatomy of the *Masdevallia*. The accompanying illustrations provide a view of the whole plant, with the key features of the

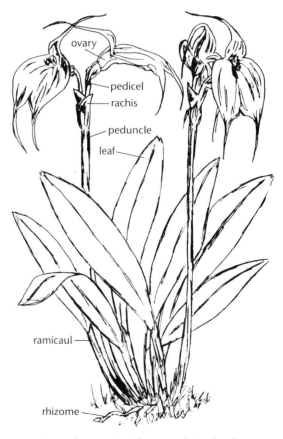

General anatomical features of *Masdevallia*

plant labeled, and a dissection of a typical *Masdevallia* flower and column, and it points out the anatomical parts that are mentioned many times in this book. The distinguishing features of masdevallias are listed here:

- Ramicauls, or leaf-bearing stems, shorter than the leaves they bear
- Inflorescences borne laterally from the ramicaul with an annulus (an ill-defined ring) a considerable distance below the leaf-stem abscission layer
- Petals callous (hardened and thickened) and unusually small in most species
- Lip hinged flexibly to a curved extension from the end of a column-foot
- Shaft of the column semiterete (semicylindrical and tapering) with a ventral anther, rostellum, and stigma
- One pair of pollinia

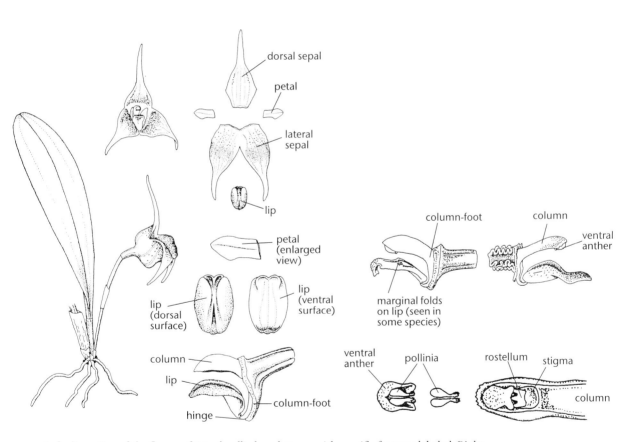

Left, dissection of the flower of *Masdevallia bourdetteana* with specific features labeled. Right, detailed morphology of a *Masdevallia* flower. Both reproduced (with permission from Missouri Botanical Garden) from *A Treasure of Masdevallia* (Luer 1997).

CHAPTER 2

The History of the Genus *Masdevallia*

No book about orchids can overlook the intriguing and varied history of this group of plants. Orchids are found on every continent except Antarctica, and in wide, varied climates. For centuries, orchids have been used as sources of food, medicine, and aphrodisiacs by cultures throughout the world. Tropical orchids began to be imported to Europe in the early 1700s, although their potential as a commercial "crop" was not realized until Messrs. Loddiges established their first orchid nursery in London in 1812. Many of the Latin names of orchids honor the early orchid connoisseurs—for example, in *Cattleya loddigesii*, the genus is named after William Cattley, a horticulturist interested in plants collected from the mountains of Brazil, and the species epithet derived from the Loddiges. The Sander family of England was one of the early large orchid growers, and their collectors searched worldwide for plants to send back to England. In 1894, they employed more than 100 people and had nearly 2 million plants under their care. Today, the "Sander's List" is the definitive record of registered orchid hybrids in the world. A number of orchids are named in honor of one or more members of the Sander family, including *Macodes sanderiana* and *Vanda sanderiana* (now *Euanthe sanderiana*). Many orchids are named for Messrs. Veitch, another early orchid nursery, such as *Masdevallia veitchiana*. Some well-known early orchid collections were located outside of England; for example, Consul Schiller of Hamburg, Germany, had a large and diverse collection of orchids, and species named in his honor include *Cattleya schilleriana* and *Phalaenopsis schilleriana*.

The genus *Masdevallia* was named to honor an 18th century Spanish botanist and physician, Dr. Don José de Masdevall. The first recorded species of the genus *Masdevallia* was collected in 1779 by a small group of botanists dispatched by Charles III of Spain to explore the forests of Peru and Chile. This scientific expedition to the colonies of South America did not actually originate in Spain but was proposed by the Comptroller General for the French King Louis XVI, Anne Robert Jaques Turgot. At that time, the Spanish colonies of South America included what we know today as Peru, Bolivia, Chile, Argentina, and Ecuador. Turgot, perhaps under the influence of the Jussieu family, sought to organize a scientific expedition to replace the lost collections of the botanist Joseph de Jussieu, who botanized for some 35 years in Peru and South America. However, J. E. B. Clugny, not Turgot, initiated the contact with the Spanish to obtain permission for Joseph Dombey, a student of Antoine de Jussieu, to travel through Peru. A complicated contract was conceived, which required that the expedition be under Spanish leadership. Conditions concerning the organization, sharing of the collected material, and the rights to publish new species were restrictive, and Dombey was required to present all of his collected specimens first to the authorities of the *Real Jardin Botánico* in Madrid. Dombey was allowed to keep the third specimen (a duplicate) of a set of three, but which specimen he kept was to be determined by the Madrid authorities. Moreover, if only a single specimen was collected, Dombey was obliged to turn over all materials. Dombey's companions were two Spanish pharmacists with no experience in fieldwork or botanical taxonomy, Hipálito Ruiz and Antonico Pavón y Jiménez; and two artists, José Brunete and Isidro Gálvez. Ruiz, the more junior of the group, became the leader of the expedition. The expedition was plagued at the outset with problems. The two artists refused to work for Dombey, the only experienced botanist in the group. Dombey ended up doing the drawings of his collections himself, shipping the small collections in 1778 and 1779. Catastrophically, the later ship was captured by the English (which was at war with France and Spain at the time), and the entire collection of drawings, descriptions, dried plants, and personal material was captured and later auctioned in Lisbon. Fortunately, Spain was the highest bidder, so a large part of the collection came home to Madrid after all. The war also delayed the return of the expedition by several years. Dombey returned to Spain in 1785, while Ruiz and Pavón remained in Peru, but they shipped part of their collection to Spain. Unfortunately, all of this material was lost when the ship *San Pedro de Alcántara* sank before reaching Portugal. This was a serious loss, as more than 200 orchid drawings and 600 drawings of other plants went down with the ship. Further disaster struck when another large part of the collections of Ruiz and Pavón was lost in a fire at their base camp. The material of *Masdevallia uniflora*, collected in 1779, was included in the part that Dombey took back to Spain. Ruiz and Pavón left Peru in 1787 with the remainder of their collection and arrived in Cádiz in September 1788.

The first publication of the genus *Masdevallia* finally appeared in 1794 in the *Flora Peruviana et Chilensis Prodromus*. The publication was accompanied by a drawing of *M. uniflora*, although the species was not formally described. The publication of the species came several years later (1798) in *Systema Vegetabilum Florae Peuvianae et Chilensis*. It is often overlooked that the main part of the later publications of Ruiz and Pavón were based on Dombey's collections, since most of their collections were lost.

Throughout the next 70 to 80 years, explorers contributed only a few more *Masdevallia* species. Baron Alexander von Humboldt, who was characterized by Charles Darwin as "the greatest scientific traveler who ever lived," explored the Orinoco basin of Venezuela accompanied by the botanist Aimé Bonpland in 1800. This was followed by a trip to the Andes and ascents of many volcanoes, including Chimborazo in Ecuador. During this arduous expedition, Humboldt and Bonpland collected numerous botanical specimens, although many were lost or destroyed on the long, perilous ocean voyage. However, one of the species collected on their trip from the Colombia-Ecuador border at Rumichacha was published as the *Masdevallia uniflora* of Ruiz and Pavón. Reichenbach later realized this was not the same species and renamed it *M. bonplandii* in honor of Bonpland in 1855.

Two species collected by the French botanists M. Descourtilz and Justin Godot in the mountains of southern Brazil were published as *Masdevallia infracta* and *M. caudata* by John Lindley in 1833. Eduard Frederick Poeppig, a German explorer, collected *M. constricta* and *M. pumila* during his explorations of Peru and Colombia between 1829 and 1831. *Masdevallia racemosa* was first discovered in 1839 near Popayán, Colombia, by Karl Theodore Hartweg, a German collector for the Horticultural Society of London. *Masdevallia floribunda* was apparently first collected by botanists somewhere in the state of Veracruz, Mexico, around 1840. Louis Schlim collected with N. Funck for Jean Linden. Schlim and Funck followed old trails through the Eastern Cordillera during the mid-19th century and contributed two new *Masdevallia* species: *M. schlimii* was discovered in 1843 at Valle, near Mérida, Venezuela; *M. bucci-*

Masdevallia uniflora (from *Flora Peruviana et Chilensis Prodromus* by Ruiz and Pavón, published in 1794)

nator was discovered in 1848 near old gold mines at La Baja near Pamplona, Colombia. Lindley, who in the mid-1800s was considered the foremost authority on Orchidaceae, described a few more species to the genus (such as *M. coriacea*, *M. cucullata*, *M. laevis*, *M. meleagris*, *M. minuta*, and *M. triangularis*) based on collections made by other botanists, mostly from the mountains of Colombia and Ecuador.

Many of the early horticultural plants perished in cultivation, due in part to the cultural recommendations of Lindley (1830), which promoted constant, excessive humidity and as great amounts of heat as could be attained in the greenhouse. Fortunately, critical reforms in orchid culture, proposed by Joseph Paxton in particular, ex-

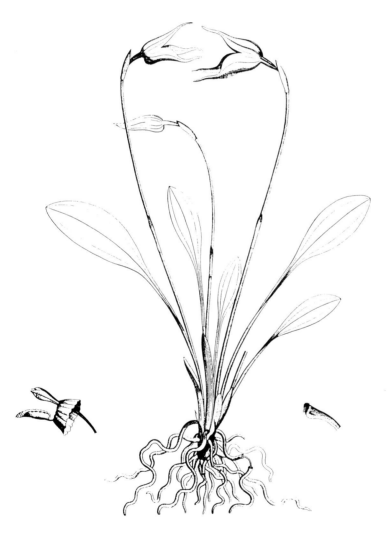

Drawing from Humboldt expedition of plant initially (and incorrectly) identified as *Masdevallia uniflora*. It was later named *M. bonplandii* by Reichenbach.

erted tremendous influence on orchid enthusiasts. Paxton's system basically recommended the following: separate houses or portions of houses for orchids from different climates, lower average temperatures, fresh air, maintenance of a humid atmosphere (not soggy pots), and better drainage. The acceptance of these cultural suggestions, as well as increased importations of species from the wild, led to the accumulation of numerous orchids in both public and private collections.

In the later part of the 19th century, an orchid craze swept England and parts of the European continent and Russia. Plants were gathered by the thousands and tens of thousands from tropical and subtropical areas (Central and South America, Southeast Asia, Africa, Australia, and New Zealand). Unfortunately, many of these collected plants had to endure very much less than ideal conditions for up to many months to survive shipping from these locations. Jean Linden once remarked (Reinikka 1995)

> The Orchids, once collected, difficulties began. It was necessary to bring them down from the mountains to the port of embarkation by roads which cannot be imagined by any who have not traversed them. At that time no steamboat had yet crossed the ocean, and the poor plants had to endure the sea-voyage at the bottom of the hold of a rough sailing vessel, after having waited, sometimes during more than a month, for a chance of carriage to a port near their destination. Packed like a herring in a barrel, the heat and fermentation worked sad havoc, and but few of them arrived alive.

The result was that tremendous numbers of these collected plants died in transit. Species from some areas were no doubt nearly or totally exterminated by these practices.

With the death of Lindley in 1865, Heinrich Gustav Reichenbach, a professor of botany as well as the director of the Botanic Gardens of the University of Hamburg, emerged as the leading authority of Orchidaceae for the remainder of the 19th century. He published descriptions of many more plants in the genus *Masdevallia*, and his enthusiasm probably contributed in a major way to the "orchid madness." New species were eagerly acquired by wealthy growers willing to pay exorbitant prices (sometimes up to thousands of dollars per plant) at auctions. This frenzy also contributed to the unscrupulous behavior of some of the early horticultural collectors, who gave incorrect or misleading geographical information relating to the sites of plant collection to conceal (or attempt to conceal) the plant sources.

Reichenbach's descriptions of new species were brief but often colorful, and many of these appeared in *The Gardeners' Chronicle* in articles published by Reichenbach from 1869 to 1878. His descriptions of the flowers often included some unusual adjectives in addition to varied and miscellaneous comments about the collector or other features of the species. For example, of *M. platyglossa* he wrote, "this curious, rather small flowered species of the *Coriaceae* group, having a light yellowish flower with short tails and a very broad singular lip, full of acute warts at the top." Of *M. chestertoni* (now *Dracula chestertoni*) he described "a decidedly new species. . . . They are of the finest orange color. . . . Thus the colours of the Austrian empire. . . . We have had nothing like it in the masdevallias." Reichenbach described *M. gargantua* as follows: "This is also in flower in Messrs. Veitch's nursery. The flowers have certainly a very remarkable appearance, and emit a very disagreeable odor. . . . It belongs to the *M. velifera* group, another of the vile smelling species." Of *M. corniculata*, Reichenbach wrote "a Neo-Granadian novelty. . . . It is well known by the natives who call it the 'widow flower,' no doubt on account of its dark, apparently black-purplish color." Other notable descriptions by Reichenbach included *M. lata*, "among the plants of the late Mr. Zahn, one of the recent botanic martyrs (drowned in a stream)," and *M. barlaena*: "this is very gay scarlet-flowered *Masdevallia*, while its next sister, *M. amabilis* is deep purplish. . . . The plant turns out to be one of the new Peruvian discoveries of the very promising traveler, Mr. Davis." Of *M. davisii*, Reichenbach wrote

> This is a beautiful thing, much like *Masdevallia Harryana* and *Veitchiana*. . . . The other parts of the flower are yellowish, white and of the deepest splendid orange inside; so that it would appear to give a most welcome contrast in a group of the scarlet and vermilion and white *Masdevallias*. It was discovered by a, most probably, new collector, Mr. W. Davis. . . . I have a very good opinion of this collector, who was introduced to me by a set of new dried Orchids; so I thought it my duty to attach the name of such a promising collector to such a welcome *Masdevallia*.

Reichenbach was particularly enchanted by *Masdevallia veitchiana*, about which he states, "This is a magnificent species. . . . What is quite new is the colour of the inside of the sepals. They are of a splendid saturnine red on the inner halves of the lateral sepals. All the other surface is of a striking purplish violet hue, shining like velvet."

As a person, Reichenbach was an eccentric, sarcastic, and extremely selfish man. He would attack other botanists if he thought they were invading his private turf, and it is said that he created the genus *Aa* so his name would always appear at the top of any list of plant names. Moreover, he never allowed anyone to look at his herbarium during his life, and after his death, his will sealed the collection for 25 years. It is thought he did this to deprive Robert Alan Rolfe, a botanist working at the Royal Botanic Gardens at Kew and whom Reichenbach considered a great rival, from the opportunity of studying his herbarium. His obituary, published in *The Gardeners' Chronicle* on 18 May 1889, captured the spirit of this "Orchid King." It said he was

> possessed of a remarkably distinct individuality, which was as remarkable as his curiously cribbed handwriting which few could decipher. Short and massive in

stature till his recent illness, with a keen penetrating glance and aquiline nose, his features revealed something of the impetuous temper of the man and his occasional biting sarcasms. His devotion to Orchids amounted to a consuming passion; not a scrap, nor a note, nor a sketch, however rough came amiss to him if it related to an orchid. To him meals and clothes were necessary evils but his herbarium was a prime necessity of existence. The amount of his work was prodigious. Of its quality the botanists of the future will judge better than we.

The striking species in the group related to *Masdevallia coccinea* (for example, *M. davisii*, *M. welischii*, and *M. veitchiana*) attracted considerable attention toward the later part of the 19th century, particularly in England and Belgium, where these plants commanded extremely high prices, especially the white and yellow color forms of *M. coccinea*. This financial incentive led the firm of James Veitch and Sons (a nursery in Chelsea, England) to send a young Scotsman, Walter Davis, to collect plants of *M. coccinea*. In addition to *M. coccinea*, Davis found another unidentified *Masdevallia* species in the vicinity of Cuzco, Peru. He sent flowers to Reichenbach for identification. As mentioned earlier, Reichenbach described this new species as *M. davisii* in *The Gardeners' Chronicle*. Other commercial establishments also funded collectors in the field. For example, Messrs. Sanders at one time had 20 collectors working in various jungles throughout the world, some of whom spent up to 10 years in search of new species. Many of these collectors (for both the Sanders and other commercial enterprises), including those dispatched to the Andes (for example, J. H. Chesterton, Benedict Roezl, Gustave Wallis, and Josef Ritter von Rawicz Warszewicz), forwarded their unidentified species to Reichenbach for identification. Reichenbach attributed about 150 plants to the genus *Masdevallia*, although many were subsequently removed from the genus and moved to related genera (such as *Dracula*, *Dryadella*, *Porroglossum*, *Scaphosepalum*, and *Trisetella*) or reduced due to synonymy. Reichenbach's unexpected death in 1889 resulted in the sealing of his herbarium for 25 years (a stipulation of his will), which was then deposited in Vienna at the *Naturhistorisches Hofmuseum* (Natural History Museum).

Gustave Wallis was a famous German plant collector, born in Lünenburg in 1830. He started studying gardening when he was 16 and after his training worked in Munich. In 1856 he was sent to Brazil to establish a horticultural business for a German firm. However, the parent firm went bankrupt, and Wallis was left stranded and practically penniless. In 1858 Wallis joined the employ of Jean Linden of Brussels, for whom he worked as a plant collector. He crossed the South American continent, starting at the mouth of the Amazon, and traveled the entire length to its source. He was later commissioned by James Veitch and Sons and collected orchids for the firm in the Philippines as well as in Colombia. His last journey began in 1875, when he was no longer in Veitch's employ. He explored various parts of South and Central America, succumbing to fever and dystentry in Cuenca, Ecuador, on 20 June 1878. *Masdevallia* species discovered by Wallis include *M. angulifera*, *M. estradae*, *M. peristeria*, and *M. wallisii* (now *Dracula wallisii*), as well as several other choice species of other genera (such as *Epidendrum wallisii*, *E. pseudo-wallisii* [now both *Oerstedella*], and *Houlletia wallisii*), which commemorate Wallis's contributions to orchid biology.

A. R. Endres was an enthusiastic but little known collector engaged by Messrs. Veitch to continue the works of an earlier collector, Gottlieb Zahn, who had perished by drowning while en route to Costa Rica. Endres's origins are unclear, but his detailed and insightful descriptions suggest that he was an educated man, although at least one reference to him suggests that he was a "half-caste." Endres sent back to Reichenbach exquisitely detailed descriptions written in a beautiful, clear script along with meticulous, often colored drawings of the species he had collected, mostly from Costa Rica. The paper available to Endres must have been very limited, for often the descriptions were written on the backs of financial statements and other used papers. Samples of his writings and drawings are now part of Reichenbach's herbarium collection in Vienna. Some of the species he collected include *Masdevallia anura* (now *M. molossoides*), *M. anaristella* (now *Barbosella anaristella*), *M. carpophora* (now *Pleurothallis tripterantha*), *M. demissa*, *M. erinacea* (although Benedict Roezl was the first to collect this species), *M. pygmaea*, *M. reichenbachiana*, *M. triaristella* (now *Trisetella triaristella*), and *M. zahlbruckneri*. Nothing is known of the routes Endres took in Costa Rica, but he must have found some excellent regions, because many different species were described by Reichenbach from his collections. Moreover, numerous specimens of the material he collected on other families are included in the herbarium in Vienna, although little apparently has been published concerning them. Sadly, despite Endres's enthusiasm, he was not well remembered; a 1913 description of his work in *The Orchid World* (Vol. III, p. 263) perhaps best captures this feeling: "Endres collected *Miltonia endresi* (*Miltoniopsis warscewiczii*), *Cattleya dowiana* and many others of somewhat poor horticultural value. His connection with Messrs. Veitch terminated in April, 1873." He, like many of his fellow collectors, appears to have met an untimely end; he was apparently shot in Colombia in the vicinity of the Rió Hacha.

Josef Ritter von Rawicz Warszewicz was born in 1812 in Vilna, Lithuania, of parents of Polish extraction. He studied botany at the Berlin Botanical Garden. Warszewicz was hired by Messr. Van Houtte to accompany a Belgian colony to Guatemala in 1844. He was an industrious and intelligent man who dispatched great quantities of plants wholesale to Europe, and the descriptions of a number of orchid species he collected and drew were published by Reichenbach. He spent several years exploring and collecting in various parts of Central America, returning to Europe in 1850 after an attack of yellow fever. He worked with Professor Reichenbach for some time, describing more than 300 orchid species. Perhaps bored with this sedentary work, he returned to South America in 1851. He was robbed in Ecuador but continued to Bolivia and Peru, shipping many orchids and other plants back to botanical gardens in Cracow and Berlin. Unfortunately, a second bout with yellow fever in 1853 compelled him to leave his orchid hunting, and he returned to Cracow, where he was supervisor of the Botanical Gardens until his death in 1866. *Masdevallia* species collected by Warszewicz include *M. amabilis*, *M. buccinator*, *M. civilis*, and *M. elephanticeps*. Many orchids are named in honor of this great collector, although there is often a discrepancy in the spelling of his surname (Warszewicz, Warscewicz) and the specific names of plants honoring him— for example, *Cattleya warscewiczii*, *Catasetum warscewiczii*, *Miltonia warscewiczii*. These misspellings remain due to their early nomenclature and publication.

One of the most intrepid orchid collectors of these early years was Benedict Roezl. Roezl began his plant career as a gardener apprentice under the Count of Thun in Bohemia. He was later employed in various continental gardens, including those of Baron von Hugel at Vienna, Count Liechtenstein in Moravia, and the famous nursery of Van Houtte at Ghent. Although prestigious, these were not sufficient challenges for this adventurer. In 1854 he emigrated to Mexico, where he founded a nursery and issued a catalog of the Mexican conifers he sold. In 1861 he introduced the cultivation of the ramie (*Boehmeria tenacissima*) as a textile plant. When he was 44 years old, he lost his left arm in an accident with a machine he had invented to extract fibers from these plants. His arm was replaced by a metal hook, which was a source of great astonishment among the natives. After this unfortunate accident, he began a new career as a plant collector working for Henry Sander of Saint Albans in England. Roezl traveled extensively throughout Central and South America and the west coast of North America, and he sent home more than 10,000 orchids from Panama and Colombia in 1869. The rare *Telipogon* orchids he collected at 11,000 feet died as soon as they were brought down to warmer levels, but he sent 3000 odontoglossums to Europe. He combed the Central American Sierra Madre for orchids, 3500 of which reached London in fine condition. He went across the Isthmus of Panama to Guayra and Caracas and sent 8 tons of orchids and 10 tons of other plants back to London. Numerous *Masdevallia* species were discovered by Roezl, including *M. livingstoneana*, *M. caesia*, *M. macrura*, *M. marginella*, and *M. saltatrix*. Roezl also was the first to discover *M. erinacea*, a species later collected by Endres.

Masdevallia erinacea itself has an interesting history and several synonyms that speak to the fascination of this little species. It was also collected by Frederich Carl Lehmann (discussed a bit later), and named *M. torulosa*. Rudolf Schlecter described this species as *M. echinocarpa* in 1920, based on a plant collected in Antioquia, Colombia. This species was described again in 1960 as *M. horrida* by Henry Teuscher and Leslie A. Garay. The multiple names reflect the wide distribution of this species—from as far north as Costa Rica and south to Ecuador and Colombia. Slight differences exist in the populations, with the southern Andean population having somewhat wider and shorter leaves.

The earliest attempt to subdivide the genus *Masdevallia* was made in 1861 by Reichenbach, who listed groups under the names of the species with which they seemed most closely related. Later contributors to the classification of masdevallias included E. Pfitzer (1888), James Veitch (1889), botanical artist Florence H. Woolward (1890–1896), and Fritz W. L. Kränzlin (1925), who succeeded Reichenbach after the professor's death in 1889.

A 1896 monograph *The Genus Masdevallia* by Woolward included 87 lithographic reproductions in natural size. She was both author and illustrator of this grand tome in elephant folio format. This popular work is renowned for its beautifully hand-colored lithographs. One of the late 19th century connoisseurs of orchids was the Marquis of Lothian. His collection of cultivated orchids was one of the finest and most complete at that time, and beginning in 1880, he commissioned Woolward to paint portraits of his specimens as they came into flower. She had numerous, life-size paintings in full color in gouache (a watercolor medium), and those species classified at the time in the genus *Masdevallia* were chosen for serial publication. Descriptions and text were provided by Woolward, with notes by Lehmann. This became the most notable pictorial guide to masdevallias, although it contributed to the erroneous naming of several species for nearly a century. In *The Gardeners' Chronicle* of 25 October 1890, the following announcement was published:

> *The Genus Masdevallia.* The first part of the Marquess of Lothian's Monograph of species growing in his collection at Newbattle, is announced as nearly ready. The work will contain hand-coloured lithographs and engravings of every available species. The descriptions and plates are by Miss Woolward, with notes by Consul Lehmann. The work will be issued in parts of imperial quarto size, at the price of 110 (pounds sterling) each part, the issue being limited to 250.

The plants Woolward selected for her drawings were not chosen as fine horticultural specimens but were rather considered "on the whole, to be of fair average size and color." She endeavored to make each plate as complete as possible, giving, in all except four, a drawing of buds more or less advanced in growth, as well as several different views of the perfect flower. She stated that "in some of the Plates the colouring is not so clear and bright as I could have wished. Only a drawing direct from the flowers could give the delicate effects to be seen in nature." To ensure the accuracy of her work, she touched up the coloring of every plate sent out, numbering nearly 9000. Woolward recognized that she may have included errors in her species when she wrote

> Much doubt and uncertainty about these and other species will be set at rest only when Professor Reichenbach's vast collections of dried plants, drawings and notes come to light in the Vienna Museum, where, according to the extraordinary conditions of his will, they must remain untouched for 25 years after the date of his death, which took place in 1889. Until this period has elapsed, therefore, all arrangements of Sections and determinations of species or varieties must be made with reserve and regarded as temporary and uncertain.

Complete sets of Woolward's monograph today are extremely scarce, and those that do reach the market command astronomical prices.

John Day was an amateur artist of the late 19th century who had one of the richest and most famous orchid collections of the period. He had employed several painters, including C. B. Durham, to draw some of the plants in his collections, and Durham may also have given Day lessons in drawing. Day began sketching in 1863 and apparently made drawings up to within a few weeks of his death. The earlier ones are in ink, but in many places he later added colored sketches that included the date they were made. Although the early sketches are rough, they were botanically correct. His later work was more elegant, and he had assembled an impressive collection of drawings by the date of his death. Day's collection contains drawings of a large number of the types of Reichenbach's species, which adds greatly to its value. The drawings, many of which are *Masdevallia* species, are now part of the resources in the Orchid Herbarium of the Royal Botanic Gardens, Kew.

Frederich Carl Lehmann was a German mining engineer who as a young man emigrated to Colombia. He became the German Consul in Popayán, where he married and raised a family. During his more than 30-year career in Colombia, he searched for gold and minerals, and these expeditions led him to many remote places in both Colombia and Ecuador. He died at age 53, drowning in Colombia's Rió Timbique, while crossing the river in a boat to visit a gold mine. It is not clear whether this occurred as an unhappy accident or by malice. A tradition maintained by his family is that his death was not accidental, but rather that he was murdered and his body thrown into the river to conceal the stealing of gold from his mine. Lehmann was a highly educated man, a botanist, and a lover of plants, particularly orchids. His drawings and descriptions of new plants were accurate and appeared in *The Gardeners' Chronicle*, and he was associated with Woolward in the production of the Marquis of Lothian's monograph of masdevallias. Some light into the conditions he endured at the time may be gained by reading one of his letters from the *Kaiserlich Deutsches Konsulat in Popayán*, where he wrote

Even to send letters by post was so uncertain that the last lot of important papers I sent by express mule-rider all the way down to Buenaventura, to make sure they would get on board a mail steamer. Orchid collecting and traveling have been altogether hampered during the time of civil war. Officially it has been pronounced ended over and over again, but while reading the announcement, if you were favorably situated, you would still hear the cracking of the rifles.

Some of the more interesting masdevallias collected by Consul Lehmann include *Masdevallia angulata, M. burfordiensis* (now *M. angulata*), *M. deorsa* (now *M. caesia*), *M. lehmannii, M. rosea, M. trinema* (now *Dracula trinema*), *M. tubeana* (now *D. tubeana*), and *M. ventricularia*. Reichenbach often commented on Lehmann's excellent material and details of habitat. Lehmann had tested and recorded elevations and local peculiarities. He often hurriedly sketched drawings in the jungle, which were then finished and colored upon his return. His wife, Maria Josefa Mosquera, is also thought to have been his devoted assistant, frequently finishing the hasty sketches using samples of the flowers and leaves he would bring back. Fritz Kränzlin wrote of Lehmann that "His successes as a botanical collector will ensure him a lasting memorial, and especially so as far as Orchids are concerned. If—only to mention one genus—all of the Masdevallias he drew were to be published, they would occupy more than double the well-known work of Lord Lothian" (Taylor 1974).

Fritz W. L. Kränzlin (1847–1934) was a professor of botany and did most of his work in Berlin. He received many of his plants from Lehmann, and together they described many orchids, including a number of Colombian *Masdevallia* species. Although he was a well-liked person, he is not well remembered as a botanist, even though he published a monograph on masdevallias in 1925. Kränzlin was a careless botanist and on occasion he published the same species two or three times under different names. In his monograph he did not recognize the natural groups. Although he described 75 species, only 23 were valid, and he generated 52 synonyms.

During the latter half of the 20th century, much of the new information, taxonomy, and new species identification has been contributed by Dr. Luer, a retired surgeon, who at the age of 50 embarked on his "second career." He is associated with the 1973 founding of Marie Selby Botanical Gardens of Sarasota, Florida, and as part of the development of this new botanical garden he was encouraged by his friend and colleague, Calaway Dodson, to take on the sorting out of the pleurothallids, a project that he continues today. This became an international puzzle, requiring numerous trips to various herbaria (such as those at Harvard University, Vienna, Geneva, and Kew) to organize the pleurothallid collections, including *Masdevallia*. Probably one of the most difficult parts of this job was trying to read Reichenbach's scribbled handwriting, which was notoriously bad. Although not formally trained as a botanist,

Luer's careful study of the anatomy of the different species, the dissection of the flowers, and sketching of the organs of the flower enabled him to recognize clear similarities that assisted him in continuing the subclassification of the genus *Masdevallia*. His pivotal publications in the late 1970s and onward resulted in the reclassification of many species that were originally classified as *Masdevallia*, such that several new genera—*Dracula*, *Porroglossum*, and *Trisetella*—were created or critically redefined. Luer, with his wife, Jane, and several of his colleagues, including Walter Teague, made numerous trips to the countries of origin of the pleurothallids in Central and South America, collecting and describing scores of new species. Today Luer is the internationally recognized authority on *Masdevallia* (as well as other genera in the Pleurothallid Alliance), and unidentified plants are often forwarded to him for identification.

One of Luer's most lasting contributions are the series of books, *Thesaurus Masdevalliarum* (1983–1992, with Willibald Königer) and *A Treasure of Masdevallia* (1997). The idea for these exceptionally beautiful monographs came from several *Masdevallia* enthusiasts. At that time, there was a dearth of comprehensive literature on the genus. Individual articles, most from the previous century, had been written, but only two somewhat detailed treatments of the genus existed. One was Kränzlin's monograph of 1925, which although readily available, provided often unclear or incomplete descriptions and virtually no illustrations. The other was the monograph by Woolward, which although a literary treasure, is rare and not readily accessible. The consensus of the *Masdevallia* enthusiasts was that a modern monograph should be created in the style of Woolward. A founding team made up of Königer, Bertold Wuerstle, Charles Oertle, Othmar Sailer, and Rudolf Jenny established the format of the publication; daunting, however, was the need to engage an expert as the author, since the current state of taxonomic knowledge on the genus was inadequate. Königer had met Luer at the World Orchid Conference in Frankfurt in 1975, and it became obvious that Luer should be convinced to write the monograph. This decision was an excellent one—Luer's detailed flower analysis and drawings left no question as to the accuracy and quality of his work. The search for the best artist to paint the color plates was also difficult, because the artist had to be able and willing to portray the species with highest precision and with no artistic license. The medium was to be watercolor. Moreover, the artist had to be prepared either to work together with the contact or live sufficiently near him to permit the transfer of plants to be used as models. Jenny proposed that Luer work with Anne-Marie Trechslin, an internationally recognized expert painter of roses and camellias. Trechslin and Jenny both lived and worked in Bern, Switzerland. Trechslin's paintings are in many private collections, galleries, museums, and even with royalty. The first book she illustrated exclusively was published in 1961 (*Roses*, edition Silva). The best-known rose book she produced is *Le Moulin Roses d'Anta*, published by Editions, which contains 40 plates in large format.

Trechslin was commissioned to paint the species featured in the *Thesaurus Masdevalliarum*. Her requirements were exacting; she traveled to Paris to purchase the paper, colors, and brushes. These things were to remain identical throughout the entire project and thus had to be purchased all at once. At the time, Luer had not yet separated the genera *Dracula*, *Dryadella*, and *Trisetella*, and the group estimated about 500 plates, which was too low. Königer's decision to have only *Masdevallia* in the *Thesaurus* and exclude the other related genera made it possible to put the entire project on the same lot of paper. The species were all drawn life-size, and each drawing consisted of the single plant only, without any background or artistic flourish (Jenny 1998).

The first volumes (I, II) of the monograph were published in 1980, each with 15 plates, but the commercial response to the appearance of the *Thesaurus* was poor. Königer's stubbornness is credited with the continuation of the project despite the inadequate sales. Relations became strained within the founding team, so that successively Oertle and Sailer (1979), Jenny (1982), Wuerstle (1989), and Luer (1996) eventually dropped out. The collaboration with the artist became more difficult, and after the resignation of Jenny, the plants had to be transferred from Munich to Bern and back. Despite these difficulties, additional volumes were published, each with 15 plates. When Luer dropped out in 1996, further appearance of the *Thesaurus* seemed doomed. Fortunately, Luer decided to continue with the project, publishing additional volumes in 1997, but now named *A Treasure of Masdevallia*, again bilingual and of the same dimensions as the earlier volumes. (The name was changed due to copyright reasons, and the subsequent series was published by the Missouri Botanical Garden in St. Louis.) The illustrations were by artist Stig Dalström, and a careful examination of the plates reveals differences in how the species are displayed. Dalström's drawings have more than one plant of the same species per plate and include background (such as moss and tree branches), and the style of the drawings also differs from those of the previous artist. However, the color plates of both the *Thesaurus Masdevalliarum* and *A Treasure of Masdevallia* provide a stunning representation of the featured species.

Prior to 1975, only about 100 valid *Masdevallia* species were in existence. However, modern highways and roads into formerly isolated locales enabled new regions to be readily explored, leading to the discovery of hundreds of new orchid species and the rediscovery of old "lost" species as well. Today more than 400 species are recognized in the genus *Masdevallia*. Many of the recent discoveries have been identified and named by Luer, whose series of monographs compile much of what is known about the taxonomy, distribution, and other details of this fascinating genus. (See "References and Further Reading" at the end of this book for information.)

CHAPTER 3

Masdevallia Form and Function

The color, odor, and shape of all flowers have a singular purpose—to attract a pollinator. No group of plants has devised more diverse means to entice prospective pollinators than the orchid family. Charles Darwin captured this diversity when he wrote in 1862 that "the various contrivances and adaptation of orchids vastly transcend those which the most fertile imagination of the world's most imaginative man could dream up with unlimited time at his disposal." *Masdevallia* are no exception to this subterfuge. The principal pollinators of this genus are flies (although some of the more tubular shaped *Masdevallia* species may be pollinated by hummingbirds or moths), and perhaps because flies are neither terribly bright nor very efficient pollinators, they require special guidance to the column. The hinged lip of some *Masdevallia* species may play a role in this guidance. In some species, when the insect lands on the labellum, its own weight triggers the labellum to slam against the column, leaving only a narrow tunnel for the fly to exit from the trap. The fly squeezes through, and the sticky pollinia attach to the fly. The fly travels to the next flower and thus serves as a vehicle for pollination.

An entomologist would tell you that the compound eye of the insect would prevent it from seeing the vibrant colors of an orchid at a distance, yet it is well known that specific insects will head unerringly for flowers of a specific color. The initial attractant is not color, however—it is fragrance. When an insect approaches a flower with the "right" smell, it is ultimately guided by visual clues to a successful landing. As a genus, *Masdevallia* are not highly fragrant, at least to the human nose, but this is only because some of the odoriferous compounds released by a flower are not detectable to humans. Obviously, the insects can detect these complex substances. One of the few fragrant species, *M. glandulosa*, has been described as having a scent similar to cinnamon or clove, and this fragrance, or elements of it, are captured in many of the hybrids that have been made using this species as a parent. For example, the hybrid *M.* Confetti (*M. strobelii* × *M. glandulosa*) has a fragrance that some find similar to root beer.

A number of masdevallias (for example, many in the subgenus *Masdevallia*, section *Coriaceae*) emit a fragrance resembling rotten meat. *Masdevallia caesia* has a bizarre odor, likened by some to cat urine. These scents are powerful attractants to their pollinators (certain types of carrion flies), although it may dampen the enthusiasm of the orchid hobbyist to get too close to the flower. While the pollination of a number of orchid genera has been an area of interest for botanists, entomologists, and ecologists, the pollination habits of *Masdevallia* have largely been understudied. Undoubtedly, numerous fascinating stories remain to be told about the native pollinators of the different species and the adaptations of the *Masdevallia* to its pollinators.

CHAPTER 4

❖ ❖ ❖

Growing Masdevallias

The predominant countries where the majority of the *Masdevallia* species originate are Nicaragua, Costa Rica, Panama, Colombia, Venezuela, Ecuador, Peru, and Bolivia. However, masdevallias have also been found in Mexico, Guatemala, Honduras, Brazil, Surinam, and Paraguay. Each of these countries has unique features and geography that contribute to the diversity of orchids species that are found there.

The Natural Habitat of Masdevallias

The most important consideration in growing any orchid species is to understand the origin and habitat of the species—the elevation, rainfall amounts and distribution, temperature extremes, air circulation, and whether it grows in the soil, on rocks, on trees, and in partial to full sun or shade. Masdevallias are, for the most part, cool growers and are mostly found at high elevations in mountainous cloud forests, where they thrive in the high humidity. However, some species originate in warmer lowland areas. The geography of Central and South America generates incredible diversity in microhabitats. These features, as well as the inaccessibility and isolation of certain areas, create an environment unbelievably rich in all species, be they plant or animal. It is a tragedy, and unfortunately a continuing one, that many of these habitats have been destroyed and countless species lost forever.

An understanding of the local climates, elevations, and seasonal variations in temperature and rainfall provides an improved appreciation of the varied and sometimes demanding cultural requirements of the different species of *Masdevallia*. The geography and climates of the major countries of *Masdevallia* origination are discussed below.

Nicaragua is the largest but also the most sparsely populated Central American country. The western half includes Lake Nicaragua, the largest lake in Central America. The eastern half, the Caribbean coast, was known for two centuries as the British protectorate of Mosquito Coast. The Caribbean side has a broad plain and a coastal region of lagoons, beaches, and river deltas. Rainfall here is heavy. Inland and eastward, mountain ranges are broken by basins and valleys. On the western side and to the south is a broad depression that contains the lakes Managua and Nicaragua. A string of volcanoes, including the active Momotombo, overlooks the lakes.

This geography creates four major habitats. First, the dry tropical forest and tropical savannah is found in the regions around Managua and the central part of the country. This ecosystem is considerably warmer than other parts of the country and has two distinct seasons: the rainy winter season (June through October) and the dry summer (when no rain may fall for six to seven months). Second, the rain forest region of Nicaragua is a relatively small, isolated area south of the port town of Bluefields, on the Caribbean coast, and near the border with Costa Rica. This region receives more

Central America

than 4000 mm of rain per year. Third, the remainder of the Caribbean coast, from Bluefields to north of the Honduran border, is called a monsoon forest. This region has a pronounced dry season and less rainfall than points south. Finally, the cloud forest regions are relatively cool and high (more than 800 m). Most of the orchid species of Nicaragua are found in the cloud forest.

South America

Costa Rica lies on the Central American isthmus, between its neighbors Nicaragua to the north and Panama to the south. Volcanic mountain ranges form the backbone of this country, splitting it into halves, the Pacific side and the Caribbean side. The northern Cordillera de Guanacaste extends from the border of Nicaragua to meet the Central Cordillera. This spectacular chain of volcanoes includes several that are taller than 3000 m. Further to the southeast is the Cordillera de Tilarán, which includes the cloud forest preserve of Monteverde and just to the north, the active and continually erupting Volcán Arenal (1633 m). The Cordillera de Tilarán runs into the Central Cordillera, which has two very high and semi-active volcanoes: Volcán Poas (2704 m) and Volcán Irazu (3432 m). The most southeasterly mountains form the Cordillera de Talamanca, which is much higher, more remote, and considerably more rugged than the other mountain ranges. In this range are 16 peaks in excess of 3000 m. Between the Central Cordillera and the southern Cordillera de Talamanca is a temperate region known as the Meseta Central.

The lowlands of Costa Rica on both the Pacific and Caribbean coast are densely forested and rich in wildlife. The Pacific side is relatively dry, whereas the Caribbean lowlands receive extremely heavy rains. The Pacific side is considerably more rugged and rocky, and the north is bordered by dry tropical forests that receive no rainfall at all for several months of the year. In contrast, the Caribbean side is characterized by year-round rain, mangroves, and coastal swamps. Forests on the upper slopes of the mountains are frequently draped in mists and clouds, the cloud forests. This constant cool, humid environment creates a habitat hospitable to lichens, mosses, algae, ferns, orchids, and numerous other plant species.

Panama is a unique country that bridges two oceans and two continents. Bordered by Costa Rica to the north and Colombia to the south, it consists of a narrow neck of land connecting Central and South America. Most of Panama, including 750 offshore islands, is less than 700 m in elevation and swelters in tropical heat and humidity. The region has extensive lowland rain forests, with abundant wildlife and some of the wildest, untouched areas in the world. With a range of tall mountains (around 3000 m), the Serrania de Tabasara (Cordillera Central) runs west of the canal along the isthmus. These mountains are separated from the southern Peninsula de Azuera by a fairly extensive plain. East of the canal are two more ranges of mountains that form arcs running parallel to the Pacific and Caribbean coasts. Thus Panama has two major orchid habitats: rain forest and cloud forest, with the climate on the Pacific side of the mountains somewhat dryer than the Caribbean side.

Colombia straddles the northwestern part of the South American continent immediately south of the isthmus of Panama. It is the only South American country with coastlines on both the Caribbean Sea and Pacific Ocean. The mainland territory is divided into four major geographic regions: Andean highlands (comprising three mountain ranges and intervening lowland valleys), Caribbean lowlands, Pacific lowlands, and the Llanos of eastern Colombia. The hot, wet Pacific lowlands run south from the Panamanian border and merge to the north with drier lowlands along the Caribbean. The Andean highlands are an inland region defined by the parallel Andean ranges (the western, known as the Cordillera Occidental; the middle, Cordillera Central; the eastern, Cordillera Oriental), which have a general north-south orientation. The Eastern Cordillera is complex and varied. It consists of short, discontinuous ridges that follow a north-south direction, with some of the ridges running parallel to one another. The Eastern Cordillera is quite high with extensive areas that are snow-covered year-round. The Eastern Cordillera also has a number of high basins. The Central Cordillera is the highest of the Andean ranges in Colombia with many peaks in excess of 5500 m, including a number of active volcanoes, the highest of which is Volcán Tolima (5215 m). Toward its northern end, this cordillera separates into several branches that descend toward the Caribbean coast. The Central Cordillera has many small, populated valleys but as a whole is quite sparsely inhabited. In contrast, the Eastern Cordillera is much lower (the highest peak is just over 3000 m) and the range descends gently into Caribbean coastal plain. The deep, mostly narrow valley of the Rió Cauca runs between the Western and Central ranges; this area and some adjoining valleys are the most populated areas of this region of Colombia. The relatively low elevation of the Western Cordillera is conducive to dense vegetation, which on the western slopes is truly tropical. The lowlands along the Caribbean coast consist primarily of a low-lying, flat alluvial plain formed by the extensive deposition and accumulation of sediments carried down by the Rió Cauca, Rió Magdalena, and a few smaller rivers. This region also has a number of south-north oriented hills that are descending spurs of the Andes. The Guajira Peninsula, in the extreme north, is a semi-arid region, quite different from the rest of the Caribbean lowlands. In the southern part rises the Sierra Nevada de Santa Marta, an isolated mountain system with peaks reaching heights of more than 5700 m. The extensive lowlands of the east, which cover nearly two-thirds of Colombia, belong to two large drainage basins: that of the Orinoco River in the north and the Amazon River in the south. Two natural landscape regions are present: the Llanos (plains) in the north and the Selvas (forests) in the south. Elevated regions (spurs of the Andes) give the vast, undulating plain most of its topographical variety. The rivers are a dominant feature of both the physical as well as human landscapes and most of the population of the eastern lowlands lives on or near river banks.

Colombia is a country with striking variations in temperature and precipitation, resulting primarily from differences in elevation. There is, however, little seasonal variation in temperature. For example, the average annual temperature at Bogotá is 15°C, with the difference between the average of the coldest and the warmest months less than 1°C. Greater, however, is the daily variation in temperature, from 5°C at night to 17°C during the day. Colombia has three major climatic zones: the area lower than 900 m is called the hot zone (*tierra caliente*), that from 900 to 1800 m is the temperate zone (*tierra templada*), and areas with elevations from 1980 to 3500 m are the cold zone (*tierra fría*). The upper limit of the cold zone marks the tree line, and the treeless regions above this are high bleak areas called the *páramos*. Elevations above 4500 m tend to be permanently snow-covered.

Venezuela lies on the north coast of South America. A spur of the northern Andes divides the Basin of the Maracaibo from the valley of the Orinoco River to the east. In the east, the lowland plains of the Llanos are found, best known as savannah country for cattle grazing. During the wet season, much of the Llanos floods, but it is dry for the rest of the year. The southern part of Venezuela has the vast granite plateau of the Guyana highlands. The rain forest habitat is limited to the Federal Amazonas territory in the far south of the country, where the headwaters of the Orinoco and Rió Negro originate. These are low-elevation, hot forests on fairly flat terrain. These forests tend to be dense and comparatively devoid of orchids. The cloud forest is found in most of the mountainous regions of Venezuela and generally covers most of the country's higher ground, except the bare-rock tops of the great sandstone massifs of the Guyana and Amazonas regions. Dunsterville (1988) described the cloud forests of Venezuela as "plums in a plumcake," with the size and quality of each "plum" highly variable and dependent on local factors such as variations in soil, local and prevailing winds, the steepness of the slope, and the elevation.

Ecuador, home to many, if not the majority, of the known *Masdevallia* species, is a relatively small country bordered by Colombia to the north and Peru to the south and east. Despite its size, this country has some of the most diverse habitats and varied plant and animal life in the world. One of the most impressive statistics about Ecuador is that it has more species per square mile than any other country in the world; in fact, more than 30 percent of the known orchid species of the Western Hemisphere can (or were) found in this tiny country (Hirtz 1990). Unfortunately, Ecuador has in recent years suffered extensively from deforestation, and the decline in orchid as well as other species habitat has been devastating. It also has the distinction of being the most densely populated country of South America. With the equator basically bisecting the country (*Ecuador* is Spanish for equator), little seasonal variation occurs as a consequence of the angle of light from the sun. However, despite the even "seasons," critical differences occur in light, humidity, soil, and other components of the local ecology.

Ecuador has three major geographical areas: the Pacific coastal lowlands, the highlands, and the eastern lowlands (part of the Amazon River basin). Some of the highest mountain ranges in the region run north to south, dividing the country. Two major mountain ranges, the Western and Eastern Cordilleras, and two minor cordilleras complete the four mountain chains that cross Ecuador. The Western and Eastern ranges are separated by a series of 10 basins that form part of a long rift valley, and the intense and ongoing volcanic activity along this valley produced the discontinuities that form the basins. Rising along the basins are 30 volcanoes, many of which are still active, and these are some of the world's highest snowcapped cones. The eastern lowlands are part of the Amazon basin and are characterized by an undulating plain that slopes gently eastward. This region is drained mainly by the Rió Putumayo (which flows along part of the boundary with Colombia), Rió Napo, and Rió Pastaza and their tributaries. This region is covered almost entirely by dense, tropical rain forest. Most of it is uninhabited with settlements confined to the foot of the Andes and to small areas along the banks of the main rivers, where some agriculture is practiced. Distance, elevation, and inhospitable climates created powerful barriers in Ecuador, and

Masdevallia xanthina ssp. *pallida* growing *in situ* in Ecuador. Photograph by John Leathers.

up to 80 percent of the species described in Ecuador appear to occur in highly isolated populations.

The presence of two currents off the coast of Ecuador, the cold Humboldt Current and the warm California Current, creates impressive variety in climate from year to year and decade to decade. These currents produce the clouds, wind, and rain that collide with the mountain chains and the evaporation from the Amazon basin. These climatic collisions result in variation in the strength, duration, and degree of winds and rain and create incredibly varied microhabitats. Thus it might rain in one valley, while an area a short distance away may be experiencing drought. Distinct climate belts, noted by Alexander Humboldt at the beginning of the last century, are the classical rain forest from 1000 to 2500 m, the cloud forest from 2500 to 3500 m, the tundra from 3500 to 4500 m, and the Amazonas region. In an additional region, southeastern

Cloud forest habitat of Ecuador. Photograph by John Leathers.

Ecuador, the influence of the Humboldt Current has produced desertification. This region has savannah and Kapok trees but is in transition since once the Kapok trees are established, they trap humidity and rapidly colonize with epiphytes. What is characteristic of Ecuador (and other countries in this region) is that literally thousands of microhabitats exist. A small change in elevation, sunlight, winds, humidity, temperature ranges, and associated vegetation and potential pollinators (insects and hummingbirds) creates a microhabitat that fosters the evolution of entirely new species. Thus, sadly, the clearance of even a small patch of land may destroy a species forever (Hirtz 1990).

Geographically, Peru encompasses the magnificent Andes mountains, a wide strip of desert and coastal areas, and a lowland rain forest. The latter makes up about half of the country and a substantial portion of the Amazon basin. The coastal area is quite arid. To the north is a low, flat, but extremely faulted plateau of land. In the south, a narrow coastal mountain range rises just behind the shore of the Pacific. This area is very rugged, covered by bare, hard rock and deep, narrow gorges. Troughlike basins running parallel to this range separate it from the Andes. The highlands in Peru have two parallel mountain ranges, the Western Cordillera (Occidental) and Eastern Cordillera (Oriental), which extend northwest to southeast. Both the western and eastern ranges have peaks higher than 6000 m. In addition, numerous volcanoes are localized to the more southern part of the highlands. A series of high (3000 to 4500 m) valleys and basins separate the two mountain ranges and broaden into the Altiplano, where Lake Titicaca and a few smaller lakes are located. The eastern lowlands of Peru are generally divided in the *selva alta*, the higher hilly areas at the foot of the Andes, and the *selva baja*, the lower areas farther east (especially in the northeast) that slope toward the boundaries of Colombia and Brazil. The *selva alta* is dominated by low, gently sloping eastern spurs of the Andes (300 to 1000 m), with broad valleys. This gradually transitions into the *selva baja*, a much lower undulating plain, where the relief is dominated by a dense network of rivers and river terraces. It slopes gently northeastward from approximately 300 to 100 m. The eastern lowlands are covered with dense tropical rain forest, much of which is so dense that access is possible only via the rivers.

The southernmost species of masdevallias are found in Bolivia, a landlocked country bordered by Chile and Peru to the west, Brazil to the north and east, and Paraguay and Argentina to the south. Climatically and structurally, Bolivia has two major regions: the highlands and the eastern lowlands. The highlands of Bolivia can be subdivided into three distinct components: the Western Cordillera, the Altiplano, and the Eastern Cordillera. The Western Cordillera features many active volcanoes, part of a line of volcanoes that runs from southwest Peru to Chile. The southern part of the Eastern Cordillera is more arid than the northern region and almost uninhabited. The northern region has some high valleys, with altitudes of up to 4200 m. The Western Cordillera has peaks rising higher than 6000 m, steep slopes, and much volcanic activity. The Altiplano region is a high plateau, ranging from 3600 to 4000 m, that lies between the Occidental and Oriental ranges. This region is divided into basins by spurs of the Andes. The northernmost basin is partly occupied by Lake Titicaca, which straddles the border with Peru. In contrast to the Western Cordillera, the structure of the Eastern Cordillera is quite varied and complex, with distinctly different landscapes and habitats in the northern region (which rises abruptly to great heights above the Altiplano with snow-capped peaks higher than 6400 m). The eastern slopes of this region are densely covered by forest and are known as the Yungas; they are the wettest region of the Bolivian Andes. The southernmost part of the Eastern Cordillera rises abruptly from the Altiplano as a precipitous escarpment, but the uppermost regions are less rugged and slope gently toward the eastern lowlands. This creates a high level surface at 3600 to 4260 m, which is surmounted by shorter mountain ranges with higher peaks. This region is known as the Puna. The eastern lowlands of Bolivia also differ in their natural features. The northeast, the Llanos de Mamore, slopes gently into the Amazon basin, receives considerable rainfall, and is richly forested; the southeast region, the Gran Chaco, slopes toward the Rió Pilcomayo and Rió Paraguay and is semi-arid with dry scrub, savanna, and occasional pockets of forest.

Masdevallia yungasensis growing *in situ* in Bolivia. Photograph by Walter Teague.

Culture of Masdevallias

As discussed, the natural habitats of different *Masdevallia* species vary quite widely. However, fortunately for the hobby grower, the general growing conditions for masdevallias can be subdivided into three broad categories: cold to cool, intermediate, and warm. In the accompanying table, note that temperatures provided are rounded off to whole numbers.

Recommended growing conditions for masdevallias

GROWING CONDITION	NIGHTTIME TEMPERATURES	DAYTIME TEMPERATURES
Cold	4 to 7°C (40 to 45°F)	10 to 16°C (50 to 60°F)
Cool	7 to 12°C (45 to 53°F)	10 to 17°C (50 to 63°F)
Intermediate	10 to 13°C (50 to 56°F)	13 to 20°C (55 to 68°F)
Warm	16 to 18°C (60 to 65°F)	20 to 27°C (68 to 80°F)

Cool- to cold-growing masdevallias

These *Masdevallia* species tend to require nighttime temperatures ranging from 4 to 12°C and daytime temperatures not reaching much above 17°C, although many will tolerate short periods of somewhat higher daytime temperatures if high humidity levels (60 to 80 percent) can be maintained. Most *Masdevallia* species prefer a temperature change of at least 6 to 7°C between day and night, and plants grown under cooler conditions are generally sturdier. Cool evenings also help to reduce the heat stress of warmer days.

The cultural requirements of these cool-growing orchids can be somewhat demanding. If you live in California's Bay Area (the coast side), they can be grown outside for most if not all of the year, in lath houses or other exterior growing areas. Even in areas where the natural conditions are appropriate for *Masdevallia* culture, weather extremes can occur and the grower should have some type of backup systems and plans for such periods. In warmer or drier areas, *Masdevallia* growers will require additional investments in evaporative coolers, fogging or misting equipment, and other humidifying systems to meet these cultural requirements. In areas with colder winters but warmer summers (such as the midwestern or northeastern United States), provisions for maintaining appropriate temperatures will have to be made year-round.

Cool-growing masdevallias will rapidly perish in hot weather, direct sun, or dry conditions; thus, limiting heat stress is a critical issue when growing these plants. Signs of heat stress include leaf drop and abortion of new growths and flowers. During times of heat stress, the roots of the plants should be kept drier—the roots can quickly rot if a wet medium is combined with high temperatures. Elevating humidity, increasing air movement, misting the plants, and reducing light levels are additional strategies to reduce heat stress.

Intermediate-growing masdevallias

A number of *Masdevallia* species, primarily those that originate in warmer, lower elevations, can be grown under conditions in which the winter nighttime temperatures range from 10 to 13°C and daytime temperatures range from 13 to 20°C. Many species listed here will grow just as well cool (see Appendix II). As with the cooler growing masdevallias, to avoid heat stress during periods of high temperatures, it is important to maintain a humid environment with good air circulation, provide additional shading, and if possible provide significantly cooler night temperatures. A list of intermediate-growing species is provided here:

M. abbreviata	*M. brachyantha*	*M. cucullata*	*M. floribunda*
M. adamsii	*M. brachyura*	*M. cuprea*	*M. foetens*
M. aenigma	*M. brenneri*	*M. curtipes*	*M. formosa*
M. agaster	*M. bryophila*	*M. datura*	*M. frilehmannii*
M. ×alvaroi	*M. bucculenta*	*M. decumana*	*M. fuchsii*
M. amaluzae	*M. calagrasilis*	*M. deformis*	*M. fulvescens*
M. amplexa	*M. caloptera*	*M. delphina*	*M. garciae*
M. ampullacea	*M. calura*	*M. deniseana*	*M. geminiflora*
M. anachaeta	*M. campyloglossa*	*M. descendens*	*M. glandulosa*
M. anceps	*M. cardiantha*	*M. dimorphotricha*	*M. glomerosa*
M. andreettana	*M. carruthersiana*	*M. discoidea*	*M. gnoma*
M. angulata	*M. caudata*	*M. discolor*	*M. goliath*
M. angulifera	*M. chasei*	*M. dorisiae*	*M. guayanensis*
M. aphanes	*M. chimboensis*	*M. dynastes*	*M. guerrieroi*
M. ariasii	*M. chontalensis*	*M. echo*	*M. gutierrezii*
M. asterotricha	*M. chuspipatae*	*M. encephala*	*M. guttulata*
M. attenuata	*M. citrinella*	*M. ensata*	*M. hartmanii*
M. aurea	*M. cocopatae*	*M. erinacea*	*M. helenae*
M. auropurpurea	*M. collantesii*	*M. eumeces*	*M. helgae*
M. aurorae	*M. collina*	*M. eurynogaster*	*M. herradurae*
M. bangii	*M. concinna*	*M. excelsior*	*M. heteroptera*
M. belua	*M. constricta*	*M. exquisita*	*M. hymenantha*
M. bicolor	*M. corazonica*	*M. falcago*	*M. impostor*
M. bicornis	*M. coriacea*	*M. filaria*	*M. infracta*
M. bottae	*M. corniculata*	*M. flaveola*	*M. ingridiana*

M. irapana
M. iris
M. ishikoi
M. isos
M. klabochiorum
M. kuhniorum
M. lamprotyria
M. lankesteriana
M. lansbergii
M. lappifera
M. laucheana
M. lehmannii
M. lenae
M. lilianae
M. limax
M. loui
M. lucernula
M. luziae-mariae
M. lychniphora
M. maduroi
M. mallii
M. maloi
M. manta
M. marginella
M. marthae
M. mejiana
M. melanopus
M. melanoxantha
M. menatoi
M. mezae
M. minuta
M. molossoides

M. monogona
M. mooreana
M. morochoi
M. ×mystica
M. navicularis
M. nicaraguae
M. nidifica
M. norops
M. odontocera
M. odontopetala
M. omorenoi
M. ophioglossa
M. ortalis
M. os-viperae
M. panguiënsis
M. papillosa
M. paquishae
M. patchicutzae
M. patriciana
M. patula
M. persicina
M. pescadoënsis
M. phoenix
M. picturata
M. pinocchio
M. pleurothalloides
M. plynophora
M. ×polita
M. polysticta
M. porphyrea
M. portillae
M. pozoi

M. princeps
M. prodigiosa
M. pteroglossa
M. pumila
M. purpurella
M. pygmaea
M. pyknosephala
M. rafaelliana
M. reichenbachiana
M. rhodehameliana
M. richardsoniana
M. ricii
M. rigens
M. rima-rima alba
M. robusta
M. rodolfoi
M. rolfeana
M. rubiginosa
M. rufescens
M. sanctae-fidei
M. sanctae-inesiae
M. scabrilinguis
M. schizopetala
M. schizostigma
M. schroederiana
M. schudelii
M. scopaea
M. segrex
M. sernae
M. setacea
M. stenorhynchos
M. stirpis

M. strattoniana
M. striatella
M. strobelii
M. sulphurella
M. theleüra
M. thienii
M. torta
M. tovarensis
M. triangularis
M. tricallosa
M. trochilus
M. tubulosa
M. urosalpinx
M. utriculata
M. velella
M. venatoria
M. venezuelana
M. ventricularia
M. verecunda
M. vidua
M. virens
M. virgo-cuencae
M. wageneriana
M. walteri
M. weberbaueri
M. wendlandiana
M. whiteana
M. wurdackii
M. xanthina
M. zahlbruckneri
M. zebracea

Warm-growing masdevallias

Some truly warm-growing *Masdevallia* species do not do well under intermediate conditions. A list of these species is provided here. The ideal nighttime range for these species is 16 to 18°C and the daytime range is from 20 to 27°C. The flowering habit of some of the warmer growing species is of concern. Specifically, for those species that produce an abundant display of flowers near the base of the plant, the faded and dead flowers should be removed immediately so that the dead flowers do not develop a fungal infection, which can quickly debilitate or even kill the plant.

M. anfracta	*M. demissa*	*M. naranjapatae*	*M. tonduzii*
M. ayabacana	*M. lata*	*M. norae*	*M. tubuliflora*
M. bennettii	*M. livingstoneana*	*M. sprucei*	*M. vieriana*
M. crescenticola	*M. martiana*		

Light

In nature, most masdevallias grow in shady areas (about 1200 foot-candles), although some species are found in areas with higher light (greater than 3500 foot-candles). A general rule of thumb is that plants with softer, thinner leaves prefer the shadier conditions, whereas those with thicker, heavier leaves require more light. There are, however, exceptions; for example, several high-light species such as *Masdevallia barlaena* and *M. davisii* have softer, thinner leaves. Light for all species should be filtered or diffused, and in no case should the plants be exposed to direct sun. (In the following sections of the book, where specific species and/or hybrids are discussed, more detailed cultural information is provided.) During warmer periods (such as heat waves), providing increased shade will help the plants survive these stressful periods. Stressed plants may drop all their leaves (even within a single day). However, the plants may recover if the plants are shaded, provided high humidity, and given plenty of air circulation.

Humidity

Masdevallias require high humidity (ideally, at least 70 percent) and plenty of air circulation. During heat waves, leaf tips may turn brown or become spotted, which is stress-related. If grown in a greenhouse, the plants should be placed as close as possible to evaporative coolers. Unlike many orchids that have pseudobulbs, masdevallias do not have much water storage capacity, and a moist atmosphere is necessary to prevent their dehydration. Some growers spray (mist) their plants every morning and wet the staging under the plants as well. Masdevallias also require very clean water—many growers find that distilled water, rainwater, or water obtained by reverse osmosis is necessary to grow healthy plants. The potting medium should be kept moist but not soggy. This means that in the summer, masdevallias may require watering two to three times a week (depending on the temperature and humidity). In cooler weather, the plants will require less frequent watering. Overwatering can lead to a soggy medium, which may facilitate fungal growth.

Potting mix

A variety of potting mixes can be used successfully. However, different mixes have different properties—such as retention of water and salts, rate of decomposition, as well as differences in cost and availability. One simple rule followed by many growers is to use the same mix for all of their masdevallias. This simplifies watering, feeding, and repotting schedules. However, other growers base their choice of potting mix on the type of roots provided by their plants. For example, fine-rooted species such as *Masdevallia decumana* are potted in New Zealand sphagnum moss, while thicker rooted types such as *M. tovarensis* or *M. ignea* are potted in bark/perlite blends.

Several different possible potting mixtures are provided in the accompanying table, with comments about their properties. Note that plants ideally should be repotted in the late winter to early spring, and not in the heat of the summer, which may unduly stress the plant. Additionally, all potting media should be premoistened prior to using. A useful rule of thumb is to soak bark 24 hours in water before mixing with other components. Sphagnum moss should also be presoaked in water, as it can take some time to hydrate properly. To keep track of the repotting date, write the date on the back of the plant label.

The frequency of repotting varies with the potting mix as well as the environment, but as a general rule, masdevallias should be repotted every one to two years. When repotting, plants can be divided. Some species tend to accumulate dead spots in the center of the plants. These plants should be divided and the dead shoots removed. The

Suggested potting materials for masdevallias

POTTING MEDIA	COMMENTS
Pure New Zealand sphagnum moss	Holds an incredible amount of water. Depending on growing conditions may break down rapidly; best to repot yearly.
1 part fir bark 1 part sphagnum moss	Medium may last a little longer (up to 2 years). Good quality medium fir bark is necessary.
3 parts fir bark 1 part #3 perlite	Tends to dry out more quickly in heat spells; addition of chopped spagnum moss or shredded coir (coconut bark) will improve water retention. Medium lasts up to two years. Addition of charcoal may be beneficial.
6 parts fir bark 1 part #3 perlite 1 part shredded tree fern 3/4 part sphagnum moss	May be a more useful mix in areas with high heat and humidity. Addition of charcoal may be beneficial.
Mounted on tree fern or cork slabs	Plants will require daily watering (or even several times a day) and high humidity.

plants will be more attractive and are likely to bloom more vigorously. However, plants should not be divided into pieces that are too small—they are less likely to thrive and bloom the following year. Another common error made by novice orchid enthusiasts is to repot their orchids into pots that are too large. Masdevallias do better kept "crowded"—when repotted, use a pot of similar size or only slightly larger than the original pot. Moreover, the choice of pot should be based on the mass of the roots, not the leaves.

Fertilizing

Masdevallias are light feeders and do well on a more dilute mix of fertilizer than other orchids. Recommendations on frequency vary, but generally the plants do well with a feeding of $\frac{1}{4}$- to $\frac{1}{2}$-strength fertilizer (20-10-10 or 20-20-20) once or twice per month, although some growers fertilize their plants every week with a weaker solution of fertilizer. It is important that water is flushed thoroughly through the medium before fertilizing, and plants should be flushed with water every time they are watered. This will prevent salt buildup that can cause brown to black tips on the leaves. If this occurs, the plants should be watered without fertilizer for several months. Some growers suggest that plants grown in sphagnum moss or tree fern should be fertilized less frequently (once a month) than plants grown in a fir bark mixture (biweekly). The frequency of feeding should be reduced during the winter months.

Pests and diseases

The culture of masdevallias, like that of any plant group, is complicated by many of the usual pests. In the following sections, some of the more common problems—such as snails, aphids, scale, and disease—and potential solutions are discussed.

Insects and mollusks

The most serious insect pests are aphids, scale, mealy bugs, mites, and thrips. Snails and slugs can also do serious damage to an orchid collection. Which pests are present and, moreover, which present the greatest problems probably depends on where the plants are grown (outside, in a greenhouse, or in the house). An important first rule to avoid disaster is to inspect your orchids diligently and regularly (daily if possible) for thrips, scale, aphids, and ants. Weeds (such as oxalis and ferns) that may be growing along with your orchids should be removed because they can harbor pests and diseases. Plants look unhealthy for a reason. Look carefully under the leaves, on the stems of the plants, and on the buds of the flowers. The presence of ants is a warning that an aphid or scale infestation may be imminent or may have already occurred. Ants are known to introduce scale and aphids to many plants, and orchids are no exception.

Many insect pests are small and difficult to see. Aphids are small, green, white, yellow, black, or pink insects that live and feed in colonies on young growth (new leaves and buds). They can also be vectors for virus, so it is critical to eliminate them as soon as possible. Mealy bugs are small, white, cottony insects that often look like a tiny ball of fuzz. They are usually found at stem joints and near the base of leaves (usually on the underside) as well as in young, new growth. Scale are small insects protected by hard shells that attach to stems and leaves. Immature scale, which are more difficult to detect, are yellowish and tend to group along the midveins and leaf edges. When mature, they look like small, brown warts on the underside of the leaves or on the stems. Spider mites are almost impossible to see (you need a magnifying glass) but are suspected if plants develop fine, silvery gray stippling on leaves with fine, silvery webs on the underside.

If you see insects, treat your orchids immediately, and follow-up treatment is also required to eliminate these pests completely. If you have a small collection or prefer not to use pesticides, a spray solution of rubbing alcohol (isopropanol) or a Q-tip or cotton ball moistened with rubbing alcohol can be used. Stems and leaves should be scrubbed. This process, while labor-intensive, is less toxic to the environment and yourself. Alcohol will dehydrate flowers or buds, but it is generally not harmful to the plant *per se*. The pesticide of choice depends on availability and the labeling of the pesticide for certain insects. Often the best way to determine which pesticide to use is to consult local orchid growers or county extension agents for specific recommendations. Alternating products will help to prevent the build-up of resistant insect populations to a single product. As for any pesticide, it is important to read and follow the manufacturer's directions, and moreover, never spray when temperatures are warmer than 27°C. Certain insecticides work better than others on specific pests, and this information is provided on the product label. If spraying in a closed area, such as a greenhouse, a respirator will be required, and the area should be well ventilated before reentering.

Slugs and snails can be detected by the holes they leave in the leaves and the slime trails they leave behind. These mollusks feed at night and hide on warm days. They may be eliminated by hand picking, use of traps (sunken containers with an attractant such as beer), or use of snail or slug bait. Snail bait should not be placed on the plant media, but rather under the bench or on the surface where the pots are placed. Some snail baits are toxic to birds and pets, so it is important to read the label carefully and use appropriately.

Fungus

The most important step in preventing a fungal infection is to keep the growing area as clean as possible. Plastic pots used for repotting should preferably be new or well scrubbed, soaked in a bleach solution (10 percent bleach in water) overnight, and well rinsed. Used potting mix should be discarded. Another important preventative measure is good air circulation. The easiest method to move air is to use fans—overhead, oscillating, blower, or exhaust fans will all do the job.

Tiny spots are often observed on *Masdevallia* leaves. These can be caused by fungus, but a more likely cause is environmental stress (excessive heat on cool growers or cold on warmer growers), which results in mesophyll collapse on the soft new growth of the plants, as well as the buildup of a dark pigment that may appear as tiny, black spots. Application of a fungicide may be useful in diagnosing and resolving the problem. If a fungus is the culprit, subsequent new growths should be clean (though the spots will stay on the old leaves). Most fungicides are highly toxic to the environment as well as to the orchid hobbyist and should be handled carefully and as suggested by the manufacturer. Again, check with local authorities for recommended fungicides for your growing area.

Another cause of fungal or bacterial infections is overwatering. Planting media that stays soggy or wet is a friendly environment for fungal and bacterial growth, which can manifest itself very quickly and rapidly kill a plant. Infected plants can be treated with an appropriate fungicide or bactericide. Removal of dead or dying leaves is important to reduce potential sources of infection—fungal spores can be transmitted to other plants if splashed in water droplets. Stagnant air is also conducive to fungal spores settling and developing; thus the use of fans to provide air circulation (lots of it) is an important preventative measure.

Prevention is half the cure. Once or twice a year, the growing area should be cleaned and sprayed with a product such as Physan (following the recommended dilutions on the package insert), or if you have removed the plants, a 10 percent bleach solution can be used.

Virus

Unfortunately no treatment is available for plants infected with virus, and the best solution is to discard an infected plant or at the very least isolate it from the rest of the orchid collection. Virus can be hard to detect—it may appear as either chlorotic or blackened streaks, as mosaic or color breaks on young leaves, as surface irregularities on older leaves, and as deformed or disfigured foliage and flowers. Sometimes these symptoms can result from other causes, such as stress or insecticide burn, making definitive identification difficult. Other infected plants may show no outward symptoms at all. If suspected of viral infection, plants should be isolated and tested for infection by a commercial service. (Check with your local orchid society or search for such services on the Internet.)

Aphids can spread bean yellow mosaic virus, which is particularly harmful to masdevallias, and thus aphid infestation of any plant should be dealt with immediately. Bean yellow mosaic virus and other viruses can be spread by cutting tools, potting media, and even reuse of plant stakes. If a pot came from a plant suspected to be virused, discard it—why chance losing a prized plant over a pot that costs next to nothing? Cutting tools should be sterilized by heat treatment or soaking in a 10 percent bleach solution or used once and discarded. A razor blade is a convenient and inexpensive disposable "sterile" cutting tool, used for only one plant and safely discarded after use. Wooden plant stakes are best discarded after use (or use them on your other flowers in the garden; just don't reuse them on another orchid). Heat (over a propane torch, for example) or soak in a 10 percent bleach solution to sterilize wire plant stakes prior to reuse. When repotting, new or sterilized (washed carefully, and then soaked in 10 percent bleach solution overnight) pots should be used. Use of disposable rubber gloves during repotting will also help to avoid spreading viruses. Some growers lay down newspaper as a working surface and change the paper and disposable gloves between each plant to avoid spreading potential viruses. An additional and important preventative measure is to avoid the purchase of any plants that look suspect. When purchasing new orchids, it is also a good idea to isolate them from the rest of your collection for a short period to avoid possible transfer of any pests, diseases, or viruses from the new plant(s).

Purchasing Masdevallias

Masdevallias are sold at many orchid shows, orchid nursery open houses, and by mail order (or Internet). A partial listing of nurseries featuring *Masdevallia* species and/or hybrids for sale is provided at the end of this book. (Many more can be found by using a search engine on the Internet.) In addition, you may receive plants from other growers or win them at a raffle table at a local orchid meeting. However obtained, new orchids should not be immediately introduced to the rest of your collection. It is a good idea to keep them separate for two or three weeks, checking for possible insect or disease presence, and treating if necessary. Many growers also repot their new plants into their own potting mix, which will simplify watering requirements. When purchasing a plant, inspect it carefully for good, sturdy growth and possible signs of disease. Plants should be well rooted in the potting mix, not wiggling around. Purchasing a larger, more established plant, even if it costs a little more, is often a better investment as such plants are likely to thrive and bloom more quickly.

CHAPTER 5

✧✧✧

Masdevallia Propagation: Hybridization

Masdevallias are typically propagated by two methods: division and hybridization through selfing or sibling crosses. Mericloning, or meristemming, which is used to propagate other orchid species, has not, to the best of our knowledge, been used for masdevallias. *Division* simply means to split a plant into two or more parts, and this is very simple to do with masdevallias, which can be readily separated into multiple parts when taken out of the potting media. Divided plants should have at least several leaves and preferably one or more new growths. Smaller divisions may reduce the strength of the plant. Plants should be divided in the late winter to early spring, and division is often done when repotting.

Hybridization of orchids, either naturally or by humans, has yielded a vast number of new plants. More than 100,000 orchid hybrids have been registered, and this number will continue to grow due to the intense hybridization activities by commercial and hobby growers. However, in contrast to many plants, the hybridization of orchids has some unique challenges. While it is simple to take the pollinia from one flower and deposit it on another, the difficulty lies in the germination of the seeds. The orchid fruit, or capsule, does not carry the required nourishment to feed the seedling as it germinates (in contrast to a seed, such as a bean, which provides a store of food in the endosperm). In nature, orchid seeds are associated with a mycorrhizal fungus that produces the necessary nutrients to allow the orchid embryo to develop. The seeds of orchids are very tiny, and when the capsule is opened, a fine white "powder" spills out— each fine grain is a single seed.

Growing orchid seeds has been likened to a science project. It requires sterile technique, a special mixture of agar and nutrients in sterile flasks, and a laminar flow hood or other setup to allow sterile work. This can require a heavy investment in equipment and, more importantly, time. *Masdevallia* hybridization has further challenges. The flowers of the tiny, delicate *Masdevallia* have smaller "essential organs" and almost colorless pollinia. A steady hand and jeweler's loupe are required to place the minute pollinia on the translucent stigma. Each hybridizer has his or her own "secrets"; for example, sometimes it is necessary to carve away part of the sepaline tube, and some hybridizers prefer to use the newest inflorescences for pollination.

After pollination, a *Masdevallia* capsule will require about 90 days to mature. During this time, the capsule will enlarge rapidly. When the capsule dehisces (splits open), it often occurs near the base, and this may be preceded by a lightening or yellowing of the capsule sutures. Photographs of seed pods are shown in the illustration.

Although the ideal workstation is a laminar flow hood (or tissue culture hood), these are expensive and bulky. An alternative is to make a sterile work box. Plexiglas is a fairly inexpensive and easy-to-use material that can be used to create a box about 2 ft. tall, 2 ft. deep, and 3 ft. wide, with a partial opening in front. The surfaces of the box can be disinfected with a 10 percent bleach solution or sprayed with a solution of 70 percent alcohol. Sterile rubber gloves (such as surgical gloves) should be worn with sterile disposable paper sleeves over the arms, and anything that goes in the box must be "sterile." Before beginning a hybridization project, a record-keeping ledger (or file on a computer) should be established to keep track of the crosses made. An easy way is to number the crosses and keep the detailed files on selfings and crosses in the ledger. The ledger should also contain information relating to success or failure of the crosses, the plants that result, and ultimately the evaluation of the quality or other features of the flowers. A shortcut used by many hobbyists is to pay an orchid flasking

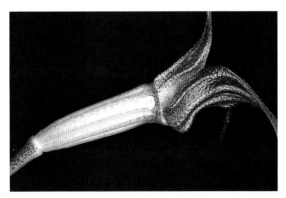 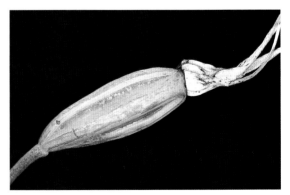

Masdevallia seed pods

service to sow the seeds and even replate the flasks. Many such services are available and can be readily found by searching on the Internet or by asking other orchid hybridizers in your area. A few sources of materials and flasking services are provided at the end of the book in "Sources: Nurseries and Flasking Services."

Intact, mature (called *green* because they have not opened yet) capsules should be surface sterilized (for example, with a 10 percent bleach solution) for 10 minutes. If multiple capsules are used, they should be labeled with indelible ink (which will not come off in the bleach solution), so that the capsules can be tracked. The capsule is opened with a sterile razor blade or scalpel and the seed sowed directly on agar medium. This is a tricky step, since it requires that the sterile seed-sowing flask also be opened (with a free hand), so that as the seed is scraped out of the opened pod, it will drop into the opened seed-sowing flask. If the capsule has already split (called *dry seeding*), it can be transferred to a clean sheet of paper and allowed to dry for 24 hours (preferably in a sterile tissue culture hood). The seed can be removed by tapping the capsule, followed by surface sterilization of the seed with the bleach solution. A number of nutrient mediums are used by hybridizers (see "Sources"), including G & B Orchid Laboratories' Mother Flask Medium V with charcoal or Phytamax Orchid Maintenance Medium. The nutrient media must be prepared and autoclaved (an alternative to an autoclave is a pressure cooker, like the type used to can fruits and vegetables from the garden) prior to use. The seeds are germinated in the light (but not direct sunlight) at room temperature. Green protocorms are usually visible within three weeks, and plantlets can be transplanted to a medium (replated), such as G & B Replate Medium or fresh Phytamax. Protocorms can be transplanted using a sterile instrument, such as a long fork (forks can be sterilized in a 70 percent alcohol or 10 percent bleach solution). Only a few protocorms should be placed in each flask to prevent overcrowding. The time required for development of protocorms into leaves and roots can vary dramatically.

Seedlings are removed from the flasks when they have developed several leaves and healthy roots. Removal must be done carefully, because bruised or torn tissues are more susceptible to fungus. Clinging medium should be rinsed off, and some growers use a fungicide at this juncture to avoid damping off, although doing this will kill any of the mycorrhizal fungi that may be developing with the seedling roots. Seedlings are planted together in small community pots with damp sphagnum moss and placed in a shady spot with plenty of air circulation. The seedlings require high humidity (a "cloud forest" can be created by misting or using an ultrasonic humidifier). Seedlings should not be allowed to dry out and should be fertilized every two weeks with a dilute liquid fertilizer. Seedlings can be moved to individual pots within 6 to 12 months and may produce their first flowers in 1 to 4 years (Barnes 1991; Staal 1993).

Ploid Shifting

In the early 1960s a technique was developed in the laboratory that enabled the doubling of the chromosome count of an orchid. Normally, all plants have two sets of chromosomes (called 2N, or diploid). However, with the aid of a chemical treatment, these chromosomes were doubled (called 4N, or tetraploid). The effect of doubling the chromosomes is to create generally bigger and better flowers and plants. Tetraploid orchids do occur spontaneously in nature and in cultivation, but only rather rarely. During the past 50 years of orchid breeding, a few orchids have stood out to be of a very high quality and exceptionally good breeders. These were later found to be chance tetraploids.

Today, most of the cultivated orchids that are tetraploid are purposely induced using colchicine or other inhibitors of mitosis. (It should be noted that colchicines are toxic and should be handled and disposed of properly.) Tetraploid plants often produce larger and more colorful flowers. The cells of the polyploid plant are larger, such that the same number of cells results in a larger, thicker flower. This technique has been used widely with cymbidiums, odontoglossums, and phragmipediums, but successes with other genera have been somewhat limited. Recently, several clones of tetraploid *Masdevallia ignea* have been produced by Bob Hamilton of Berkeley, California; as predicted, the flowers of these plants are large and thick and a striking orange-red color.

Putative tetraploid (4n) and diploid (2n) *Masdevallia ignea* 'Eureka ('Hawk Hill' × 'Strawberry Creek'). "Tetraploid" produced by Bob Hamilton (note that verification of ploidy is still pending). Grower: John Leathers. Photograph by Gerardus Staal.

CHAPTER 6

❖ ❖ ❖

What Is in a Name?

One of the most confusing aspects of the orchid to newcomers to the addiction is the seemingly complex and incomprehensible nomenclature of species, hybrids, and multigeneric crosses. The species names of many orchids utilize Latin or Greek names for roots that often describe a specific feature of the plant. All orchid species are given a binomial (two-worded) "Latinized" name that consists of the generic name (genus) followed by the descriptive species name (epithet). The generic name is written with a capital initial letter, while the epithet is written with a lowercase initial letter. Epithets illustrate certain features of the species that the original describer used to name the plant. For example, the epithet for the *Masdevallia* species *M. colossus* means huge, *M. discolor* has two colors, *M. floribunda* is profusely flowered, *M. ignea* refers to glowing or on fire, *M. princeps* means distinguished, *M. rosea* is rose colored, *M. tridens* has three teeth, and *M. ventricosa* is swollen on one side. Other epithet names honor individuals. For example, *M. reichenbachiana*, *M. rolfeana*, *M. schroederiana*, *M. veitchiana*, and *M. wageneriana* are named after the German orchidologist Reichenbach, Kew taxonomist Rolfe, English baron and orchid enthusiast Schröder, English nurseryman Veitch, and German plant collector Wagener, respectively. The ending of the epithet also provides important information relating to the name. Epithets ending in *ensis* or *ense* are named after a place (usually where the plant came from), whereas those ending in *i*, *ii*, or *ae* denote species named after the discoverer of that species (man or woman, respectively). Some species end in *iana*, which indicates that the species is named after an individual who perhaps brought the orchid to the attention of the botanist who first described the species, or otherwise to honor a specific person.

To be published validly, a botanical name must include its *author*, the person who first described the species as new to science. Thus, *Masdevallia adrianae* Luer is the correct botanical name for this species first described by Luer. Some author names are abbreviated, such as *M. caloptera* Rchb.f., a species first described by Reichenbach. The first author name may also appear in parentheses, followed by a second author name, such as *M. pachysepala* (Rchb.f.) Luer. In this case, the author in parentheses, Reichenbach, first described the species, but Luer transferred it to its currently recognized genus later on.

Sometimes minor differences occur within a species (such as color or size) that distinguish them from the typical form. In this case, the plant name would also include this information. For example, the plant *M. coccinea* var. *alba* refers to a white variation of this normally rose-colored species. If a plant has been awarded, this plant and all plants vegetatively derived from it are also given a cultivar name as well as the award name. For example, *M. coccinea* var. *xanthina* 'Seattle Gold' AM/AOS happens to refer to a named, yellow colored cultivar that won an Award of Merit (AM) from the American Orchid Society (AOS) in 1998 and was named 'Seattle Gold' by the grower. In some species of *Masdevallia*, variation has been recognized as a subspecies (abbreviated *ssp.*). Subspecies are plant or animal populations differing slightly to substantially, but consistently, in appearance (color, pattern, size, for example) from the nominate population, and they are usually geographically, altitudinally, or ecologically separated. For example, the flowers of *M. yungasensis* are quite variable in size, shape, and color. The color of the glabrous sepaline tube varies from white to rose with purple stripes, or it may be yellow with brown stripes. A pure-yellow color form also exists. But *M. yungasensis* ssp. *calocodon* has gaping, bell-shaped flowers with a red pubescence.

A plant is called a *primary hybrid* when it is produced from two species crossed together. When two different species are crossed, the resulting hybrid cross includes the name of both parents—*M. veitchiana* × *M. strobelii*. Hybrid crosses are usually given a *grex* (Greek for group, it refers to a seedling batch) name consisting of one to three words, not italicized, but beginning with a capital letter. A generic name plus epithet forms a *grex name*, and this name is applied to all the progeny directly raised from two parent plants that bear the same pair of specific or grex names, regardless of parental cultivars. A grex epithet should be a name in a modern language (that is, not Latin), although older hybrid names sometimes sound "scientific," such as *M.* Measuresiana. Thus, the cross *M. veitchiana* × *M. strobelii* was given the grex name *M.* Angel Frost. Angel Frost is the grex name of all crosses of *M. veitchiana* × *M. strobelii*, regardless of

Masdevallia coccinea var. *alba*. Grower: John Leathers.

which plant is the source of the pollinia. Moreover, all progeny of this cross are known as Angel Frost, even if specific cultivars of *M. strobelii* and *M. veitchiana* are used. Progeny from any cross can vary greatly, frequently exhibiting the full range of variation from one parent to another. Cultivar names are given to particular plants with exceptionally fine flowers. A cultivar name begins with a capital letter and is set within single quotation marks. For example, an awarded plant of the *M.* Angel Frost grex is *M.* Angel Frost 'Golden Girl', which was awarded a HCC (Highly Commended Certificate) from the American Orchid Society. All vegetative divisions from *M.* Angel Frost 'Golden Girl' HCC/AOS should bear that name on the label. When vegetatively propagated through divisions, keikis (offshoots), or mericlones, all derivatives of a cultivar will be genetically identical and will possess the same cultivar name. This permits hobbyists to know exactly what to expect from plants they purchase bearing this name.

If a hybridizer crosses *Masdevallia* Angel Frost with another species or hybrid, the progeny of that cross can be given a different grex name. For example, *M.* Angel Frost × *M. floribunda* is named *M.* Tasmanian Devil, and *M.* Angel Frost × *M.* Copper Angel is named *M.* Copper Frost. Thus a grex name might represent multiple species that have been interbred to produce the cross. Grex names are published by the Royal Horticultural Society in what is known as *Sanders List of Orchid Hybrids*. This is the definitive listing of orchid hybrids, their parentage, hybridizer, and year registered. Appendix I lists many of the registered *Masdevallia* grex names and their parentage.

The pronunciation of the Latin names of orchids is another subject altogether, and often no two growers will pronounce a name the same way. The best way to learn is to listen to other growers and attend meetings of your local orchid society. Several good publications on the subject are available, such as *An Orchidist's Glossary*, published by the American Orchid Society, and Alex Hawkes's *Encyclopedia of Cultivated Orchids* (1965).

Intergeneric Hybrids Using *Masdevallia*

Dracula is a genus related to *Masdevallia*, and species of genus *Dracula* were originally attributed to *Masdevallia* until they were moved to their own genus by Luer in 1978. More than 100 species of *Dracula* are distributed in the wet forests of southern Mexico, Costa Rica, and southward to northern Peru, with most species found in Colombia and Ecuador (if they can be found at all, due to tropical forest deforestation; some are known from only one collection). Many species are very rare and extremely localized. The blossoms are highly intriguing, with the tips of the three sepals tapering to long, slender tails. They seem to have false "eyes," which are usually the petals, looking back at the viewer from the center of the flower.

Dracula crosses with *Masdevallia* are known as *Dracuvallia*. A few of these intergeneric crosses have produced spectacular plants. For example, *Dracuvallia* Blue Boy is a cross of *D. chimaera* with *M. uniflora*. At least one clone of this cross has been awarded, *Dracuvallia* Blue Boy 'Cow Hollow' AM/AOS.

Another closely related genus that has had limited success in intergeneric hybridization with the *Masdevallia* is *Porroglossum*. Intergeneric crosses are given the name *Porrovallia*. One awarded cross is *Porrovallia* Monica, which is the name given to the cross *M. veitchiana* × *Porroglossum echidna*. A clone of this cross named 'Free Spirit' was awarded an HCC/AOS

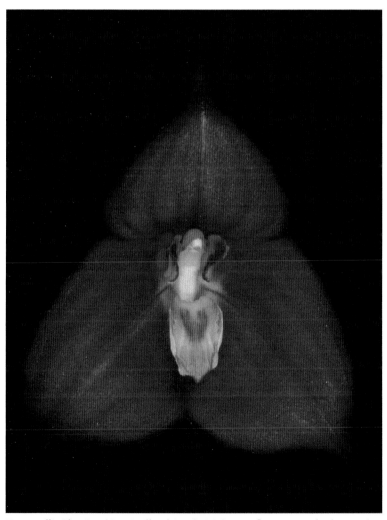

Dracuvallia Blue Boy 'Cow Hollow' AM/AOS (*M. uniflora* × *Dracula chimaera*). Grower: Anna Chai.

CHAPTER 7

Showing Masdevallias

One of the most rewarding and enjoyable aspects of growing orchids is entering a plant into an orchid show. Many local orchid societies sponsor annual shows, offering the opportunity for such endeavors. Most offer classes for novice, intermediate, and advanced growers (used for ribbon judging), as well as trophy judging (based on rules set by the local society sponsoring the show, or in some cases national or regional groups that also have named trophies). If the show has been approved by the American Orchid Society, plants can also be considered for AOS awards, discussed below.

Preparation of an orchid for exhibition should begin before the blooms are actually open to encourage the flowers to open to their fullest potential and present themselves in the best way possible. The first step is to remove any distracting hardware, such as old stakes, twist ties, or clips. Old plant spikes or remnants should be removed, and unsightly leaves should either be removed or the damaged parts cut off with a sterile razor blade. Purists will also remove some of the flowers (if the plant has lots) that might be older or unattractive for some reason. All cuts to healthy plants should be dressed with a fungicide to discourage infection. (However, if most of the leaves look unhealthy, it may be best not to show that plant. Diseased or infested plants are not permitted at shows.) For masdevallias, small stakes can be made using straight pieces of floral wire. The floral wire can also be bent with pliers and looped at the end to make an almost closed C-shape, in which the flowering stem, just below the flower bud, can be inserted when the spike becomes more mature, and moreover, cut to the right size. The straight end of the wire is inserted close to the bottom of the flowering growth. Carefully move the stake such that it will support the inflorescence. (Moving the spike to stake can also work with most masdevallias since the floral stems are quite flexible—but be careful not to break the spike.) If this is done while the flower spikes are quite young, the stakes will provide support and enable the spike to grow up straight and display the flower. The stakes can be fastened to the spike with a twist tie or thin wire. (An inexpensive source of thin-coated wire is phone wire—peel away the outer heavy plastic coating, and you'll see numerous, thin, plastic-coated wires.) The objective is to support the inflorescence as the buds develop and become heavy, and also allow the flowers to open naturally. Staking also helps to protect the flowers during transport. Many species and hybrids of *Masdevallia* may not require staking, as their flowers are borne on short stems, the stems are strong enough to bear the weight of the flowers, or the flowers are diminutive and don't require support. Every plant presents a unique challenge; the key is to prepare the plants slowly and carefully.

Chemical residues can be removed by cleaning the leaves with a 50:50 mixture of whole milk and water; this can also leave a wonderful healthy sheen on the orchid's leaves. Any weeds should be pulled out. If the old mix looks ugly, remove a half inch or so off the top and add fresh mix or sphagnum on top to provide a fresh appearance. If white marks (signs of mineral or salt buildup) appear on the outside of the pot, they can be removed using a toothbrush and a solution of Epsom salts (1 tablespoon per gallon water).

After you have transported your plant to the show, many of the ties and clips (not necessarily the stakes) should be removed so that they do not detract from the plant. A small pot can be placed inside a larger or more attractive pot or basket, and the base of the plant can be dressed with a little Spanish or sphagnum moss. Some growers use beautiful ceramic pots to house the smaller utilitarian pots; this looks more attractive and improves the impact at the show. (Don't count on this influencing the judges, however! They are judging the quality of the flowers, not the pot.) Plants on slabs or small plants may require an additional "prop" to display them most attractively. Some growers use tree branches or wire mesh grids to hang slabs, and others use risers to raise the level of the small plant to catch the eye of the viewers.

Orchid Awards

National and even regional orchid societies have established criteria of excellence by which orchid plants are evaluated. Scores are based on a possible total of 100 points. (See the following table for specifics for orchids of the Pleurothallid Alliance.) For example, the AOS recognizes individual orchid plants (cultivars or clones) with flower quality awards such as the First Class Certificate (FCC, 90+ points), Award of Merit

(AM, 80 to 89 points), or Highly Commended Certificate (HCC, 75 to 79 points). Orchids that show distinctive characteristics recognized for good features outside of the traditional flower qualities are acknowledged by an affirmative vote of at least 75 percent and may also be awarded a Judges Commendation (JC). Other awards may be given to the grower for achievement in culture, the Certificate of Cultural Merit (CCM) and Certificate of Cultural Excellence (CCE); and to the plant for botanical novelty, the Certificate of Botanical Recognition (CBR) and the Certificate of Horticultural Merit (CHM). The Award of Distinction (AD) and Award of Quality (AQ) are awarded to the hybridizer as well as exhibitor and recognize worthy new trends (AD) and improved quality (AQ) for a specific hybrid.

As mentioned, in addition to the AOS, many plant societies around the world present awards for orchids, including the Royal Horticultural Society (RHS), Japanese Orchid Grower's Association (JOGA), and Australian Orchid Council (AOC).

Masdevallia judging by the AOS uses the pleurothallid scale

FORM (35 pts total)	COLOR (35 pts total)	OTHER CHARACTERISTICS (30 pts total)
General form (20)	General color (20)	Size of flower (10)
Dorsal sepal (4)	Dorsal sepal (5)	Substance/texture (7)
Lateral sepals (8)	Lateral sepals (10)	Habit/arrangement (5)
Caudae (3)		Floriferousness (8)

CHAPTER 8

❖ ❖ ❖

Genera Related to *Masdevallia*

Masdevallias are part of a larger group (called a *subtribe*) of orchids, which are named the Pleurothallidinae. All plants in this subtribe are referred to as pleurothallids. Most pleurothallid species are small to miniature plants with a diversity of the flowers that defy a general floral description. Moreover, some of the genera so closely resemble each other that many taxonomists have difficulty in sorting and classifying them. Several genera that are related to *Masdevallia* are discussed here.

Dracula

Plants of this genus were originally classified as *Masdevallia* but were moved to a new genus by Luer. The name *Dracula* means little dragon. The more than 100 species of this genus are found in the wet forests of southern Mexico, Nicaragua, Costa Rica, Colombia, Ecuador, and Peru. Most of the species are rare and tend to be highly localized. The plants are similar to masdevallias in appearance but are distinguished by their thin, keeled, conduplicate (folded together at the base) leaves. The flowers also have three large sepals, but the small petals have divided tips or end in knobs. *Dracula* are grown in baskets to accommodate the pendant inflorescences. The lip is two-part, often mobile, and shell-shaped and thought to mimic fungi. The pollinators of these species are fungus gnats. These plants are best grown under cool to intermediate conditions with lots of humidity. Many of the flowers are bizarre; the tiny petals can look like eyes and give the flowers a "monster" appearance. Exposure to heat and/or dry air will cause the flowers to close. As noted earlier, intergeneric hybrids of *Dracula* and *Masdevallia* are called *Dracuvallia*.

Dryadella

This group of species was also removed from *Masdevallia* and placed into a separate genus by Luer. The name of the genus is derived from the word *dryad*, a nymph or divinity of the woods. *Dryadella* range from southern Mexico to Brazil and northern Argentina. The leaves are narrow, channeled, and fleshy. The sepals have a callus (thickened fold) near the base and are joined below the callus to form a mentum (a chinlike structure) below the column-foot. The lip of *Dryadella* is long and tonguelike. The small flowers, often hidden by the foliage of the plant, may bloom singly or successively or in massive flushes. The flowers have a protective coloring, and their buds are shaped like birds' heads, which has resulted in their nickname, "pheasant in the grass." Many of the flowers have a foetid odor, and generally *Dryadella* are somewhat drought tolerant.

Porroglossum

The name of this genus derives from the Greek word *porroglossa*, meaning a distantly held tongue, which alludes to the spoon-shaped lip characteristic of this genus. *Porroglossum* comprises about 30 small epiphytic or lithophytic (plants that grow on rocks) species from the Andean cloud forests and montane forests in Colombia, Ecuador, Peru, and Venezuela. A single species has been found in Bolivia. A successive flowering raceme of small to medium-sized flowers characterizes the genus. The tips of the sepals end in a knob or tail. The leaves are finely pitted and/or reticulated. The flowers are distinguished by their lip, which is S-shaped, and hinged to the column-foot by a long, slender claw. The outer lobe of the lip is triangular and edged with hairs. The lip hangs down when open, and when the callus on its center hump is touched (by an insect, a drop of water, or an instrument held by a human hand), the lip rises up against the petals, forming a chamber. If an insect is the instigator, it is trapped in the chamber until it pushes its way out through the side, effectively collecting or depositing the pollinia. *Porroglossum* are cool to intermediate growing and prefer roots that are drier than most of the related genera, and they can flower throughout the year.

Trisetella

Species of this genus were also removed from *Masdevallia* and placed in new genus *Trisetella* (three bristles) by Luer. This genus has just more than 20 dwarf epiphytic species that range from Mexico to Bolivia. The species produce a raceme that bears relatively large and odd-looking, successively blooming flowers. For most species, the sepals taper to long tails. *Trisetella* are characterized by a very tight caespitose growth, forming a pin cushion–like plant.

CHAPTER 9

❖ ❖ ❖

Subclassification of *Masdevallia*

The first attempt to subdivide the genus *Masdevallia* was made in 1861 by Reichenbach, who listed groups of species under the name of the species with which they seemed to resemble most closely. Later contributors to the classification of the genus included Pfitzer (1888), Veitch (1889), Woolward (1896), and Kränzlin (1925). However, the present classification used today is based on Luer's 1986 monograph *Icones Pleurothallidinarum II. Systematics of Masdevallia*. He defined five subgenera, two of which were further subdivided into sections and subsections. Further updates of the classification were published in 2000, 2001, 2002, and 2003.

While morphological characteristics have remained the mainstay of orchid classification, the ability to sequence DNA has led to refinements and controversies in the classification of orchids and other plants. This has occurred at the same time that a shift occurred in cladistic (a method of grouping animals or plants by measurable likeness) theories from phenetic theories to parsimony algorithms. *Phenetic analysis* groups organisms based on their overall similarity. *Parsimony analysis* groups organisms based on shared evolutionary characteristics. DNA analysis often confirms traditional classification schemes, although when it does not, new classification schemes may result. Morphological-based classification, while extremely useful as an end-user tool for plant identification, may be vulnerable to the phenomenon known as "convergent evolution." Thus, similarity in a given morphological characteristic can be due to common ancestry, or it can have independent origins but occur as a consequence of similar selection pressures (such as pollinators, climate, and other factors). A recent publication based on DNA sequencing by Alex M. Pridgeon, Rodolfo Solano, and Mark W. Chase (2001b) sampled representative species from the *Masdevallia* subgenera, sections, and subsections proposed by Luer (as well as other pleurothallid genera). It should be noted, however, that for the most part only a single species per subclassification category was sampled. These authors concluded that a low level of molecular divergence occurred among the *Masdevallia* species sampled, but they did not propose further changes to the finely split generic subclassifications of Luer. However, this analysis did challenge the creation of the monospecific genus *Jostia*, which was proposed by Luer (2000b) to accommodate *M. teaguei* solely based on the morphological characteristic of its actively mobile lip (that, when disturbed, flips suddenly upward to a position beneath the column, then returns to the down position after about 15 minutes). Based on DNA sequencing analysis and the *Masdevallia* species sampled, *M. teaguei* was most closely related to *M. racemosa* and did not segregate into a separate clade (a group that shares genetic features inherited from a common ancestor), and clearly this type of mobile lip has arisen independently in other pleurothallids.

In contrast, the DNA sequencing data supported Luer's creation of the genera *Trisetella*, *Dracula*, and *Porroglossum*. Interestingly, *Masdevallia erinacea*, which was classified as one of the species in the *Masdevallia* subgenera *Pygmaeia* (see below), is distinguished morphologically from other species of *Masdevallia* by its carinate (keeled) and echinate (bristly) or papillose (warty) ovaries. DNA sequencing evidence segregated *M. erinacea* into a separate group, suggesting that at least this species and possibly its relatives warranted generic status. Pridgeon and Chase (2001a) proposed a new genus, *Diodonopsis*, and included the former *Masdevallia* species *M. anachaeta*, *M. erinacea*, *M. hoeijeri*, *M. pterygiophora*, and *M. pygmaea*. Full agreement on this classification has not occurred, however, and for the purposes of this book, the *Diodonopsis* species are included under Luer's classification as the *Masdevallia* subgenus *Pygmaeia*. The current subclassification scheme of *Masdevallia* is likely to evolve further as additional DNA sequencing information becomes available.

The complex infrageneric scheme of *Masdevallia* does enable identification of different species and thus is a useful tool for the orchid hobbyist; it is detailed in the following pages. The descriptions of the sections and type species that follow are based on the original publications of Luer (1986 and 2000a), and the reader is referred to these monographs for more detailed botanical descriptions. The species upon which the description of the subgenus, section, or subsection is based is called the *type* and is the basis for applying names in botany. In the table, the classification scheme is outlined. A key to identifying the different subcategories is also provided.

Subclassification of *Masdevallia* (adapted from Luer 2000a; 2003)

SUBGENUS	SECTION	SUBSECTION	TYPE SPECIES	PEDUNCLE	RACEME	FLORAL BRACT INFLATED	OVARY	CONNATION OF SEPAL	SEPALINE TAIL	PETALS	LIP DIVIDED
Amanda			*M. amanda*	terete	SI	+	C	+	+	–, mostly serrate	+ (–)
Cucullatia			*M. cucullata*	terete	U	+	C	+	+	–, tip verrucose	+
Fissia			*M. picturata*	terete	U	–	L	free	+/–	T	+
Masdevallia			*M. uniflora*								
	Coriaceae		*M. coriacea*	terete	U	–	n/a	+	+/–	–	V, –
	Dentatae		*M. collina*	terete	SC	–	n/a	+	+	T	BC, –
	Durae		*M. dura*	terete	SC	–	n/a	+	+	–	V, –
	Masdevallia		*M. uniflora*								
		Caudatae	*M. caudata*	terete	U	–	Sm	+	+	+, T	H, –, (some Os)
		Coccineae	*M. coccinea*	terete	U	–	n/a	+	+	+	–
		Masdevallia	*M. uniflora*	terete	U	–	n/a	+	+	+	–
		Oscillantes	*M. wageneriana*	terete	U	–	Sm	+	+	+	W, H, Os
		Saltatrices	*M. saltatrix*	terete	U	–	n/a	+ CT	+	+/–	–
	Minutae		*M. minuta*	terete	U, SI, SC	–	n/a	+	+	+, T, P	BC, –
	Racemosae		*M. racemosa*	terete	SI	–	n/a	+	–	–	–
	Reichenbachianae		*M. reichenbachiana*	terete	U, SC	–	n/a	+	+	–	–
	Triotosiphon		*M. bangii*	terete	U	–	n/a	+	–	–	–
Meleagris			*M. meleagris*	terete	SC	–	Co	free	+	–	–
Nidificia			*M. nidifica*	terete	U	–	C	+	+	T	+
Polyantha			*M. schlimii*								
	Alaticaules		*M. melanoxantha*								
		Alaticaules	*M. melanoxantha*	triq.	SC	–	Sm	+	+	+/–	+
		Coaetaneae	*M. sceptrum*	triq.	SI	–	Sm	+	+	+/–	+
	Polyanthae		*M. schlimii*								
		Polyanthae	*M. schlimii*	terete	SC	–	Sm	+	+	–	+
		Successiviflorae	*M. lata*	terete	SI	–	Sm	+	+	–	+
Pygmaeia			*M. pygmaea*								
	Amaluzae		*M. amaluzae*								
		Amaluzae	*M. amaluzae*	terete	SC	–	Sm, R, LC	+	+	–	–
		Zahlbrucknerae	*M. zahlbruckneri*	terete	SC	–	Sm/Co	+	+	–	–
	Aphanes		*M. aphanes*								
		Aphanes	*M. aphanes*	terete	U, SC	–	C/V	+	+/–	–	–
		Pterygiophorae	*M. pterygiophora*	terete	U	–	W	+	+	–	–
	Pygmaeae		*M. pygmaea*	terete	U, SC	–	Sp/Pa	+	+	T	–
Scabripes			*M. bicornis*	scab.	SC	–	n/a	+	+	T	–
Volvula			*M. caudivolvula*	terete	U	–	n/a	+	+ twisted	–	+

Key

+ yes – no n/a not applicable

PEDUNCLE **terete** round in cross section; **triq.** triquetrous, triangular in cross section; **scab.** scabrous, rough to the touch with small points or scales

RACEME **SI** raceme simultaneously flowered; **SC** raceme successively flowered; **U** peduncle bears single flower

OVARY **C** carinate or crested; **L** lamellate; **V** verrucose; **Sm** smooth; **LC** low costate; **R** ribbed; **Sp** spiculate; **Pa** papillose; **Co** costate; **W** winged

CONNATION OF SEPALS **CT** cylindrical tube

SEPALINE TAIL + with tails; – without tails

PETALS – no marginal process; + with a marginal process; **T** tooth; **P** pointed

LIP + lip divided by marginal folds into an epichile and hypochile; **BC** bicarinate; – lip not divided by marginal folds into two parts; **H** hinged; **Os** oscillates; **W** winged; **V** verrucose

Key to the Subgenera and Sections of *Masdevallia*

The genus *Masdevallia* has been divided into 10 subgenera, 13 sections, and 13 subsections. The classification is based on various structural features of the plant. A key to the classification is provided here, adapted from Luer (2000a, 2000c, 2001, 2002, 2003).

1 Lip undivided, with or with out calli (go to 2)
1 Lip divided by marginal folds into two parts, epichile and hypochile (go to 19)
    2 Rhizome elongated, plant repent (go to 3)
    2 Rhizome abbreviated, plant caespitose (go to 4)
3 Inflorescence racemose, lateral sepals tailless . . . . subgenus *Masdevallia* section *Racemosae*
3 Inflorescence single-flowered, sepals caudate . . . .
    . . . . .subgenus *Masdevallia* section *Masdevallia* subsection *Masdevallia*
    4 Peduncle scabrous . . . . subgenus *Scabripes*
    4 Peduncle smooth (go to 5)
5 Single-flowered inflorescence (go to 6)
5 Two or more flowered inflorescence (go to 12)
    6 Ovary variously ornamented (go to 7)
    6 Ovary not ornamented, may have low carinae (keels) or ribs (go to 8)
7 Ovary carinate-crested, sepals tailless or contracted into short tails . . . .
    . . . . subgenus *Pygmaeia* section *Aphanes*
7 Ovary spiculate to papillose, sepals caudate . . . . subgenus *Pygmaeia* section *Pygmaeae*
    8 Petals without a protruding process (go to 9)
    8 Petals with a protruding process (go to 11b)
9 Sepals deeply connate into a tube, constricted above the middle . . . .
    . . . . subgenus *Masdevallia* section *Triotosiphon*
9 Sepals not connate into a constricted tube (go to 10)
    10 Lip thick, verrucose at the apex . . . . .subgenus *Masdevallia* section *Coriaceae*
    10 Lip thin, smooth, or microscopically verrucose at the apex (go to 11a)
11a Small, weak plant with membranous sepals . . . . subgenus *Pygmaeia* section *Amaluzae*
11a Strong, robust plant with fleshy sepals . . . . subgenus *Masdevallia* section *Reichenbachianae*
    11b Petals with a small callus above or along the margin . . . .
    . . . . subgenus *Masdevallia* section *Minutae*
    11b Petals with a protruding marginal process . . . . . subgenus *Masdevallia* section *Masdevallia*
12 Free sepals, with the bases of the lateral sepals forming a shallow cup with a curved column-foot; lip entire or with ill-defined marginal folds . . . . subgenus *Meleagris*
12 Sepals variously connate (go to 13)
    13 Ovary variously ornamented (go to 14)
    13 Ovary not ornamented; may be costate, ribbed, or smooth (go to 15)

14 Ovary crested, lateral sepals tailless . . . . subgenus *Pygmaeia* section *Aphanes*

14 Ovary and sepals echinate, sepals caudate-clavate . . . . subgenus *Pygmaeia* section *Pygmaeae*

  15 Petals with two distinct or two joined, descending basal processes . . . .
  . . . . subgenus *Masdevallia* section *Dentatae*

  15 Petals without a descending basal process (go to 16)

16 Sepals thickly rigid, lip thick, verrucose at the apex, with basal concavities . . . .
  . . . . subgenus *Masdevallia* section *Durae*

16 Sepals not thickly rigid, lip thin to thick, smooth or microscopically verrucose at the apex, not with basal concavities (go to 17)

  17 Inflorescence more or less lax, prostrate, horizontal or ascending, rarely erect . . . .
  . . . . subgenus *Masdevallia* section *Amaluzae*

  17 Inflorescence more or less congested, always erect (go to 18)

18 Petals without a protruding callus above or along the margin between the middle and basal thirds . . . . subgenus *Masdevallia* section *Minutae*

18 Petals with or without a low, marginal callus . . . subgenus *Masdevallia* section *Reichenbachianae*

  19 Inflorescence single-flowered (go to 20)

  19 Inflorescence double or many-flowered (go to 24)

20 Floral bract greatly inflated, engulfing pedicel, ovary, and base of the flower; petals with verrucose tips . . . . subgenus *Cucullatia*

20 Floral bract not engulfing base of the flower, petals not with verrucose tips (go to 21)

  21 Ovaries with tortuous, undulate lamellae; sepals nearly free; petals sharply tridentate . . . .
  . . . . subgenus *Fissia*

  21 Ovaries not with tortuous, undulate lamellae; sepals variously connate; petals not sharply tridentate (go to 22)

22 Ovaries not carinate . . . . few exceptions in subgenus *Polyantha* section *Polyanthae*

22 Ovaries carinate (go to 23)

  23 Ovaries carinate-crested; sepals connate into a tube inflated below the middle with a long, curved, column-foot . . . . subgenus *Nidificia*

  23 Ovaries carinate; sepals not connate into an inflated tube, with thick, twisted tails . . . .
  . . . . subgenus *Volvula*

24 Peduncle triquetrous . . . . subgenus *Polyantha* section *Alaticaules*

24 Peduncle terete (go to 25)

  25 Ovary carinate-crested; raceme simultaneously flowered; petals serrated or with a marginal callus . . . . subgenus *Amanda*

  25 Ovary not carinate; raceme simultaneously or more commonly successively flowered; petals with a marginal callus, never serrated . . . . . . subgenus *Polyantha* section *Polyanthae*

Subgenus *Amanda*

Species of this subgenus are characterized by a simultaneously flowered raceme with one to several flowers. The peduncle is terete (round in cross section), the ovaries are carinate (keeled) or crested, the sepals are variously fused (connate) into a cup or tube, the petals are relatively thin and variously toothed, and the lip is more or less divided by marginal folds into a hypochile (the basal portion) and an epichile (the terminal portion). This group contains more than 20 species and most of the species are endemic to Ecuador, although some are found in Costa Rica, Colombia, and Peru.

Type species *Masdevallia amanda*

The epithet for this species derives from the Latin *amandus*, meaning lovable. This species is variable in size and coloration and is found through all three cordilleras of Colombia to southeastern Ecuador at elevations ranging from 1700 to 2400 m. In the wild, this species is found on exposed rock faces and tree branches in cool cloud

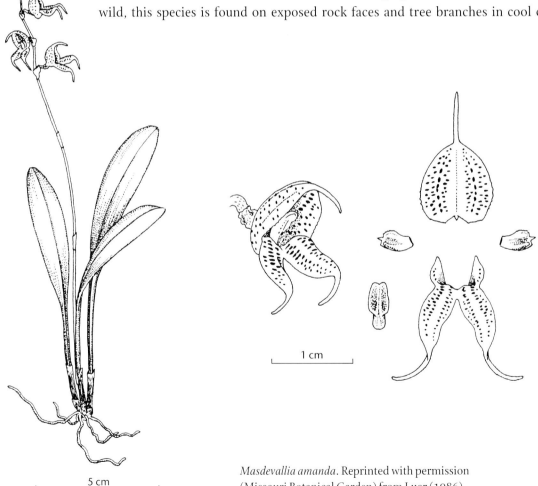

5 cm

1 cm

Masdevallia amanda. Reprinted with permission (Missouri Botanical Garden) from Luer (1986).

forests. This cool- to cold-growing small epiphyte grows in dense clumps. The ramicauls are very short and almost inconspicuous, with oblong-elliptic leaves that attenuate to the shortly petiolate base. The leathery, clear green leaf has a rounded, slightly indented apex. The plant blooms on an erect, scapose raceme, 12 to 16 cm long, bearing three to four flowers held well above the leaves. The campanulate (bell-like) flowers appear mostly in the winter and spring. This species can be separated from others by its racemose inflorescence, the shortly connate (having similar parts joined) sepals, the strongly arched dorsal sepal, and the keeled petals that are tridentate and serrulate.

Species attributed to subgenus *Amanda*

M. abbreviata Rchb.f.

M. ×alvaroi Luer and Escobar

M. amanda Rchb.f. and Warsc.

M. anceps Luer and Hirtz

M. bulbophyllopsis Kränzl.

M. caloptera Rchb.f.

M. chaestostoma Luer

M. corazonica Schltr.

M. dalstroemii Luer

M. delphina Luer

M. densiflora Luer

M. dimorphotricha Luer

M. graminea Luer

M. hydrae Luer

M. lehmannii Rchb.f.

M. leptoura Luer

M. melanopus Rchb.f.

M. microsiphon Luer

M. ova-avis Rchb.f.

M. pachyura Rchb.f.

M. polysticta Rchb.f.

M. porphyrea Luer

M. pozoi Königer

M. pulcherrima Luer and Andreetta

M. rafaeliana Luer

M. segrex Luer and Hirtz

M. sertula Luer and Andreetta

M. spathulifolia Kränzl.

M. staaliana Luer and Hirtz

M. tentaculata Luer

M. tridens Rchb.f.

M. vittatula Luer and Escobar

M. xanthodactyla Rchb.f.

M. zygia Luer and Malo

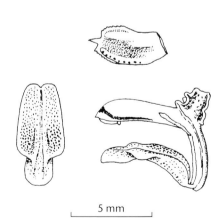

5 mm

Subgenus *Cucullatia*

The subgenus *Cucullatia* is characterized by single flowers and scapes, a terete peduncle, carinate ovaries, and a large and inflated floral bract that encloses the pedicel, the ovary, and part of the flower. The petals are callous or channeled at the apex and the lip is divided by marginal folds.

Type species *Masdevallia cucullata*

The name for this species derives from the Latin *cucullatus*, meaning hooded, in reference to the large, cucullate floral bract. The species is found in both Colombia and Ecuador at elevations ranging from 1600 to 2700 m. This cool-growing epiphyte blooms in the spring and summer on a solitary flowered inflorescence, 15 to 20 cm long, with a hooded flower held at leaf height and a large bract at the base of the sepaline tube. The glabrous sepals are a deep red to purple color, somewhat yellowish toward the base, with prominent external veins.

Species attributed to subgenus *Cucullatia*

M. cerastes Luer and Escobar	*M. delhierroi* Luer and Hirtz
M. corniculata Rchb.f.	*M. hercules* Luer and Andreetta
M. cucullata Lindl.	*M. vidua* Luer and Andreetta

Subgenus *Fissia*

This small subgenus contains three species (and one subspecies) that are characterized by solitary flowers, inflated floral bracts, curled or undulate ovarian crests, sepals free nearly to the base, a lip divided into a hypochile and an epichile, and a short column-foot. The epithet for this section is derived from the Latin *fissus*, meaning cleft, which refers to the free sepals of this subgenus. The type species is *Masdevallia picturata*.

Type species *Masdevallia picturata*

This miniature species is found over a wide range in Bolivia, Colombia, Costa Rica, Guyana, Peru, and Venezuela in the wet cloud forests, where it grows on tree trunks. It is found at elevations of 1500 to 2450 m. It blooms on an erect, 4 cm long, single-flowered inflorescence that holds the flowers above the leaves. Two natural varieties have been identified—a large, colorful form that occurs at high elevations and a dwarf form

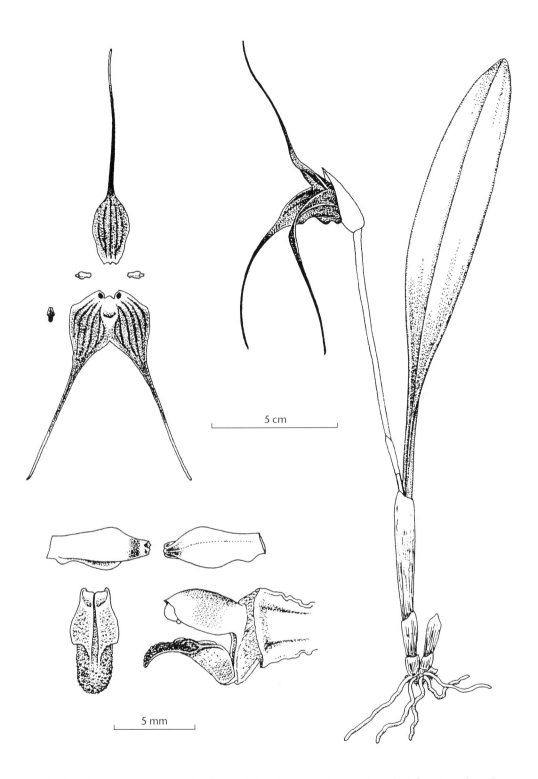

Masdevallia cucullata. Reprinted with permission (Missouri Botanical Garden) from Luer (1986).

5 cm

5 mm

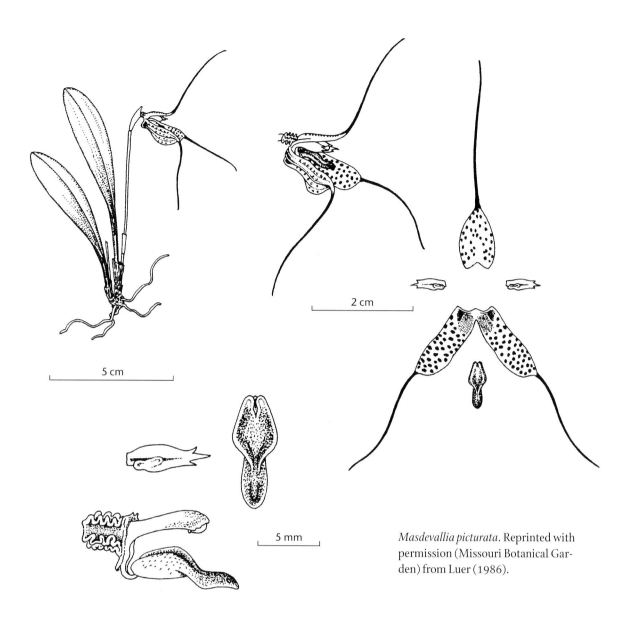

5 cm

2 cm

5 mm

Masdevallia picturata. Reprinted with permission (Missouri Botanical Garden) from Luer (1986).

with more pallid flowers that occurs at lower altitudes. This cool to intermediate growing species prefers partial shade and blooms in fall to winter.

Species attributed to subgenus *Fissia*

M. mutica Luer and Escobar   *M. picturata* ssp. *minor* Rchb.f.
M. picturata Rchb.f.   *M. pleurothalloides* Luer

Subgenus *Masdevallia*

This subgenus contains the majority of the species in the genus. Species in this subgenus are characterized by single or successive flowers borne by a terete peduncle. The sepals are variously connate into a widely spread or tubular flower. The petals are variable and callous with or without a protruding process. The lip is entire, with or without calli, but not divided by marginal folds. This subgenus is divided into eight sections and five subsections. The type for this subgenus, by definition, is the same as the type for the genus, *Masdevallia uniflora*.

Section *Coriaceae*

The name for this section derives from the Latin *coriaceus*, meaning leathery, referring to the texture of leaves and possibly the flowers of species assigned to this section. The type species is *Masdevallia coriacea*. This is a large section of interrelated species, many of which have fleshy, often malodorous flowers. The petals are cartilaginous without a tooth, but an obtuse angle may be present. The lip is thick and ligulate, undivided by lateral folds, and the usually rounded apex is verrucose. The base is often more or less cordate with the basal lobes concave and possibly nectariferous. The species of this section are single flowered and wholly Andean in origin.

Type species *Masdevallia coriacea*

This plant is medium- to large-sized and terrestrial (although it can be, but rarely is, epiphytic). It has an inflorescence characterized by a solitary, large, waxy, pale green flower borne by a stout, suberect to erect peduncle, 10 to 24 cm long, more or less spotted with purple. This species is locally common in the grassy páramos of the Eastern Cordillera of Colombia, at elevations ranging from 2100 to 3300 m. A similar but smaller plant with a much greater distribution was described by Reichenbach as *Masdevallia bonplandii*, which was later classified as a subspecies of *M. coriacea*. More recently, *M. bonplandii* has been returned to species status.

Species attributed to subgenus *Masdevallia* section *Coriaceae*

M. angulata Rchb.f.
M. atahualpa Luer
M. belua Königer and D. D'Alessandro
M. bonplandii Rchb.f.
M. bourdetteana Luer
M. cacodes Luer and Escobar
M caesia Roezl
M. campyloglossa Rchb.f.
M. civilis Rchb.f. and Warsc.
M. colossus Luer
M. coriacea Lindl.
M. elephanticeps Rchb.f. and Warsc.
M. foetens Luer and Escobar
M. fractiflexa Lehm. and Kränzl.
M. fragrans Woolward
M. gargantua Rchb.f.
M. hylodes Luer and Escobar
M. hystrix Luer and Hirtz
M. lappifera Luer and Hirtz
M. leontoglossa Rchb.f.
M. lilianae Luer
M. macroglossa Rchb.f.

M. macrura Rchb.f.
M. maloi Luer
M. misasii Braas
M. mooreana Rchb.f.
M. murex Luer
M. oscarii Luer and Escobar
M. pachyantha Rchb.f.

M. pachysepala (Rchb.f.) Luer
M. pardina Rchb.f.
M. peristeria Rchb.f.
M. picea Luer
M. platyglossa Rchb.f.
M. rigens Luer
M. sanctae-rosae Kränzl.

M. semiteres Luer and Escobar
M. spilantha Königer
M. strumosa Ortiz and Calderón
M. sumapazensis Ortiz
M. torta Rchb.f.
M. velella Luer
M. velifera Rchb.f.

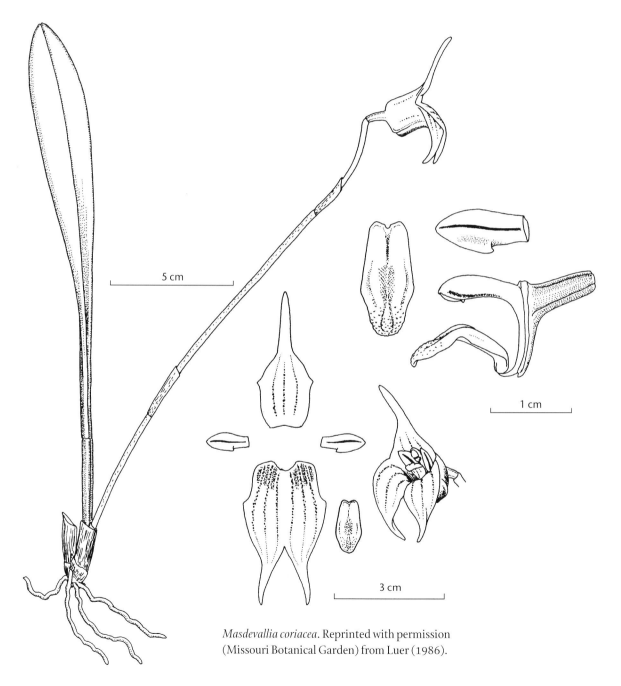

Masdevallia coriacea. Reprinted with permission (Missouri Botanical Garden) from Luer (1986).

Section *Dentatae*

Together with the section *Durae* of the subgenus *Masdevallia*, and section *Polyanthae* of the subgenus *Polyantha*, the section *Dentatae* of subgenus *Masdevallia* is distinguished by a successively flowered inflorescence; a terete peduncle; and thick, fleshy sepals that are variously connate into a sepaline cup or tube. The petals are thickly callous below the middle, with a descending process, and the base of the lip is without cavities. Currently, only four species meet the criteria for this section. The first described was *M. collina*.

Type species *Masdevallia collina*

This species was first discovered in Panama by Paul Allen, when he was botanically exploring for the *Flora of Panama* in 1940. It is endemic to central Panama, growing at 900 to 1000 m, and it is also known as one of the species that will epiphytically colonize cultivated orange groves. This species is characterized by a congested, successively flowered raceme on a terete peduncle. The flowers are rigid with short tails on the lateral sepals, and they are purple and glossy in appearance.

Species attributed to subgenus *Masdevallia* section *Dentatae*

M. collina L. O. Williams	*M. macrogenia* (Arango) Luer and Escobar
M. dryada Luer and Escobar	*M. zapatae* Luer and Escobar

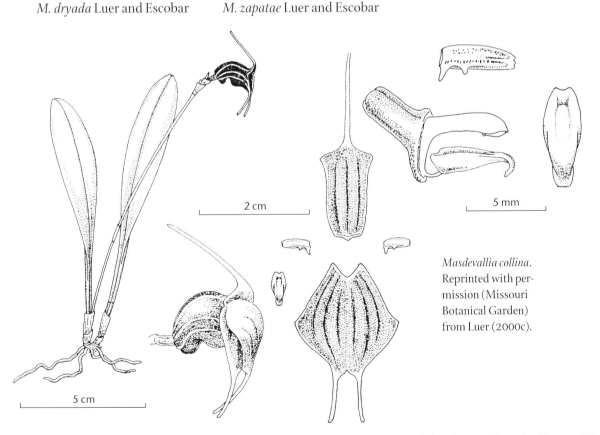

2 cm

5 mm

5 cm

Masdevallia collina. Reprinted with permission (Missouri Botanical Garden) from Luer (2000c).

Section *Durae*

This section is named after the Latin *duras*, meaning hard, which refers to the texture of the flowers. Most of the species are Andean in origin, although *Masdevallia utriculata* is Panamanian. This section contains some of the most spectacular species in the genus *Masdevallia*, although none of the more spectacular species were known to exist prior to 1978. *Masdevallia dura*, one of the more drab members of this section, was first collected by Hübsch in 1884 or thereabouts. These species have a successively flowered inflorescence; thick, fleshy sepals; and thick, callous petals. The lip is thick, oblong, and obtuse, with deeply concave basal lobes.

Type species *Masdevallia dura*

This species occurs locally, but abundantly, in the cold cloud forests of southern Ecuador at elevations of about 3000 m. Accumulations of hundreds of plants may be found on the trunks of old, fallen trees. The plant has unusually hard, rigid, long-lasting flowers that are produced successively in pendent racemes. The successive habit and ever-lengthening racemes allow the plants to remain continuously in flower for years. The sepals are connate into a short, nondilated, cylindrical tube, from which the rigid tails spread.

Species attributed to subgenus *Masdevallia* section *Durae*

M. ayabacana Luer	*M. princeps* Luer
M. dura Luer	*M. regina* Luer
M. goliath Luer and Andreetta	*M. robusta* Luer
M. newmaniana Luer and Teague	*M. titan* Luer
M. panguiënsis Luer and Andreetta	*M. utriculata* Luer

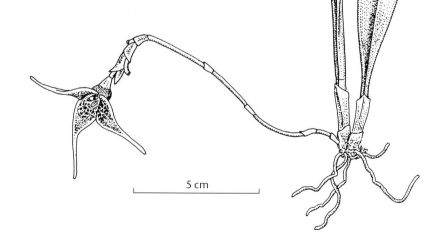

5 cm

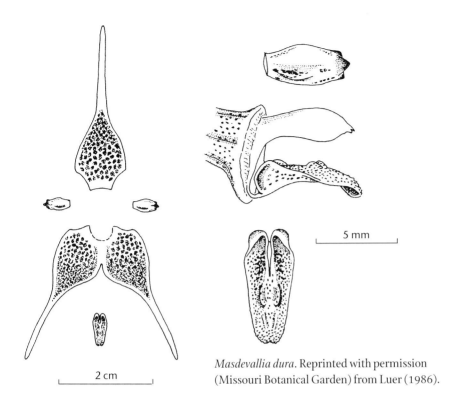

Masdevallia dura. Reprinted with permission (Missouri Botanical Garden) from Luer (1986).

Section *Masdevallia*

Subsection *Caudatae*

This subsection is characterized by sepals that are connate basally, forming a short, gaping, sepaline cup, with the free portions widely spread. The column, petals, and lips are exposed, and the petals have a well developed basal process.

Type species *Masdevallia caudata*

The epithet for this species is from the Latin *caudatus*, meaning with tails, which refers to the caudate sepals of this species. The flowers are very large, to 16 cm (tall) or even larger. The species is found in western Venezuela, Colombia, Ecuador, and Peru. It is a cool to intermediate growing, tufted epiphyte found in cloud forests at elevations of 2000 to 2500 m and has blackish, slender, erect ramicauls. The plant blooms in the late autumn through early spring with an arching, short, slender, 12 to 13 cm long inflorescence arising from low on the ramicaul. The flowers are fragrant and variable in color.

Species attributed to subgenus *Masdevallia* section *Masdevallia* subsection *Caudatae*

M. acaroi Luer and Hirtz
M. alismifolia Kränzl.
M. antonii Königer
M. apparitio Luer and Escobar
M. arminii Linden and Rchb.f.
M. asterotricha Königer
M. boliviensis Schltr.
M. bottae Luer and Andreetta
M. brockmuelleri Luer
M. caudata Lindl.
M. cloesii Luer
M. cordeliana Luer
M. cyclotega Königer
M. cylix Luer and Malo
M. decumana Königer
M. discolor Luer and Escobar
M. estradae Rchb.f.
M. eucharis Luer
M. eumeliae Luer
M. expansa Rchb.f.
M. harlequina Luer
M. hubeinii Luer and Würstle
M. icterina Königer

M. immensa Luer
M. instar Luer and Andreetta
M. iris Luer and Escobar
M. klabochiorum Rchb.f.
M. leonii D. E. Benn and Christenson
M. ludibunda Rchb.f.
M. ludibundella Luer and Escobar
M. lychniphora Königer
M. mandarina (Luer and Escobar) Luer
M. marizae Luer
M. nivea Luer and Escobar
M. pandurilabia C. Schweinf.
M. papillosa Luer
M. pernix Königer
M. phlogina Luer
M. pileata Luer and Würstle
M. polychroma Luer
M. prodigiosa Königer
M. purpurella Luer and Escobar

M. renzii Luer
M. replicata Königer
M. rhinophora Luer and Escobar
M. rufescens Königer
M. sanctae-inesiae Luer and Malo
M. schizantha Kränzl.
M. schmidt-mummii Luer and Escobar
M. setacea Luer
M. stigii Luer and Jost
M. triangularis Lindl.
M. tricallosa Königer
M. valenciae Luer and Escobar
M. venatoria Luer and Malo
M. vexillifera Luer
M. wuelfinghoffiana Luer and J. J. Portilla
M. wurdackii C. Schweinf.
M. xanthina Rchb.f.
M. zamorensis Luer and J. J. Portilla

Subsection *Coccineae*

The species of this subsection are found in the Andean mountains of Colombia, Ecuador, and Peru and make up some of the largest and showiest of the genus. Most of the species are characterized by a very long peduncle, which bears a large, solitary, intensely colorful flower. The sepals are connate into a slender, cylindrical sepaline tube, but beyond the orifice the lateral sepals are expanded and are much larger and broader than the dorsal sepal. The petals and lip are out of sight, hidden deep within the sepaline tube.

Type species *Masdevallia coccinea*

Masdevallia coccinea is found in Colombia and possibly Peru (information from Peru may be false, based on a misidentified specimen of *M. amabilis* that was collected at elevations of 2400 to 2800 m). It is a cold-growing, terrestrial species with erect leaves, and it blooms in the spring. It has short ramicauls enveloped by two or three closed, tu-

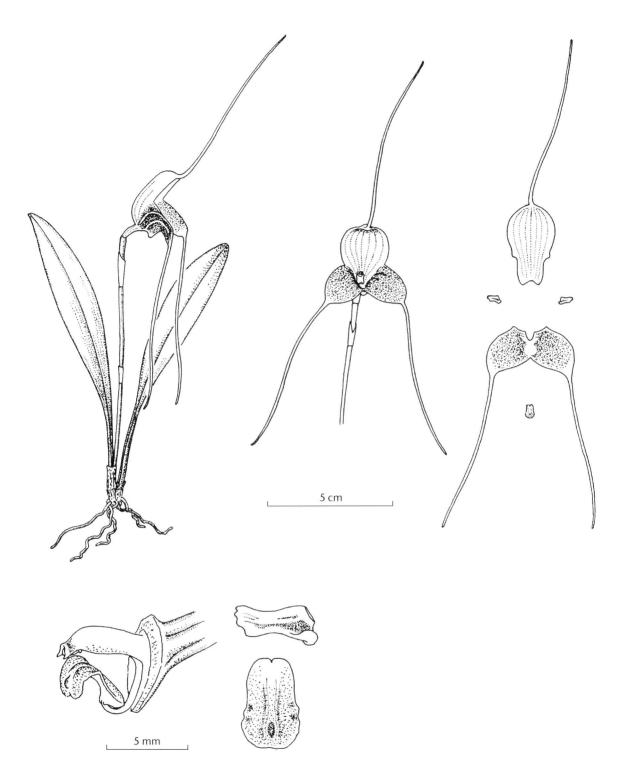

Masdevallia caudata. Reprinted with permission
(Missouri Botanical Garden) from Luer (1986).

bular sheaths. The leaves are oblong-lanceolate to spathulate, petiolate, and rounded and minutely tridentate at the apex. Solitary flowers bloom on a slender, erect inflorescence, to 30 cm long, and slightly flexous. The bract is spotted at each node, and the waxy, variable-sized flowers are held higher than the leaves. This species comes in many different color forms.

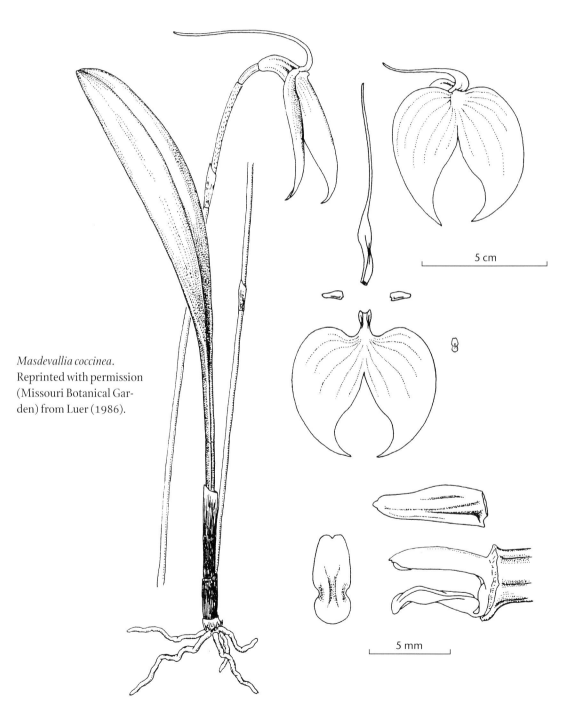

Masdevallia coccinea. Reprinted with permission (Missouri Botanical Garden) from Luer (1986).

Species attributed to subgenus *Masdevallia* section *Masdevallia* subsection *Coccineae*

M. amabilis Rchb.f. and Warsc.	*M. echinata* Luer	*M. stumpflei* Braas
M. barlaena Rchb.f.	*M. idea* Luer and Arias	*M. veitchiana* Rchb.f.
M. coccinea Linden ex Lindl.	*M. ignea* Rchb.f.	*M. venusta* Schltr.
M. davisii Rchb.f.	*M. niesseniae* Luer	*M. welischii* Luer
M. deformis Kränzl.	*M. rosea* Lindl.	

Subsection *Masdevallia*

This large subsection has many dissimilar plants, but in general it is characterized by single flowers, smooth ovaries, petals with a prominent process, and a comparatively thin lip. The sepals are variously connate from below the middle to near the apex and form cups or noncylindric tubes. The petals have a prominent, marginal process.

Type species *Masdevallia uniflora*

This species, the original *Masdevallia* identified in the late 18th century, is found in Ecuador and central Peru at elevations of 2500 to 3000 m. It is a medium-sized, caespitose terrestrial that can be found among rocks, or it grows epiphytically on scrub trees in cloud forests. The plants are characterized by short, slender, erect ramicauls enveloped by two to three loose, tubular bracts. The leaves are erect, coriaceous, elliptic, long petiolate, and acute at the apex and gradually narrow into the petiole. The flowers, which bloom in the winter, are borne on an erect, 22 cm tall, wiry, single-flowered inflorescence that arises low on the ramicaul with a bract below the middle and an acute, tubular bract with the campanulate flower held well above the leaves. Distinguishing factors of this species are the fuchsia-colored flowers, the relatively short sepal tails, the prominent basal petal lobes, and the elongate column-foot.

Species attributed to subgenus *Masdevallia* section *Masdevallia* subsection *Masdevallia*

M. assurgens Luer and Escobar	*M. datura* Luer and Vásquez	*M. gilbertoi* Luer and Escobar
M. burianii Luer and Dalström	*M. deniseana* Luer and J. J. Portilla	*M. glandulosa* Königer
M. calocalix Luer	*M. dreisei* Luer	*M. glomerosa* Luer and Andreetta
M. carpishica Luer and Cloes	*M. dudleyi* Luer	*M. guayanensis* Lindl. ex Benth.
M. chaparensis Hashimoto	*M. elachys* Luer	*M. hartmanii* Luer
M. clandestina Luer and Escobar	*M. elegans* Luer and Escobar	*M. heideri* Königer
M. cleistogama Luer	*M. encephala* Luer and Escobar	*M. helenae* Luer
M. condorensis Luer and Hirtz	*M. ensata* Rchb.f.	*M. hians* Rchb.f.
M. corderoana Lehm. and Kränzl.	*M. exquisita* Luer and Escobar	*M. hieroglyphica* Rchb.f.
M. cranion Luer	*M. falcago* Rchb.f.	*M. hymenantha* Rchb.f.
M. crassicaudis Luer and J. J. Portilla	*M. figueroae* Luer	*M. ionocharis* Rchb.f.

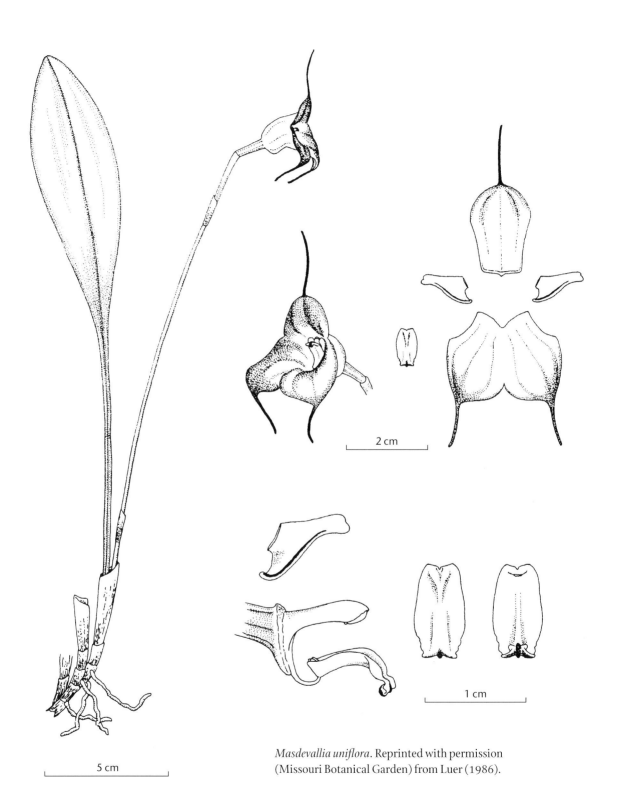

Masdevallia uniflora. Reprinted with permission
(Missouri Botanical Garden) from Luer (1986).

M. ishikoi Luer

M. juan-albertoi Luer and Arias

M. karineae Nauray ex Luer

M. laevis Lindl.

M. lamprotyria Königer

M. leonardoi Luer

M. leucantha Lehm. and Kränzl.

M. lewisii Luer and Vásquez

M. lilacina Königer

M. lineolata Königer

M. lucernula Königer

M. macropus Lehm. and Kränzl.

M. manaloi Luer and Arias

M. mastodon Rchb.f.

M. medinae Luer and J. J. Portilla

M. melanoglossa Luer

M. midas Luer

M. nebulina Luer

M. nitens Luer

M. norops Luer and Andreetta

M. odontocera Luer and Escobar

M. os-viperae Luer and Andreetta

M. paivaëana Rchb.f.

M. patriciana Luer

M. phacopsis Luer and Dalström

M. picta Luer

M. popowiana Königer and J. G. Wein

M. pumila Poepp and Endl.

M. quasimodo Luer and Teague

M. repanda Luer and Hirtz

M. rimarima-alba Luer

M. roseola Luer

M. scandens Rolfe

M. schoonenii Luer

M. selenites Königer

M. soennemarkii Luer and Dalström

M. solomonii Luer and Vásquez

M. ×strumella Luer

M. strumifera Rchb.f.

M. strumosa Ortiz and Calderón

M. suinii Luer and Hirtz

M. terborchii Luer

M. tinekeae Luer and Vásquez

M. trautmanniana Luer and J. J. Portilla

M. truncata Luer

M. tubulosa Lindl.

M. uncifera Rchb.f.

M. uniflora Ruiz and Pavón

M. urceolaris Kränzl.

M. ustulata Luer

M. vasquezii Luer

M. verecunda Luer

M. yungasensis Hashimoto

M. yungasensis ssp. *calocodon* (Luer & Vásquez) Luer

M. zebracea Luer

Subsection *Oscillantes*

This subsection, according to Luer, is closely allied to subsection *Caudatae*. The significant difference is the lip with winglike, lateral margins that may be modified into lobes, and a base that is delicately hinged or balanced by a thin, flat, straplike extension from the column-foot. This hinge allows the lip to move, or oscillate, upon exposure to a slight motion or breeze. Some species have a lip intermediate between subsections *Oscillantes* and *Caudatae*, which makes their classification into either of the two subsections unclear. Species with intermediate lips that are included in *Oscillantes* are *Masdevallia amoena*, *M. ariasii*, *M. dalessandroi*, and *M. josei*.

Type species *Masdevallia wageneriana*

This species is named after the German plant collector Herman Wagener. This small, tufted, epiphytic species with suberect leaves and slender roots is endemic to a coastal range of mountains in northern Venezuela, at elevations of 1400 to 2200 m. The leaves are coriaceous and the inflorescence, to 5 cm long, consists of a single flower borne by a suberect to horizontal pedicel. This was the first of the species with an oscillating lip to be described. The complicated, delicately hinged but balanced lip protrudes from the little gaping sepaline cup. This species grows cool to warm and blooms in the spring, summer, and fall.

Species attributed to subgenus *Masdevallia* section *Masdevallia* subsection *Oscillantes*

M. albella Luer and Teague
M. amoena Luer
M. andreettana Luer
M. ariasii Luer
M. castor Luer and Cloes
M. catapheres Königer
M. citrinella Luer and Malo
M. cretata Luer
M. dalessandroi Luer
M. ejiriana Luer and J. J. Portilla
M. formosa Luer and Cloes

M. josei Luer
M. manta Königer
M. microptera Luer and Würstle
M. nikoleana Luer and J. J. Portilla
M. ortalis Luer
M. persicina Luer
M. phasmatodes Königer
M. pollux Luer and Cloes
M. pteroglossa Schltr.

M. rhodehameliana Luer
M. rodolfoi (Braas) Luer
M. rubeola Luer and Vásquez
M. rubiginosa Königer
M. sulphurella Königer
M. tricycla Luer
M. wageneriana Linden ex Lindl.
M. ×wübbenii Luer
M. zongoënsis Luer and Hirtz

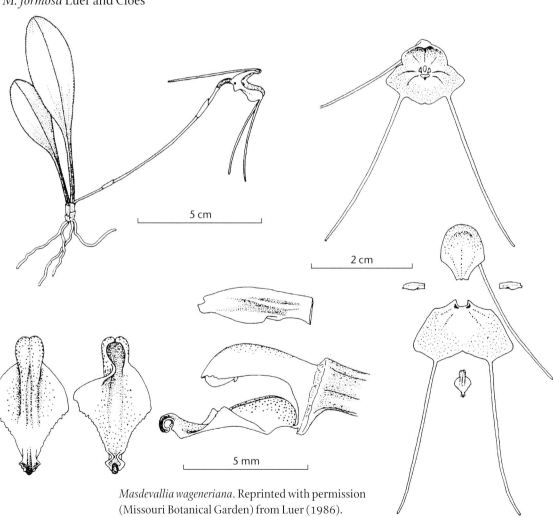

Masdevallia wageneriana. Reprinted with permission (Missouri Botanical Garden) from Luer (1986).

Subsection *Saltatrices*

This subsection is characterized by species with sepals deeply connate into a long, sepaline tube that is more or less constricted above the middle or below the free segments and more or less ventricose below the constriction. The species of this subsection are found in the Andes of Colombia, Ecuador, and Peru.

Type species *Masdevallia saltatrix*

This species is endemic in the region around Frontino in the Western Cordillera of Colombia. The first specimen was collected by Roezl in 1884 at an elevation of 2000 m. This small, epiphytic, caespitose species has slender, erect, 1 to 2 cm ramicauls enclosed by two or three loose, tubular sheaths. The inflorescence consists of a solitary flower borne by a slender, erect to suberect peduncle 2 to 6 cm long, with a bract near the base. The sepals are glossy red-purple externally, yellow dotted with red, and cellular pubescent within. The dorsal sepal is oblong, connate to the lateral sepals for 2 to 3 cm, forming an erect, curved, ventricose, cylindrical tube that is constricted below the ostium.

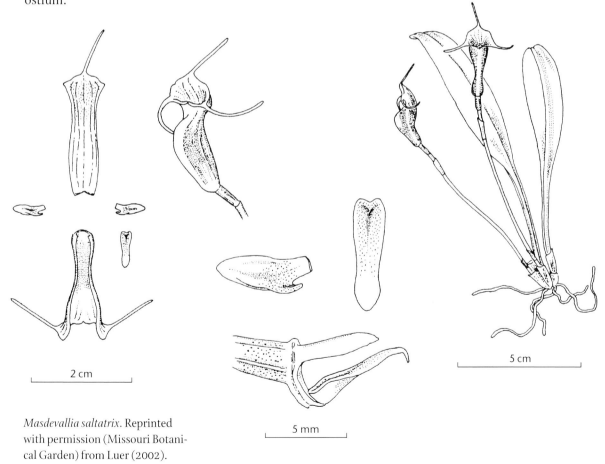

2 cm

5 cm

5 mm

Masdevallia saltatrix. Reprinted with permission (Missouri Botanical Garden) from Luer (2002).

Species attributed to subgenus *Masdevallia* section *Masdevallia* subsection *Saltatrices*

M. agaster Luer

M. ampullacea Luer and Andreetta

M. anemone Luer

M. angulifera Rchb.f. ex Kränzl.

M. aurea Luer

M. calosiphon Luer

M. chuspipatae Luer and Teague

M. constricta Peopp. and Endl.

M. eurynogaster Luer and Andreetta

M. filaria Luer and Escobar

M. fuchsii Luer

M. hirtzii Luer and Andreetta

M. ×ligiae Luer and Escobar

M. limax Luer

M. marthae Luer and Escobar

M. maxilimax Luer

M. mendozae Luer

M. morochoi Luer and Andreetta

M. ×mystica Luer

M. notosibirica Maekawa and Hashimoto

M. os-draconis Luer and Escobar

M. rex Luer and Hirtz

M. ricii Luer and Vásquez

M. saltatrix Rchb.f.

M. siphonantha Luer

M. strobelii Sweet and Garay

M. tubata Schltr.

M. ventricularia Rchb.f.

Section *Minutae*

Reichenbach first designated the subgeneric category *Minutae* for a single species, *Masdevallia minuta*. Florence Woolward, in her 1896 monograph *The Genus Masdevallia*, proposed the section *Minutae*, describing it as a collection of small, miscellaneous species not readily classified into any other group. Later revisions reclassified many of the species Woolward had included in this section, but Luer has classified 20 species originating from Mexico to Bolivia, based on their morphological characteristics, to section *Minutae*. Most of the species in this section are found in Central America. Luer recognizes that there is potential "overlap" with section *Reichenbachianae*, since several species of that section, namely *M. lankesteriana* and *M. mejiana*, have intermediate characteristics between the two sections. Section *Minutae* is characterized by single flowers or (more commonly) a successively few-flowered raceme. The peduncles are terete. The petals are distinguished by a protrusion from the callus between the middle and lower thirds that may occur above or along the labellar margin. The lip is more or less oblong, with a longitudinal pair of more or less converging calli on or above the middle third of the disc.

Type species *Masdevallia minuta*

The species epithet comes from the Latin *minutus*, meaning very small, which refers to the habit of the plant. This species was first collected by Splittgerben in 1842. This widely distributed species is found in the forests of the mountain lowlands surrounding the Amazon basin. The miniature plants come from Venezuela, Surinam, Guyana, French Guiana, Colombia, Ecuador, Peru, and Bolivia, where they grow terrestrially or epiphytically at elevations of 220 to 1000 m. The length of leaves, peduncles, and pedicels of this species are somewhat variable. The plant has slender, erect ramicauls that are enveloped basally by two to three tubular sheaths and carries a single, apical, erect, coriaceous, narrowly obovate, subacute leaf that gradually narrows below into an indistinct petiolate base. *Masdevallia minuta* grows best under intermediate conditions and blooms in the summer and fall.

Species attributed to subgenus *Masdevallia* section *Minutae*

M. adamsii Luer
M. arangoi Luer and Escobar
M. attenuata Rchb.f.
M. chontalensis Rchb.f.
M. crescenticola Lehm. and Kränzl.
M. flaveola Rchb.f.
M. floribunda Lindl.

M. geminiflora Ortiz
M. gutierrezii Luer
M. herradurae Lehm. and Kränzl.
M. laucheana Kränzl.
M. livingstoneana Roezl and Rchb.f.
M. minuta Lindl.

M. nicaraguae Luer
M. pescadoënsis Luer and Escobar
M. scabrilinguis Luer
M. tokachiorum Luer
M. tonduzii Woolward
M. tubuliflora Ames
M. wendlandiana Rchb.f.

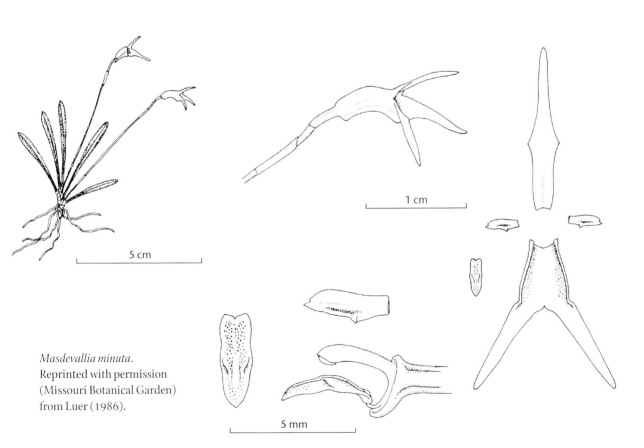

Masdevallia minuta.
Reprinted with permission (Missouri Botanical Garden) from Luer (1986).

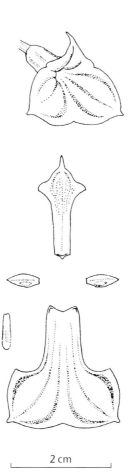

Section *Racemosae*

This section consists of a single Colombian species and is set apart from all of the other *Masdevallia* subgenera and sections by its habit: a long, creeping, or ascending rhizome and a loose inflorescence that produces several flowers simultaneously and successively. The sepals are tailless.

Type species *Masdevallia racemosa*

This unique species is the only long-repent species in the genus *Masdevallia*. It is endemic in the subpáramo forests at high elevations (3000 m) in southern Colombia. It grows in the shade of large trees in loose, leafy humus. The successively flowered racemes usually bear no more than two scarlet flowers at any time, but as many as eighteen may be produced. The sepaline tube is cylindrical below the middle, where the broad, obtuse, tailless sepals expand abruptly.

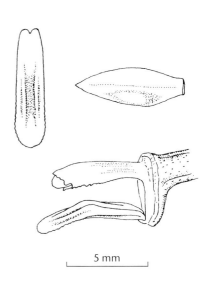

5 mm

Masdevallia racemosa. Reprinted with permission (Missouri Botanical Garden) from Luer (1986).

5 cm

2 cm

Section *Reichenbachianae*

This section was first proposed by Woolward in her 1896 monograph on *Masdevallia*. In the original description of the section, Woolward included seven closely allied Central American species, to which Luer added five additional species. As mentioned, this section is closely allied to the section *Minutae*. Species of this section are medium-sized plants with terete peduncles. The plants are characterized by single flowers or a successively few-flowered raceme. The sepals are slender-tailed and usually not as fleshy as those in section *Coriaceae*. The petals have a marginal callus without a descending process and a more or less callous but undivided lip.

Type species *Masdevallia reichenbachiana*

The section and type species are named in honor of Heinrich Gustav Reichenbach, the orchidologist of the Hamburg Botanical Garden who in the late 19th century con-

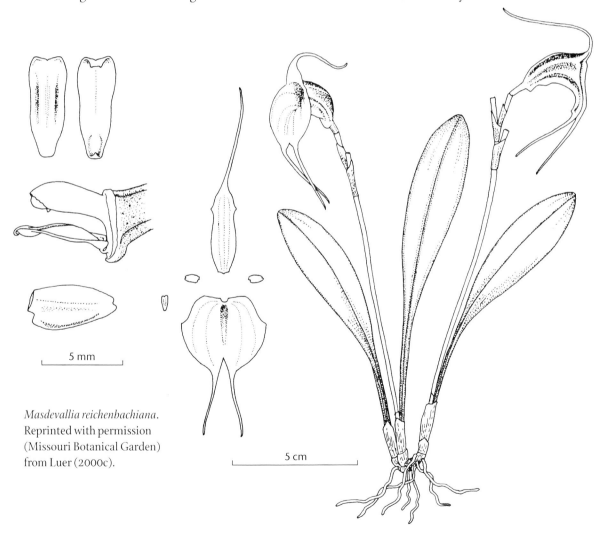

5 mm

Masdevallia reichenbachiana.
Reprinted with permission
(Missouri Botanical Garden)
from Luer (2000c).

5 cm

tributed many species to the genus *Masdevallia*. This species was first discovered in 1875 by Endres, who sent living plants back to Europe with the request that the species be named after his friend, Professor Reichenbach. This medium-sized, warm- to cool-growing epiphytic species is endemic to the dense, wet cloud forests of Costa Rica, where it grows low on mossy tree trunks at elevations of 1500 to 2200 m. The plant has terete stems of 1.2 to 2.6 cm long, enveloped by two to three thin, tubular bracts. The leaf is fleshy, oblanceolate, coriaceous, keeled below, and minutely triden- tate apically. The plant blooms successively in spring and summer with a slender, erect, 17.5 to 20 cm long, terete, bright green inflorescence that carries one to three flowers held above the leaves.

Species attributed to subgenus *Masdevallia* section *Reichenbachianae*

M. calura Rchb.f.

M. chasei Luer

M. demissa Rchb.f.

M. eburnea Luer and Maduro

M. enallax Königer

M. fulvescens Rolfe

M. gloriae Luer and Maduro

M. lankesteriana Luer

M. marginella Rchb.f.

M. mejiana Garay

M. ×polita Luer and Sijm

M. reichenbachiana Endres ex Rchb.f.

M. rolfeana Kränzl.

M. schroederiana Sander ex Veitch

M. walteri Luer

Section *Triotosiphon*

The section *Triotosiphon* is characterized by small flowers with sepals that are connate into a tube that is constricted above the middle. The apices are equal, more or less elongate, but tailless. The petals lack a protruding process.

Type species *Masdevallia bangii*

This tiny species was named in honor of its discoverer, Miguel Bang, a famous early 20th century plant collector in Bolivia. The plant originates from Ecuador to central Bolivia, where it grows in tufts on the mossy branches of small trees at elevations of 1000 to 2000 m. This species grows abundantly in cool, moist forests. The tiny leaves vary in length in different populations (shorter or longer than the inflorescence). The whitish sepals are connate into a tube that is constricted above the middle, with the short, thick, free portions spread. The petals and lip are hidden within the tube and are also quite variable between populations. The lip is constant in the presence of a pair of longitudinal calli, which end in marginal angles above the middle.

Species attributed to subgenus *Masdevallia* section *Triotosiphon*

M. bangii Schltr.

M. gnoma Sweet

M. irapana Sweet

M. kyphonantha Sweet

M. lansbergii (Rchb.f.) Schltr.

M. venezuelana Sweet

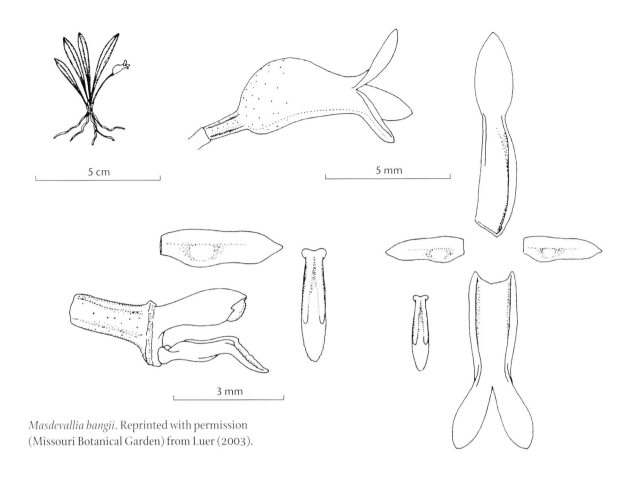

Masdevallia bangii. Reprinted with permission
(Missouri Botanical Garden) from Luer (2003).

Subgenus *Meleagris*

The subgenus *Meleagris* is characterized by a successively flowered raceme, terete peduncle, costate ovaries, free sepals, petals with a low callus, and lips with ill-defined marginal folds.

Type species *Masdevallia meleagris*

The name for this species derives from the Latin *meleagris*, a guinea fowl or peacock, which refers to the colorful flowers. The plant is medium in size and grows epiphytically. It was first collected by Hartweg in the first half of the 19th century in the Eastern Cordillera of Colombia. It is characterized by a short, successively flowered raceme that is borne on a peduncle that is round in cross section. The dorsal sepal is free, and the lateral sepals are free nearly to the column-foot. The lip is hinged over the edge of the foot. This species is difficult to grow, as are most of the other species in this subgenus.

Species attributed to subgenus *Meleagris*

M. alexandri Luer   *M. meleagris* Lindl.

M. anisomorpha Garay   *M. parvula* Schltr.

M. heteroptera Rchb.f.   *M. segurae* Luer and Escobar

M. hortensis Luer and Escobar

Masdevallia meleagris. Reprinted with permission
(Missouri Botanical Garden) from Luer (1986).

Subgenus *Nidificia*

The five species of this section are endemic to the mountains of Central America, Colombia, and Ecuador. This section is characterized by the single-flowered inflorescence; more or less inflated floral bract; carinate or crested ovary; sepals connate into a short or cylindrical sepaline tube with a bulbous or broad base created in part by a long, curved column-foot; and a lip divided into a hypochile and an epichile that stands erect within the flower. The type species is *Masdevallia nidifica*.

Type species *Masdevallia nidifica*

Masdevallia nidifica is found from Costa Rica to Ecuador. The epithet derives from the Latin *nidificus*, meaning built like a nest, in reference to the caespitose (growing in

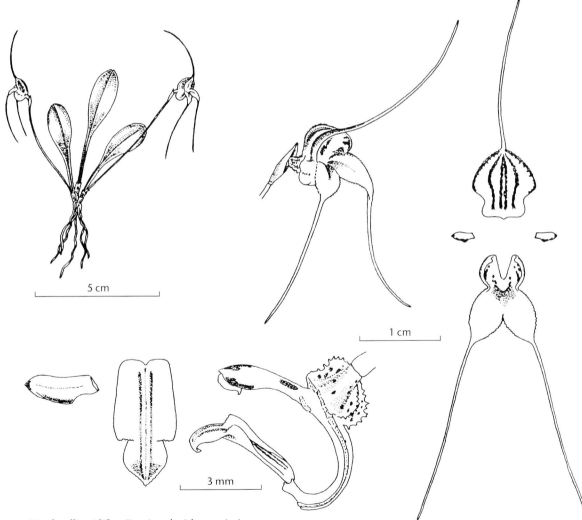

5 cm

1 cm

3 mm

Masdevallia nidifica. Reprinted with permission (Missouri Botanical Garden) from Luer (1986).

dense tufts) habit of the plant. This dwarf epiphytic species can grow cool to warm. It is found in windy, lower montane cloud forests on slender branches at elevations of 500 to 2000 m. This species is solitary flowered, with an arching inflorescence of 1.5 to 5 cm long, held at or above the leaves. The plant blooms in the winter and summer.

Species attributed to subgenus *Nidificia*

M. dynastes Luer *M. nidifica* Rchb.f.
M. molossoides Kränzl. *M. ventricosa* Schltr.
M. molossus Rchb.f.

Subgenus *Polyantha*

This group of species was recently reclassified as a subgenus by Luer (2000a). Subgenus *Polyantha* is characterized by racemes of flowers that may be either successive or simultaneous in blooming. The petals are smooth and the lips divided near the middle by marginal folds into an epichile and a hypochile. (Note that all other taxa of *Masdevallia* with divided lips are single-flowered.) The leaves are thickly coriaceous, borne by short, stout ramicauls. Species of this subgenus are found throughout the Andes of South America, with a few species in Central America.

Section *Alaticaules*

This large section is distinguished by having triquetrous (triangular in cross section) peduncles. The sepals are more or less fleshy, usually with tails, and variously connate into a cup or tube. This section is subdivided into two subsections based upon the raceme, which can be simultaneously flowered or successively flowered.

Subsection *Alaticaules*
Species in subsection *Alaticaules* are successively flowered.

Type species *Masdevallia melanoxantha*
The epithet is from the Greek *melanoxanthos*, meaning dark yellow, referring to the color of the flower. Two collectors, N. Funck and Louis Schlim, collected plants in Venezuela and Colombia for Jean Linden between 1846 and 1852, and this species was one of the many discoveries made by the pair. (Linden and his son Lucien were renowned commercial orchid growers in Belgium.) The species is endemic in the northern part of the Eastern Cordillera of Colombia (1100 to 2800 m) and adjacent Venezuela. This is a medium to large epiphytic species with thickly coriaceous leaves and coarse roots. The slender, 20 to 30 cm, triquetrous peduncle is much longer than

the leaves and bears a succession of rigidly fleshy flowers. The sepaline tube is short. The dorsal sepal, greenish in color, ends in an erect, narrowly triangular, purple-suffused tail. The synsepal is dark purple, velvety, and ends in a pair of acute, approximate apices. The lip is characterized by finlike callous folds that demarcate the two halves. The petals are yellow and the lip light yellow flecked with purple. The species can be grown warm to cool and blooms in the summer.

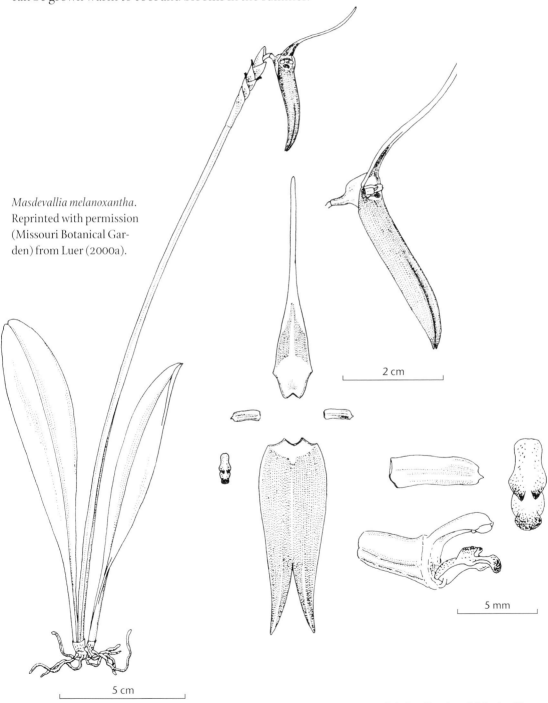

Masdevallia melanoxantha. Reprinted with permission (Missouri Botanical Garden) from Luer (2000a).

Species attributed to subgenus *Polyantha* section *Alaticaules* subsection *Alaticaules*

M. acrochordonia Rchb.f.

M. adrianae Luer

M. aguirrei Luer and Escobar

M. ametroglossa Luer and Hirtz

M. amplexa Luer

M. anfracta Königer and J. J. Portilla

M. barrowii Luer

M. bennettii Luer

M. brachyura Lehm. and Kränzl.

M. brockmuelleri Luer

M. bryophila Luer

M. calagrasalis Luer

M. cardiantha Königer

M. carruthersiana Lehm. and Kränzl.

M. cocapatae Luer, Teague, and Vásquez

M. cuprea Lindl.

M. deceptrix Luer and Würstle

M. descendens Luer and Andreetta

M. don-quijote Luer and Andreetta

M. dorisiae Luer

M. draconis Luer and Andreetta

M. echo Luer

M. excelsior Luer and Andreetta

M. forsterae Luer

M. frilehmannii Luer and Vásquez

M. garciae Luer

M. guerrieroi Luer and Andreetta

M. guttulata Rchb.f.

M. helgae Luer and J. J. Portilla

M. impostor Luer and Escobar

M. ingridiana Luer and J. J. Portilla

M. kuhniorum Luer

M. lenae Luer and Hirtz

M. lintriculata Königer

M. loui Luer and Dalström

M. luziae-mariae Luer and Vásquez

M. maculata Klotzsch and H. Karsten

M. mallii Luer

M. martineae Luer

M. martiniana Luer

M. mascarata Luer and Vásquez

M. melanoxantha Linden and Rchb.f.

M. monogona Königer

M. navicularis Garay and Dunst.

M. norae Luer

M. obscurans Luer

M. odontopetala Luer

M. omorenoi Luer and Vásquez

M. oscitans Luer

M. pastinata Luer

M. patchicutzae Luer and Hirtz

M. phoenix Luer

M. pinocchio Luer and Andreetta

M. plynophora Luer

M. portillae Luer and Andreetta

M. posadae Luer and Escobar

M. prolixa Luer

M. prosartema Königer

M. receptrix Luer and Vásquez

M. rechingeriana Kränzl.

M. recurvata Luer and Dalström

M. richardsoniana Luer

M. rolandorum Luer and Sijm

M. sanctae-fidei Kränzl.

M. sanguinea Luer and Andreetta

M. schudelii Luer

M. scitula Königer

M. scobina Luer and Escobar

M. serendipita Luer and Teague

M. sprucei Rchb.f.

M. stenorrhynchos Kränzl.

M. stirpis Luer

M. ×synthesis Luer

M. theleüra Luer

M. trochilus Linden and André

M. tsubotae Luer

M. vargasii C. Schweinf.

M. venus Luer and Hirtz

M. virens Luer and Andreetta

M. virgo-cuencae Luer and Andreetta

M. vomeris Luer

M. weberbaueri Schltr.

M. whiteana Luer

M. xylina Rchb.f.

M. zumbae Luer

Subsection *Coaetaneae*

Species in subsection *Coaetaneae* are simultaneously flowered.

Type species *Masdevallia sceptrum*

The name for this species derives from the Latin for a royal staff, which refers to its elegant inflorescence. This is a robust species, first collected near the gold mines at La

Baja near Pamplona, Venezuela, on the Funck and Schlim expedition of 1846–52. It is found in Venezuela and Colombia as a large, caespitose epiphyte that grows at elevations of 2400 to 3900 m. The plant is characterized by stout, erect ramicauls enveloped by two to three loose, tubular sheaths. The solitary leaf is erect, thickly coriaceous, elliptic-obovate, subacute to obtuse, and is narrowly cuneate from the basal petiole. The inflorescence is stout, erect, 15 to 30 cm long, loose to

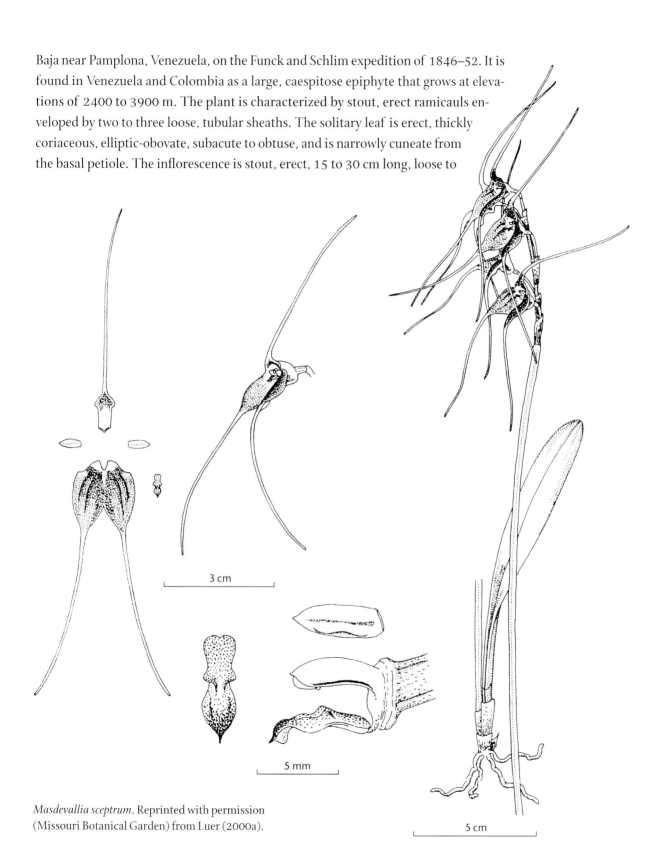

Masdevallia sceptrum. Reprinted with permission (Missouri Botanical Garden) from Luer (2000a).

congested, simultaneously few to several-flowered, and borne on a triquetrous peduncle. The flowers are held above the leaves. The sepals are glabrous and minutely verrucose within. The dorsal sepal is yellow, suffused with brown above the middle. The sepals are connate to form a short sepaline tube, and the apices are subacute, contracted into slender tails 4 to 6 cm long. In nature, this species is found in conjunction with *Masdevallia buccinator* and can be confused with *M. schlimii*, which has a terete inflorescence, basal processes on the petals, a longer hypochile, and no prominent keel on the lip. This species grows cold to cool.

Species of subgenus *Polyantha* section *Alaticaules* subsection *Coaetaneae*

M. aenigma Luer and Escobar	*M. concinna* Königer	*M. medusa* Luer and Escobar
M. bicolor Poepp. and Endl.	*M. dunstervillei* Luer	*M. mezae* Luer
M. buccinator Rchb.f.	*M. empusa* Luer	*M. sceptrum* Rchb.f.
M. cinnamomea Rchb.f.	*M. infracta* Lindl.	*M. sernae* Luer and Escobar
	M. isos Luer	*M. tovarensis* Rchb.f.

Section *Polyanthae*

Section *Polyanthae* is characterized by a simultaneously or successively flowered raceme borne on a terete peduncle. The flowers are similar to those of section *Alaticaules*, with the sepals more or less rigidly fleshy, usually with tails, and variously connate into a tube or cup. The thick lip is divided by marginal folds near the middle into an epichile and hypochile, and the petals are callous along the lip. The petals rarely form a protruding process. Similar to section *Alaticaules*, Luer has divided the section *Polyanthae* into two subsections.

Subsection *Polyanthae*

Species in subsection *Polyanthae* are simultaneously flowered.

Type species *Masdevallia schlimii*

This species is named in honor of Louis Schlim, Jean Linden's traveling companion and half brother, who discovered this species on an orchid collecting trip to New Granada, Colombia, in 1843. This is a Colombian and Venezuelan, large-sized, caespitose, epiphytic species that is a cold- to cool-grower found at elevations of 1800 to 2500 m. The ramicauls are stout and erect and are enveloped by two to three tubular sheaths carrying a single, erect, thickly coriaceous, elliptic, obtuse leaf that is narrowed below into a petiolate base. The plant blooms in the spring and early summer with an erect, 25 to 37.5 cm long, simultaneously four- to seven-flowered, purple-dot-

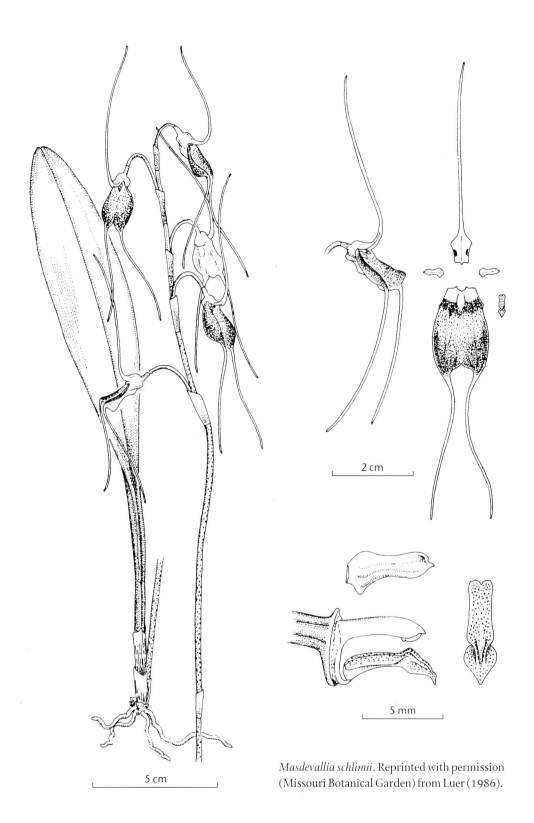

Masdevallia schlimii. Reprinted with permission
(Missouri Botanical Garden) from Luer (1986).

ted inflorescence arising from near the base of the ramicaul with two to three distinct bracts. The floral bracts hold the flowers at or above leaf height.

Species attributed to subgenus *Polyantha* section *Polyanthae* subsection *Polyanthae*

M. brachyantha Schltr.	*M. schlimii* Linden ex Lindl.	*M. wuerstlei* Luer
M. menatoi Luer and Vásquez	*M. striatella* Rchb.f.	*M. zumbuehlerae* Luer
M. oreas Luer and Vásquez		

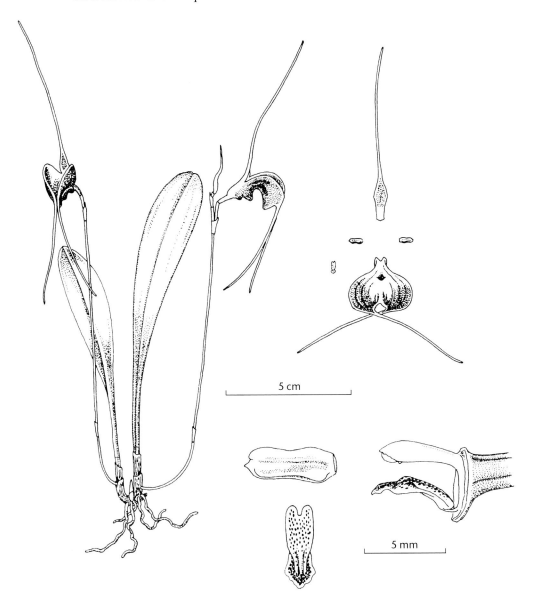

Masdevallia lata. Reprinted with permission (Missouri Botanical Garden) from Luer (2000a).

Subsection *Successiviflorae*

Species in subsection *Successiviflorae* are successively flowered.

Type species *Masdevallia lata*

This species was discovered in Costa Rica by a collector named Zahn, who apparently drowned soon thereafter. The plants were imported to Europe by the Veitch firm, and a flowering sample was sent to Reichenbach for identification in 1876. *Masdevallia lata* occurs occasionally in the low, moist forests of the Pacific watershed of Costa Rica and western Panama (100 to 500 m), where it is usually found growing in the branches of trees overhanging streams. *Masdevallia lata* is characterized by the long, slender, terete, ascending peduncle and successive flowers with broadly rounded, more or less compressed, approximate lateral sepals that are deeply arched beneath. The petals are oblong with a rounded basal callus, and the lip is divided by marginal folds.

Species attributed to subgenus *Polyantha* section *Polyanthae* subsection *Successiviflorae*

M. cosmia Königer and Sijm	*M. eumeces* Luer	*M. mayaycu* Luer and Hirtz
M. cupularis Rchb.f.	*M. jarae* Luer	*M. pyxis* Luer
M. curtipes Barb. Rodr.	*M. lata* Rchb.f.	*M. thienii* Dodson
M. discoidea Luer and Würstle	*M. maduroi* Luer	

Subgenus *Pygmaeia*

This subgenus is characterized by the small habit, papillose or spiculate ovaries with the processes often extending onto the sepals, sepals with or without tails, petals with or without a protruding callus, and a lip with a pair of keels. Luer (2000c, 2003) has defined three sections in this subgenus: *Amaluzae*, *Aphanes*, and *Pygmaeae*. *Amaluzae* and *Aphanes* have been further divided into subsections.

Section *Amaluzae*

The type species of this section, *Masdevallia amaluzae*, is named for the community of Amaluza in the province of Azuay, Ecuador. This section is distinguished by small to very small plants with successively flowered racemes, borne on a terete peduncle. The peduncle is slender, ascending, and may be horizontal to descending. The ovaries are smooth, with low ribs that may sometimes be undulate (subsection *Amaluzae*) or smooth and slightly costate (subsection *Zahlbrucknerae*). The sepals contract into slender tails. The callous petals are mostly without a protruding process and the lips are more or less oblong, with a pair of longitudinal calli that may be somewhat variable. This section is subdivided into two subsections, *Amaluzae* and *Zahlbrucknerae.*

Subsection *Amaluzae*

Species in subsection *Amaluzae* are characterized by ovaries that are smooth with undulate ribs.

Type species *Masdevallia amaluzae*

This species occurs in the wet forests of southern Ecuador at 1200 to 2450 m, and it is named after the region in which it is found (Amaluza). The small, yellow flowers are large for the size of the plant and are borne on successively flowered, horizontal racemes. The dorsal sepal has three prominent stripes. The free portion of the synsepal, which is longer than the sepaline tube, is lightly marked with brown and protrudes before it divides into the caudate apices. The petals are narrowly acute at the apex and unguiculate (clawed) at the base. The lip is narrow, oblong, and marked with three prominent red veins.

Species attributed to subgenus *Pygmaeia* section *Amaluzae* subsection *Amaluzae*

M. amaluzae Luer and Malo
M. audax Königer
M. aurorae Luer and M. W. Chase
M. carmenensis Luer and Malo
M. chimboënsis Kränzl.

M. manchinazae Luer and Andreetta
M. mataxa Königer and H. Mend.
M. merinoi Luer and J. J. Portilla

M. paquishae Luer and Hirtz
M. patula Luer and Malo
M. sanchezii Luer and Andreetta
M. schizostigma Luer

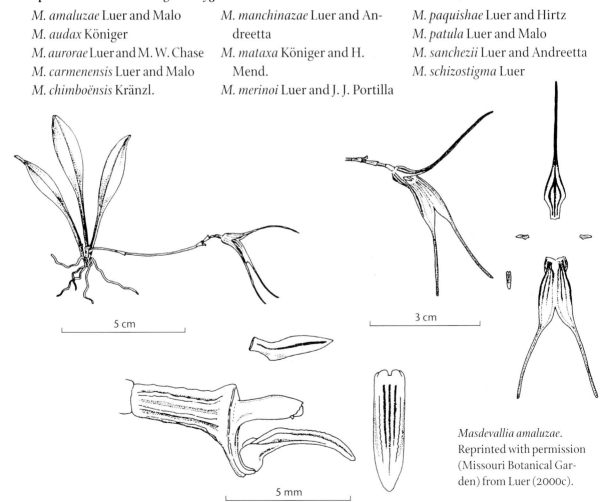

5 cm

3 cm

5 mm

Masdevallia amaluzae. Reprinted with permission (Missouri Botanical Garden) from Luer (2000c).

Subsection *Zahlbrucknerae*

This subsection is characterized by smooth or slightly costate ovaries and petals with a protruding, marginal callus or process. The lips are more or less oblong, with variations of a pair of longitudinal calli. The successively flowered raceme is borne by a terete peduncle, which may be ascending, horizontal, or descending.

Type species *Masdevallia zahlbruckneri*

This species is unusual for masdevallias in that it is a hot- to warm-growing epiphyte. It is found from Costa Rica to coastal Ecuador and central Bolivia in montane rain forests in deep shade on larger tree branches at elevations of 400 to 1700 m. Endres collected the first specimen in 1870 in Costa Rica, and he forwarded it with a detailed

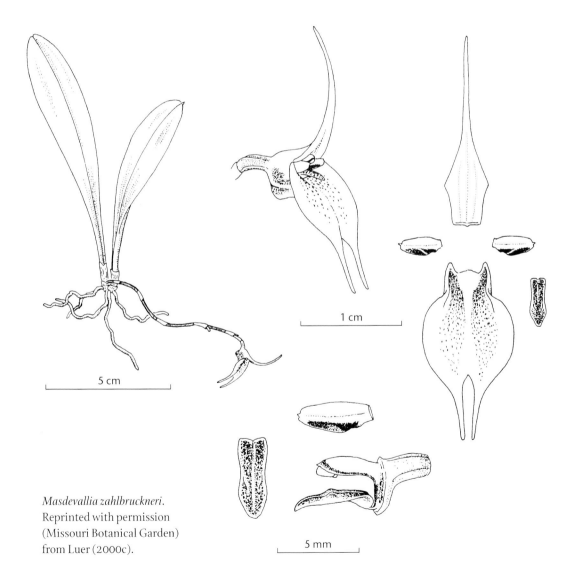

Masdevallia zahlbruckneri.
Reprinted with permission
(Missouri Botanical Garden)
from Luer (2000c).

illustration to Reichenbach. Apparently Reichenbach forgot about it, and it lay unnamed in his herbarium for many years. It was finally named by Kränzlin in 1920 in honor of Councilman Dr. Al. Zahlbruckner of Vienna, Austria. Zahlbruckner supplied many of Reichenbach's herbarium specimens to Kränzlin. *Masdevallia zahlbruckneri* blooms in the spring and has a prostrate to descending inflorescence, 3 to 7 cm long, with successive single flowers held well below the leaves. The flowers are variable in size, in the length of the tails, and in the shape of the red-purple calli on the petals.

Species attributed to subgenus *Pygmaeia* section *Amaluzae* subsection *Zahlbrucknerae*

M. naranjapatae Luer	*M. vieriana* Luer and Escobar
M. schizopetala Kränzl.	*M. zahlbruckneri* Kränzl.

Section *Aphanes*

This section is characterized by costate, crested, or verruculose ovaries, obtuse to acute sepals usually without forming a tail (although a few species have short tails), and petals without a descending process. The successively flowered raceme is borne by a slender, ascending, horizontal to descending, terete peduncle. Species of this section also have lips that are more or less oblong. The disc may be featureless or sulcate between the calli. This section is further subdivided into two subsections, *Aphanes* and *Pterygiophorae*.

Subsection *Aphanes*

Subsection *Aphanes* is distinguished from *Pterygiophorae* by the presence of carinate, or winged, ovaries.

Type species *Masdevallia aphanes*

Masdevallia aphanes is the type species for both the section *Aphanes* and the subsection *Aphanes*. The species epithet comes from the Greek, meaning obscure, and refers to the inconspicuous, tiny plant. *Masdevallia aphanes* is thought to have been discovered by Consul Lehmann, whose watercolor of this small species, now more than a century old, is conserved in the herbarium of the Royal Botanic Gardens, Kew, in England. Where the species was first discovered is unknown, but it has been discovered more recently in Ecuador and northern Peru in montane cloud forests at 2000 m. The plant is characterized by erect, coriaceous leaves and an inflorescence that bears one flower (often followed by a second) that is borne on a slender, suberect peduncle, 3 to 5 cm in length. The sepals are thick, more or less verrucose externally, and a dull yellowish green, diffusely spotted and suffused with brown. The dorsal sepal is ovate, 13 to 14 mm long, 5 mm wide, and connate for 4 to 5 mm to the lateral sepals to form a short, broad sepaline tube. This species will grow under either cool or intermediate conditions.

Species attributed to subgenus *Pygmaeia* section *Aphanes* subsection *Aphanes*

M. aphanes Königer
M. berthae Königer
M. collantesii D. E. Benn and
 Christenson
M. expers Luer and Andreetta
M. henniae Luer and Dalström

M. hoeijeri Luer and Hirtz
M. indecora Luer and Escobar
M. mentosa Luer
M. plantaginea (Poepp. and
 Endl.) Cogn.
M. pyknosepala Luer and Cloes

M. scalpellifera Luer
M. scopaea Luer and Vásquez
M. setipes Schltr.
M. smallmaniana Luer
M. strattoniana Luer
M. trifurcata Luer

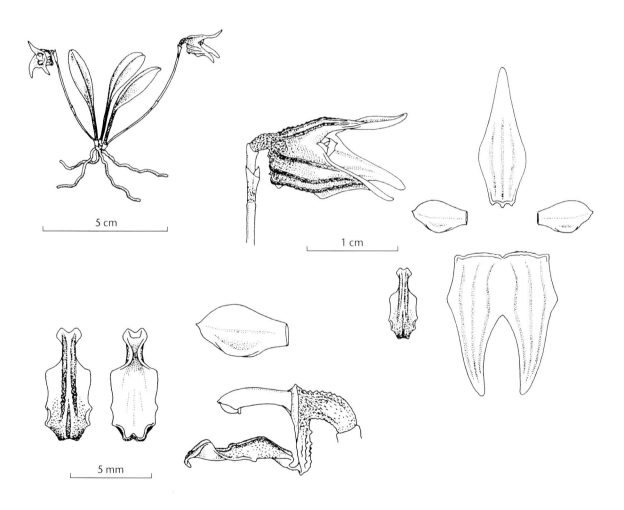

5 cm

1 cm

5 mm

Masdevallia aphanes. Reprinted with permission
(Missouri Botanical Garden) from Luer (2002).

Subsection *Pterygiophorae*

This recently described subsection (Luer 2003) apparently includes only one species, *Masdevallia pterygiophora*.

Type species *Masdevallia pterygiophora*

The species epithet comes from the Greek word *pterygiophoros*, which means bearing a little wing, and refers to the winged ovary of this species. *Masdevallia pterygiophora* was first collected by Rodrigo Escobar and Janet Kuhn in the Antioquia region of Colombia in 1975, at an elevation of 2000 m. It is quite rare, difficult to find, and has been found growing only on the twigs of small trees in a single valley. This species bears a single flower on a slender, weak, suberect peduncle, 15 to 25 mm long. The solitary flower is large for the size of the plant. The glabrous sepals are light yellow or light green with red-purple veins. The dorsal sepal is ovate and connate to the lateral sepals for 3 mm to form a broadly cylindric tube. The lateral sepals are also ovate, with the apices of the sepals thickened and obtuse. The ovary is winged, with the margins overlapping the bases of the sepals.

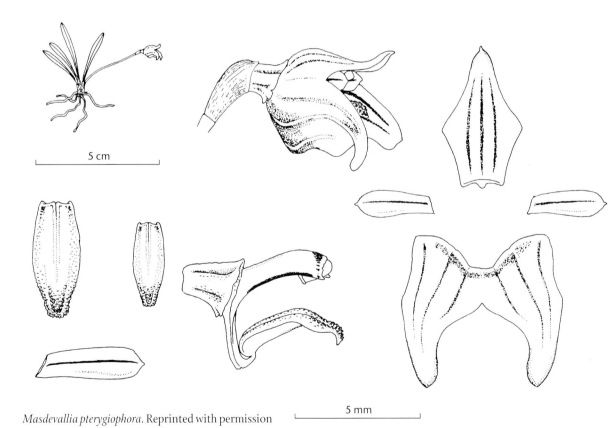

5 cm

5 mm

Masdevallia pterygiophora. Reprinted with permission (Missouri Botanical Garden) from Luer (2000c).

Section *Pygmaeae*

Species in section *Pygmaeae* are distinguished from the others in this subgenus by spiculate or papillose ovaries.

Type species *Masdevallia pygmaea*

This minute species occurs over a fairly broad range from Costa Rica to the Western Cordillera of Colombia and Ecuador. It was first collected in Costa Rica by Endres, who proposed the unpublished species name *microscopea*. This tiny species has narrow, semiterete leaves and minute, white flower with a densely papillose ovary and thickened, upturned sepaline tails. The peduncle is hairlike and shorter than the leaves. The petals bear a tooth at the base, and the simple lip is bicallous. The plant can be grown under intermediate conditions.

Species attributed to subgenus *Pygmaeia* section *Pygmaeae*

M. anachaeta Rchb.f.
M. erinacea Rchb.f.
M. pygmaea Kränzl.

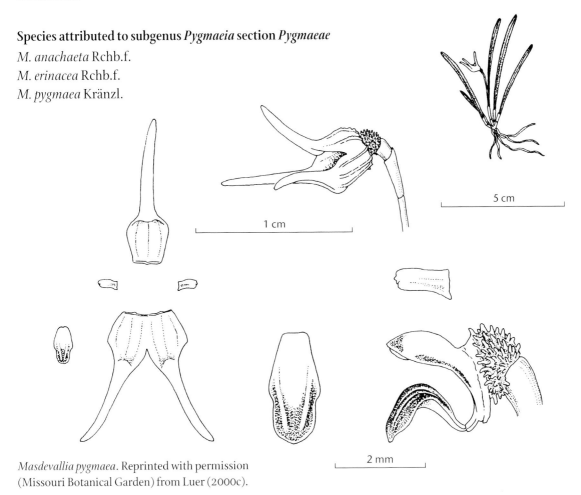

Masdevallia pygmaea. Reprinted with permission (Missouri Botanical Garden) from Luer (2000c).

Subgenus *Scabripes*

This unispecific subgenus is characterized by a scabrous peduncle.

Type species *Masdevallia bicornis*

The name for this species is derived from the Latin for two horned, referring to the labellum. This distinctive, medium-sized epiphyte is endemic in lowland (700 to 1000 m) southeastern Ecuador. *Masdevallia bicornis* is characterized by a short ramicaul and a large, petiolate leaf. This successively flowered species is distinguished from all other known members of *Masdevallia* by its long peduncle covered with branching, scaly trichomes. With the exception of the pair of tiny hornlike processes on the lip, the morphology of the flowers is similar to the subsection *Oscillantes*. The dorsal sepal is connate to the lateral sepals but does not form a tube. The sepals are long-caudate, and the laterals have subplicate veins. The petals are short, arcuate, and cartilaginous with a pointed process or tooth at the base.

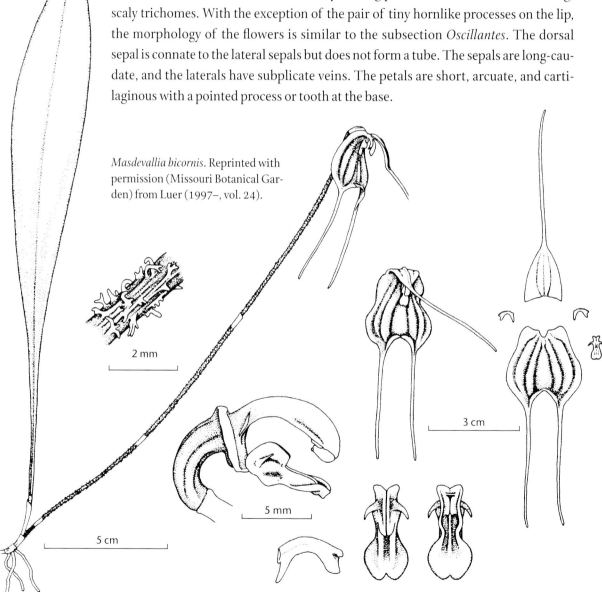

Masdevallia bicornis. Reprinted with permission (Missouri Botanical Garden) from Luer (1997–, vol. 24).

Subgenus *Volvula*

This is also a unispecific taxon, characterized by a single flower produced on a terete peduncle, with thick sepals keeled on the inside with thick, twisted tails and a divided lip.

Type species *Masdevallia caudivolvula*

The epithet is from the Latin *volvus* and means twisted intestine, and it refers to the remarkable corkscrew tails of this medium-sized epiphytic plant. The sepals of the solitary flowers are markedly thickened along the veins on the inner surfaces, and at the apices they continue into thick, rigid, twisted tails. The petals are callous without a tooth, and the lip is divided by lateral folds into a hypochile and a smoothly, although minutely, denticulate epichile. *Masdevallia caudivolvula* is restricted to, but not uncommon to, the Departments of Antioquia and Caldas in the Central Cordillera of Colombia. This species is notoriously difficult to grow in cultivation.

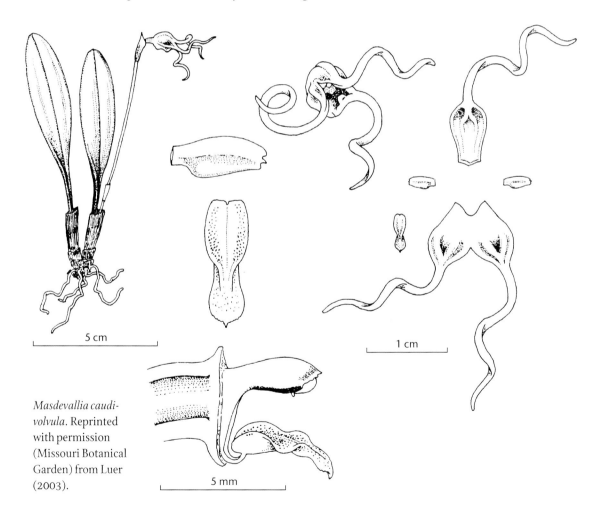

Masdevallia caudivolvula. Reprinted with permission (Missouri Botanical Garden) from Luer (2003).

5 cm

1 cm

5 mm

CHAPTER 10

❖ ❖ ❖

Featured *Masdevallia* Species

This chapter features selected *Masdevallia* species that are popular with the hobby grower, either because of the beauty of the flowers or because some other unique feature makes the plant appealing. Although many attractive species could not be included here due to space limitations, an attempt was made to include some of the more attractive or unusual species from the majority of the subgenera and subclasses of *Masdevallia* as defined by Luer. The species are discussed in alphabetical order, regardless of their classification. (The subgenus, section, or subsection of all species can be readily determined by consulting other references to the species in the index.)

It should be noted that the description of each species is brief. Rather than including all the minute details of a true botanical description, the more striking features of the flowers and/or habit of each species are discussed, along with information about the species's first collection and cultural requirements. The precise botanical descriptions of each species has been previously published in one or more of the series of monographs by Luer (1996, 2000a, 2000b, 2000c, 2000d, 2001, 2003), and the reader is referred to these sources (listed at the end of this book) for more detailed information. For the purposes of discussion, the approximate sizes of a "small" *Masdevallia* plant (not including the flowers) would be less than 10 cm tall, "medium" 10 to 20 cm tall, and "large" greater than 20 cm tall. When dimensions of a flower are provided, they describe the height of the flower unless otherwise stated.

Masdevallia amabilis

The species epithet means deserving or worthy of love and refers to the beauty of the flowers. This species originates from north and central Peru, where it occurs at elevations of 2000 to 5300 m. It was much appreciated by the Chavin culture that flourished nearly 3000 years ago in the western Andes of Peru, and their fascination with the flowers is reflected in a folktale (Rolando 1996):

> In the kingdom of Chavin there was a beautiful young princess that fell in love with a brave and handsome warrior. Once her father, the king, knew of the love affair, he prohibited any relationship between them because the princess was destined for the God Sun. When the princess took notice of the decision, she ran throughout the Andes and crying for her prohibited love turned into a "Huanganko." In this way, each time the warrior would find this flower in the Andes, he would also cry remembering his lost love.

Warszewicz was the first European to discover *Masdevallia amabilis* in about 1850, and Reichenbach described the dried specimens four years later. It was not cultivated, however, until Roezl collected plants in the same area and brought living specimens to Europe in 1872. It grows terrestrially or lithophytically in cool montane forests, as

Masdevallia amabilis. Grower: Lil Severin.

Masdevallia amabilis (pink form). Grower: Lil Severin.

well as on rocky slopes in intense sunlight (for several hours per day). In the wild, the foliage of plants growing in direct sunlight is somewhat yellowed and flowers are paler than those growing in deeper shade. The inflorescence may be up to 30 cm long and may be erect, reclining, or horizontal. This small but beautiful species is well-known for its color variations. The sepals can be bright purple, red, white, or orange; suffused or sometimes veined in red or purple; with long, slender tails that can vary considerably in length. The flowers can range from 3.6 to 10 cm tall. The purple form tends to have somewhat smaller flowers, while the white form is rare in the wild. The yellow to orange specimens are usually larger flowered. *Masdevallia amabilis* should be grown cool and can bloom in the summer, autumn, or winter. This species likes to dry out briefly between watering and has a reputation of being stubborn to flower. It needs more light than most masdevallias (1200 to 1800 foot-candles), and increasing light to the point of leaf yellowing may encourage a shy bloomer to flower.

Masdevallia ampullacea. Grower: Golden Gate Orchids.

Masdevallia ampullacea

The name from this species derives from the Latin *ampullaceus*, meaning like a flask or bottle, which refers to the shape of the sepaline tube. This species originates from cloud forests in Ecuador, where it grows epiphytically at elevations of 700 to 1500 m. The species was first discovered by Father Angel Andreetta of Cuenca, Ecuador, in August 1978. This is a captivating species, with semi-upright, 5 to 7.6 cm flowers, characterized by white and yellow-orange sepaline tubes, with varying amounts of orange on the exterior, and orange-yellow erect to reflexed tails. The internal surface of the sepals are finely pubescent. Uncommon in cultivation, this small to medium-sized, robust species grows intermediate and may bloom twice a year. When in bloom, the tubular flowers with their slender tails radiate out from the base of the plant, forming a striking display.

Masdevallia andreettana

This lovely species is named in honor of Father Andreetta. Although first discovered in southeastern Ecuador, the species also occurs in northeastern Peru. It grows epiphytically in cloud forests at elevations of 1600 to 2100 m. It has a distinctive, proportionately large, solitary, snow-white flower (sometimes with short, reddish purple stripes emerging from the base of the flower), with a typically deflexed dorsal sepal. The flowers can last six to eight weeks and appear in the autumn to early winter. The lateral sepals are wide, and when the flower is completely open it can measure more than 2.5 cm across at the widest point. The 7 to 10 cm flower blooms at or slightly above the attractive, rounded, blue-green leaves. This species is best grown under intermediate conditions (although it will also grow cool), and it has a reputation for being a challenging plant to grow. The stems on this species are somewhat weak, and thus the flowers benefit from some support to display them at their best. An appealing way to grow this species is mounted, which allows an attractive display of the flowers.

Masdevallia andreettana. Grower: Brad Cotten.

Masdevallia angulata

The species epithet is from Latin and means with angles. This species is found in southern Colombia and northwestern Ecuador as a cool, terrestrial, lithophytical or epiphytic species, at elevations of 600 to 2600 m. The first specimen of this species was collected by Consul Lehmann and forwarded to Reichenbach around 1878. The flowers of this species are variable in color, foul-smelling ("rotten meat" would be a good description), and very long lasting (months). The flowers can also exude droplets of a sugary substance, which in combination with the distinctive odor must play a role in the attraction of the pollinator of this species. The single-flowered inflorescences range from 2.5 to 6 cm in length and occur in autumn through to winter. Lasting up to several months, the flowers appear on horizontal stems, hanging around the edge of the pot. When the buds first appear, they should be adjusted if necessary so that they do not catch on the edge of the pot and rot. These plants can be grown cool to intermediate and best present themselves when grown mounted due to the short, erect to descending inflorescences.

Masdevallia angulata. Grower: Ernest Katler.

Masdevallia angulifera

The species epithet is from the Latin *angulifer*, meaning angle-bearing, which refers to the broadly angled apices of the sepals. This species was first collected by G. Wallis somewhere in Colombia in 1883 and sent to Reichenbach. However, it was not published until Kränzlin described it 36 years after Reichenbach's death. An olive-green variation of this species occurs, which was published as *Masdevallia olivacea*. *Masdevallia angulifera* occurs at elevations of 1800 to 2000 m. The upright, tubular flowers of this cool- to intermediate-growing species are held above the leaves and are characterized by a constriction above the middle, giving them a "pot belly" appearance. The flowers have triangular sepals with an attractive, velvety inner surface. The color varies from a yellow-green to rose or deep purple. A fragrance similar to banana oil (or acetone to some) is emitted by the long-lasting flowers (for up to three months if the plant is not exposed to warm temperatures). This species usually blooms in the winter or spring.

Masdevallia angulifera 'Amberina'. Grower: Ernest Katler.

Masdevallia asterotricha

The name for this species is derived from the Greek word *asterothrix*, which means a star-shaped hair, and refers to the stellate hairs on the inner surface of the sepals. This charming species was first found in 1985 by Königer in the Amazonas Province of Bongará, Peru, at an elevation of 1500 m. It is an intermediate- to cool-growing species that has a large (for the size of the plant), widely expanded, 5 to 6.5 cm tall, yellow flower with conspicuous speckles (which actually are the rose-colored stellate trichomes), particularly on the dorsal sepals. The hairs of the lateral sepals tend to be sparser and lighter in color.

Masdevallia asterotricha. Grower: San Francisco Conservatory of Flowers.

Masdevallia ayabacana

This species is named for the community of Ayabaca, Peru, where the species apparently was first collected by R. Stümple (circa 1976), although it is thought that the collection data were erroneous since subsequent efforts by many to locate the species in this region near the Ecuadoran border were without success. *Masdevallia ayabacana* is known to be a locally abundant species in the Chanchamayo valley of central Peru, elevation 1200 m. This species has striking bright green leaves. Its very large flowers are borne successively on an unusually long peduncle that may be ascending or descending and up to 20 to 35 cm in length. The sepals are fleshy, dark red to purple, smooth externally, and minutely papillose to pubescent within. The triangular dorsal sepal attenuates into a slender, somewhat reflexed, orange to green tail, and the dorsal sepal is fused to the lateral sepals for 6 to 9 mm, forming a short, conical tube. The attenuated tails of the lateral sepals typically cross over one another. This intermediate- to warm-growing species blooms from the spring to the fall. *Masdevallia ayabacana* makes a particularly pleasing display when grown in a basket, which allows the large and unusual flowers on the long peduncles to be fully appreciated.

Masdevallia ayabacana. Grower: Dan Newman.

Masdevallia barlaena

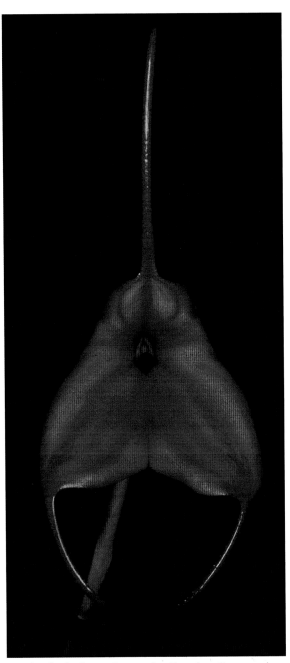

This species is named in honor of J. E. Barla, botanist and orchidologist, Consul of Brazil, and director of the Museum of Natural History in Nice, France. It was originally discovered by Walter Davis in 1865 (who was searching for *Masdevallia veitchiana* to collect for Messrs. Veitch). *Masdevallia barlaena* grows in exposed rocky habitats at high elevations (2200 to 2900 m) in southeastern Peru. This species is closely allied to *M. amabilis* (which occurs in similar habitats), and where the two species overlap, the natural hybrid *M. ×splendida* occurs. This medium-sized, terrestrial species has a characteristic solitary, showy flower, borne on an erect, reclining, or horizontal peduncle that can be 15 to 20 cm long. The sepals are a bright reddish purple and can be suffused or veined with darker red or purple; the petals, lip, and column are white. The inner surface of the sepals is minutely pubescent. This cool-growing species can be difficult to flower, and the bud, if exposed to warm temperatures when in spike, often aborts.

Masdevallia barlaena. Grower: San Francisco Conservatory of Flowers.

Masdevallia bicornis

The species epithet is from the Latin *bicornis*, meaning two-horned, which refers to the labellum, which is shallowly bilobed. *Masdevallia bicornis* is endemic to lowland (700 to 1000 m) southeastern Ecuador. It was first collected in 1996 by José Portilla and named *Portillae popoviana* by Königer and Portilla but was reclassified and included within the genus *Masdevallia* by Luer. Found in a warm region of Ecuador, it can be grown intermediate to cool. The rather large (10 cm), dark brownish red flower, with raised yellowish veins and lateral sepals that abruptly narrow into long, delicate tails, is held at or above the level of the leaves on upright to horizontal warty peduncles. An attractive way to grow this species is in baskets; when grown this way the spikes hang downward and are more readily appreciated. The successively flowered species is distinguished from all other species of *Masdevallia* by its scaly inflorescence.

Masdevallia bicornis. Grower: John Leathers.

Masdevallia buccinator. Grower: San Francisco Conservatory of Flowers.

Masdevallia buccinator

The epithet for this unique species comes from the Latin, meaning horn blower, and refers to the appearance of the inflated lateral sepals that resemble the puffed-out cheeks of some-one blowing a horn. *Masdevallia buccinator* was collected by both Schlim and Warszewicz in the mid-19th century near old gold mines in the Eastern Cordillera of Colombia at eleva-tions ranging from 2500 to 2600 m. The suc-cessively blooming 7.6 cm flowers of this spe-cies are borne two at a time, on a triquetrous (triangular in cross section) peduncle, 12 to 18 cm long. The sepals are a dull yellow-green, suffused with brown, and the lip, although hard to see, is cream-colored and faintly dotted with purple. This cool-growing species may bloom in the spring or fall.

Masdevallia caesia

The species epithet is from the Latin *caesius*, meaning sky blue, which reflects the bluish color of the leaves. This very distinct, large, epiphytic species is infrequent and endemic to southern parts of the Western Cordillera of Colombia. Benedict Roezl was the first to find this species, describing its pendent habit and large, bluish green leaves. The leaves and upside-down habit are so characteristic that this is possibly the only species of *Masdevallia* that can be positively identified even when not in bloom. The inflores-cence is a large, solitary flower, borne on a descending peduncle, 2 to 5 cm long. The sepals are dark yellow, mottled, and spotted with red-brown. The flower is quite large, measuring 12.5 to 23 cm. It grows at elevations of 1600 to 2000 m and flowers in the early spring to summer. *Masdevallia caesia* is known as the *grande dame* of mas-devallias because it has one of the largest flowers of this genus and overall makes a very attractive specimen plant. However, the stench of the flower can be detected from as far as 2 meters away and could only attract a carrion fly. One of the best fea-

Masdevallia caesia CCM/AOS. Grower: Marni Turkel.

tures of this species are the steel blue-gray leaves that can be up to 38 cm long. This plant should be grown upside down, with its leaves descending through wire mesh or a basket. It can also be grown mounted if strongly secured, as the plants can be quite heavy. When grown mounted, it requires daily watering or misting to make sure that the roots do not dry out. It should be grown cool to intermediate. This is a somewhat challenging species to grow, but specimen plants in bloom make a spectacular display. This is a must-have species if you can live with the malodorous aroma.

Masdevallia caloptera. Grower: Dick Emory.

Masdevallia caloptera

The epithet for this species means beautiful wings. This dwarf, epiphytic species is found in dense, moist forests of central Ecuador and northern Peru at 1800 to 2600 m. *Masdevallia caloptera* was first collected by Roezl somewhere in northern Peru and described by Reichenbach in 1874. The 15 cm long inflorescence has up to nine evenly spaced, white flowers, faintly to conspicuously veined in purple, with bright yellow-orange tails. The individual flowers are quite small (2 to 3 cm), but the plant in full bloom can be quite stunning. In cultivation, many plants of *M. leptoura* are mislabeled as *M. caloptera*. (Even one or two AOS awarded plants are mislabeled—for example, the clone *M. caloptera* 'Anna S. Chai' CCM/AOS is actually *M. leptoura*.) But the two species are easily distinguished. The sepals of *M. caloptera* have characteristic purple stripes, whereas those of *M. leptoura* do not; the sepals of *M. leptoura* are instead lightly spotted. This species is best grown under cool to intermediate conditions.

Masdevallia caudata

The species epithet *caudata* comes from the Latin word meaning with tails, and it refers to the long-tailed sepals of this very showy species. *Masdevallia caudata* was first collected by French botanist Justin Godot in the Eastern Cordillera of Colombia near San Fortunato in 1831 and published in 1833 simultaneously with *M. infracta* by Lindley. Thus, these two species have the distinction of being the second and third species of *Masdevallia* to have been described. The first living plants, which were

Masdevallia caudata. Grower: John Leathers.

more colorful variations than that described by Lindley, did not arrive in Europe until sent by Shuttleworth in 1874. This different color variation was named *M. shuttleworthii* but has now been reduced to synonymy. *Masdevallia caudata* is relatively frequent in nature and quite widely distributed. Specimens have been collected in western Venezuela, Colombia, Ecuador, and Peru in cloud forests at elevations of 2000 to 2500 m. It is a cool- to intermediate-growing caespitose epiphyte that blooms in the late spring to early summer on an arched, slender, 12 to 13 cm long inflorescence. Although this species may survive when grown under intermediate conditions, it will not do well if the plant is exposed to warm temperatures (for example, 26 to 27°C) for prolonged periods.

The distinctive flower, which can measure 17 to 20 cm, is fragrant and variable in color and is held slightly above, at, or slightly below the height of the leaves. All three sepals are furnished with very long, slender tails, as the name implies. More than one flower per leaf can be produced, although not simultaneously. The column, petals, and lips stand erect and exposed in the center of the flower. Typically, the dorsal sepal is white to yellow and veined, dotted, or suffused with pinkish purple or brownish and fused with lateral sepals to form a gaping sepaline cup. The lateral sepals are off-white and are usually densely dotted rose-pink to reddish brown. The rounded sepals abruptly contract into slender yellow tails. Another variety in cultivation is yellow. Some clones of this species are among the most beautiful of the genus, and plants of *M. caudata* were some of the first masdevallias to be used as parents in hybridization.

Masdevallia caudivolvula

This is a unique *Masdevallia* species. Although in bud the sepal tails are straight, upon opening the three orange-yellow sepaline tails twist like corkscrews and hence the name *caudivolvula*, derived from the Latin *cauda* for tail and *volvulus* for twisted organ. This species has a restricted distribution, in the Departments of Antioquia and Caldas in the Central Cordillera of Colombia, where it grows at 2000 to 2750 m. This species is quite common in the cloud forests of these areas, but it is difficult to cultivate. *Masdevallia caudivolvula* is grown cool and tends to bloom in the summer. Hybrids of this species have produced various offspring with curly tails, and some of the grex names reflect this feature, such as *M.* Curly George (*M. notosibirica* × *M. caudivolvula*) and *M.* Whirlygig (*M. caudivolvula* × *M. caesia*).

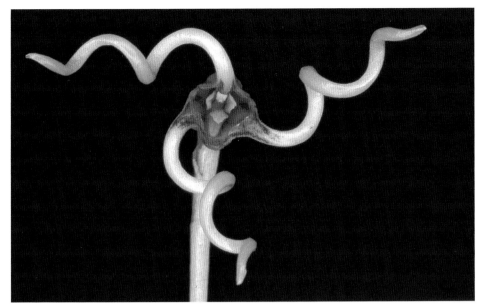

Masdevallia caudivolvula. Grower: John Leathers.

Masdevallia chaparensis

This species is named for the province of Chapare, Bolivia, where it is endemic to one humid, forested valley on the north slope of the Andes at 2400 to 2800 m. The plant is medium to large in size, with slender, erect ramicauls. This species was once also known as *M. hajekii*. The inflorescence bears one showy flower, borne on a slender, erect to suberect peduncle, 7 to 12 cm long. The 7.6 to 10 cm flower is white to light purple with darker purple spots, although color variations occur. In cultivation, this vigorous cold- to cool-growing species can produce many attractive flowers and can bloom several times a year. The stunning flowers make it an extremely desirable species to own, and many hybrids generated using this species as a parent feature unusual and eye-catching markings.

Masdevallia chuspipatae

This species was named for the locality of Chuspipata, Bolivia, where it was discovered growing epiphytically at an elevation of about 2000 m. Luer subsequently formally described the species with Walter Teague. The inflorescence bears a solitary, elegant, 10 cm flower on a slender, suberect peduncle, 6.5 to 7 cm long. The sepals are white, pubescent, and suffused with orange toward the base. The flowers have a very pleasing fragrance. Currently, this species is still quite rare in cultivation. The plant grows cool to intermediate and blooms in the summer.

Masdevallia chaparensis. Grower: John Leathers.

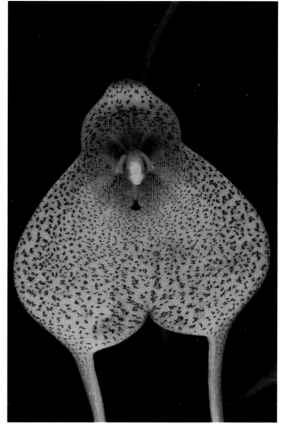

Masdevallia chuspipatae. Grower: Marni Turkel.

Masdevallia citrinella. Grower: Lil Severin.

Masdevallia citrinella

The Latin *citrinellus* means lemon yellow, which captures the essence of the delicate color of the sepals of this species. *Masdevallia citrinella* was initially discovered in 1981 by Benigno Malo, growing epiphytically in the Ecuadoran cloud forests between Loja and Zamora, at an elevation of 1900 m. This is a fairly common species found in the forests of southeastern Ecuador, easily recognized by the tan to lemon yellow, broadly expanded sepals and the tiny, oscillating lip. The charming, 3 to 6.5 cm, speckled flowers are also characterized by a reflexed dorsal sepal with dense, dark red to purple freckles. When viewed straight on, it has the appearance of a colorful spotted toad with its tongue stuck out. *Masdevallia citrinella* is a cool- to intermediate-growing species.

Masdevallia civilis. Grower: Lil Severin.

Masdevallia civilis

The species epithet is Latin for relating to civilians and refers to the drab-colored flowers of the more common variety of this species. *Masdevallia civilis* was originally discovered by Warszewicz in the mountains of northern Peru in 1853. It is quite variable both in its coloration and in the length of the sepaline tails. This cool- to cold-growing species grows as an epiphyte, a lithophyte, or terrestrially in Colombia, Venezuela, Ecuador, and Peru. It grows in cloud forests on grass-covered, rocky (limestone) slopes fully exposed to the extremes of heat in the midday tropical sun and chilly nights at elevations around 2750 to 3500 m. The malodorous, solitary flowers are borne on slender, erect to arcuate but short (10 cm) inflorescences. The thick, fleshy sepals are a dull yellow-green to dark red color with purple mottling and are glabrous externally and minutely verrucose-pubescent within. The coloration and length of the sepaline tails are variable. The plant blooms in the spring and early summer and is an easy species to grow.

Masdevallia coccinea (dark pink form). Grower unknown.

Masdevallia coccinea var. *xanthina*. Grower: John Leathers.

Masdevallia coccinea

The Latin word *coccineus* means a bright, deep red color, which describes the flowers of the more common color form of this species. It was first discovered growing terrestrially on the southern slopes of high mountains near Pamplona, Colombia (elevation 2740 m), in about 1841 by Jean Linden, and it immediately became one of the most prized species of the orchid trade. The spectacular beauty of this species caused it to be relentlessly collected for more than a century, yet miraculously it still remains locally abundant in the Eastern Cordillera of Colombia. The large, stately, solitary flowers of this species are quite variable in size and color, and moreover, the stability of the colors may vary with the clone and cultivation conditions. Some populations may produce numerous shades and tints, whereas others are more stable. The colors can vary from the more common bright red-purple to rose, yellow, orange, and pure white. The bloom times of the various color forms also differ. For example, the white

Collection of *Masdevallia coccinea*, assorted color forms. Grower: John Leathers.

Masdevallia coccinea 'Dwarf Pink'. Grower: Alek Koomanoff.

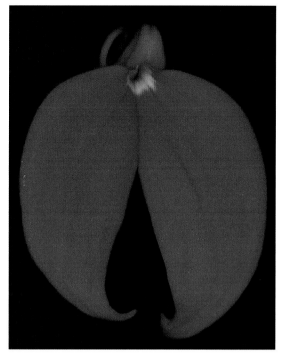

Masdevallia coccinea 'Ruth' AM/AOS. Grower: San Francisco Conservatory of Flowers.

Masdevallia coccinea var. *alba*. Grower: Alek Koomanoff.

forms may bloom somewhat later than the more highly colored varieties. A number of the Victorian cultivars were given names as varieties, including *M. approviata*, *M. armeniaca*, *M. atrosanguinea*, *M. coerulescens*, *M. conchiflora*, *M. decora*, *M. grandiflora*, *M. harryana*, *M. laeta*, *M. lateritia*, *M. lindenii*, *M. longiflora*, *M. miniata*, *M. splendens*, *M. tricolor*, and *M. versicolor*. The flowers are borne on a stout, erect peduncle ranging from 25 to 60 cm in length, most often held quite high above the leaves with a bract below the middle. The flower size is also quite variable, with smaller clones having flowers 5 cm tall and larger forms up to 13 cm tall. This species requires high humidity and must have cool conditions to do well. This can be a challenge, because this species tends to bloom in the late spring/early summer. If the flowers open during warmer weather, the tails and lateral sepals may curve under, although some clones naturally have recurved segments. (The flowers may also be smaller and less long-lasting in the heat.) Heat stress will also cause the leaf tips to blacken. *Masdevallia coccinea* has been and continues to be a very popular species for hybridizing.

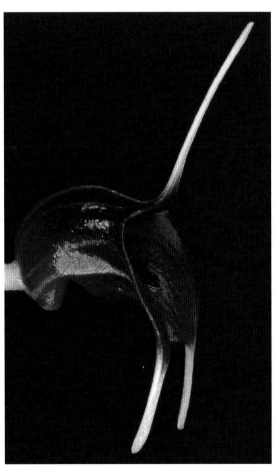

Masdevallia collina. Grower: Lil Severin.

Masdevallia collina

The Latin word *collinus* means of the hills and refers to the area above El Valle de Antón, Panama, where it was first collected by Paul Allen in 1940 while exploring for the *Flora of Panama*. This epiphytic species is endemic to cloud forests of central Panama (around 1000 m) and has the distinction of having successfully colonized cultivated orange groves. The inflorescence of this species is a congested raceme of three to five small, successive flowers, borne by an erect to suberect terete peduncle that is 6 to 11 cm in length. The 2.5 to 4.0 cm flowers have glossy, deep wine-red sepals, with rigid yellow tails. *Masdevallia collina* grows intermediate to warm.

Masdevallia colossus

As its name implies, this species is known as the "gigantic" *Masdevallia* because of its large plant and flower size. It is found in Peru and Ecuador, where it grows as an epiphyte in cloud forests at elevations of 2000 to 2500 m. *Masdevallia colossus* was discovered by Jorge Meza in 1977 near Molinopampa, in northern Peru, where it was found on the trunks and branches of mossy trees in a very limited locality near this tiny village. The pubescent flowers usually have yellowish green dorsal sepals and reddish purple lateral sepals. The fleshy, foul-smelling, 20 to 24 cm flowers are borne on a stout, suberect peduncle. The lip is large, thick, and warty. This cool- to cold-growing species prefers partial shade.

Masdevallia colossus. Grower: John Leathers.

Masdevallia concinna

The species epithet is derived from the Latin *concinnus*, which means pretty or elegant, and refers to the beauty of the flowers. The Königers and Manuel Arias discovered this species growing on a steep road embankment in 1979 between Tingo Maria and Pucallpa, Peru, at an elevation of 1700 m. It has only rarely been collected since then from other parts of central and northern Peru (900 to 1700 m) but not from the original locality. This is a medium-sized, terrestrial species. The inflorescence features a simultaneously two-flowered raceme of unusually showy flowers, borne on a slender,

Masdevallia concinna. Grower: San Francisco Conservatory of Flowers.

erect, triquetrous peduncle 10 to 11.5 cm long. The ovate lateral sepals are yellow-green, usually with a distinct transition into a purplish red about a third of the way down the length. *Masdevallia concinna* is grown cool to intermediate.

Masdevallia constricta

The name for this species is derived from the Latin *constrictus*, meaning constricted, which refers to the constricted sepaline tube. This species is perhaps more familiar to growers by its synonym, *M. urosalpinx*. This is one of the earliest identified masdeval-

Masdevallia constricta. Grower: San Francisco Conservatory of Flowers.

lias, collected by Poeppig during his explorations of Peru between 1829 and 1831. The original specimen was described as having purple stripes, but numerous subsequent collections of plants with yellow or orange sepaline tubes have failed to find one with purple stripes, suggesting the early description may have been in error. *Masdevallia constricta* grows epiphytically in cloud forests at elevations of 1500 to 1700 m and is relatively frequent in the Andes from southern Ecuador to central Peru. The inflorescence is a solitary flower, borne by a slender, erect to suberect peduncle, 4 to 6 cm long. The sepals are white, variously suffused, or veined with orange or yellow, particularly so in the middle third of the tube. The sepaline tails are thickish and a beautiful yellowish orange. Flowers of the smaller forms can be 6.4 to 7.6 cm and up to 12.7 cm in larger forms. This vigorous and floriferous species grows under intermediate conditions.

Masdevallia coriacea. Grower: Lil Severin.

Masdevallia coriacea

The Latin word *coriaceus* means leathery and refers to the tough, thick leaves of this species. *Masdevallia coriacea* grows terrestrially, on fully exposed to partially shaded, rocky and grassy slopes at elevations of 2500 to 2700 m in the Eastern Cordillera of Colombia southward to Peru. The typical form (with large, cream-colored flowers) was first collected by Hartweg in 1842 near Bogotá, Colombia. Smaller forms of the same or similar species, with more colorful spotted flowers (for example, *M. bonplandii*), were found by Humboldt and Bonpland in 1802 near the Rumichaca Bridge between Colombia and Ecuador. *Masdevallia coriacea*, like most species in its section, is foul smelling, although the scent is rather weak. The single, apical, erect inflorescence is held amid or just above the leaves. It is grown intermediate to cool, blooms in the spring and summer, and is an easy species to grow and flower.

Masdevallia cyclotega

The species epithet derives from the Greek words *cyclos* and *tegos*, meaning circular and roof, and refers to the round dorsal sepal. *Masdevallia cyclotega* was first collected by Jorge Meza above Huasahuasi, Peru, in 1978, where he found it growing in the cloud forests as an epiphyte on low, mossy tree branches as well as a terrestrial, in company with *M. uniflora* (at elevations of 2900 to 3000 m). The solitary flower is borne on an erect, slender peduncle, 12 to 14 cm long, with a bract below the middle. The sepals are rosy pink, tending toward yellow-white or light pink at the base, with yellow tails. The dorsal sepal is obovate, narrowed basally, and fused with the lateral sepals for 5 cm to form a shallow, gaping cup. *Masdevallia cyclotega* requires a cool, damp, shady environment with adequate air movement to grow and bloom well. Adding to the appeal of the beautiful flower of this species is the fragrant, raspberry-like scent.

Masdevallia cyclotega. Grower: Gerardus Staal.

Masdevallia datura

This species was first collected for herbarium specimens in the Yungas of Bolivia in the latter part of the 19th century by H. H. Rusby, but it was not published until 1983 by Luer and Vásquez. The site where the Luers and Vásquez collected the species in 1982 (elevation 2500 m) has been totally destroyed by expansion of the small community in the area. Fortunately, this species is easy to grow, and many clones are in cultivation. The spectacular flower features a large, white, funnel-shaped sepaline tube, with equally long, slender tails. The size of the flowers is 15 to 20 cm, and their weight produces arching to descending inflorescences. The species epithet is derived from the Hindu word *dhatura*, meaning giant, but this species was named *datura* based on the similarity of the flower to those of the genus *Datura* (Solanaceae or nightshade family). *Masdevallia datura* is grown cool to intermediate.

Masdevallia datura. Grower: Dan Newman.

Masdevallia davisii

This species was named by Reichenbach in honor of Walter Davis, a young Scotsman employed as a collector by the Veitch firm. In 1873, Davis had been dispatched by Veitch to collect large quantities of the highly coveted *M. veitchiana* from southern Peru. During this journey, Davis discovered many other *Masdevallia* species, including this striking species with its brilliant yellow flowers. These plants rapidly gained favor and were widely cultivated in Europe for many years, although they eventually disappeared from collections, joining the ranks of other "lost" orchid species. *Masdevallia davisii* were recently reintroduced by David Welisch of San Francisco (1978) and by Berthold Würstle of Spielberg, Germany (1980). The species grows at elevations of 3000 to 3600 m in the high mountain regions near Cuzco, Peru. *Masdevallia davisii* is grown cool and blooms in the late spring. The 6.5 to 9 cm, showy flowers hold themselves high and appear successively on an erect, slender peduncle, 25 cm long.

Masdevallia davisii 'Elena'. Grower: San Francisco Conservatory of Flowers.

Masdevallia decumana 'JK'. Grower: Ken and Jacqui Holladay.

Masdevallia decumana

The species name comes from the Latin *decumanus*, meaning of a large size, and refers to the size of the flower in comparison to the size of the plant. This attractive species was first collected in 1979 by the Königers in the Department of Amazonas in northeast Peru, where it was found growing epiphytically in cloud forests at an elevation of 2100 m. It also occurs sparingly in southeastern Ecuador. The large (7.5 to 10 cm), highly colorful, solitary flower with widespread lateral sepals is borne on a slender, horizontal peduncle 3 to 5 cm long. *Masdevallia decumana* grows cool to intermediate.

Masdevallia deformis

This species epithet is derived from the Latin for deformed, which refers to the proportions of the flower to the plant—an unfortunate epithet since this very beautiful species deserves a more charming name. The species was first discovered by the collector Hübsch in the mountains east of Loja, Ecuador, in the early part of the 20th century and described from dry herbarium material by Kränzlin in 1921 (which may explain the epithet). Although the species was originally thought to be quite rare, it was found in abundance along a new road south of Yangana, Ecuador, in 1982. (Unfortunately, most of these plants have disappeared from the regions near the highway due to extensive collection.) The glabrous sepals are scarlet to rosy red. The oblong dorsal sepal is connate to the lateral sepals, forming a cylindric sepaline tube, and the acute apex of the triangular free portion contracts into a slender, downward-directed tail. The lateral sepals form a broadly expanded synsepal beyond the sepaline tube, with rounded apices, abruptly contracting into short, slender tails. The ultimate effect of the flower form is that when well bloomed, the plant appears to have multiple pairs of vibrant pink ballerina slippers hanging down from its base. Since the 2.5 to 5 cm long flowers are pendent, the plants are best grown mounted or in baskets. *Masdevallia deformis* grows cool and does not tolerate exposure to temperatures above 24°C. A larger flowered form of this species was at one time called *M. exaltata* but has since been reduced to synonymy; this form actually grows in lower elevations and will do better under intermediate conditions.

Masdevallia deformis. Grower: John Leathers.

Masdevallia elephanticeps. Grower: John Leathers.

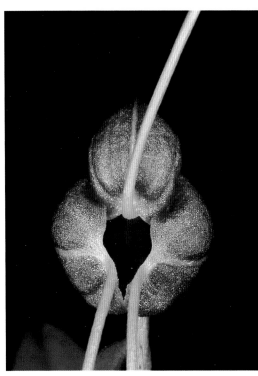

Masdevallia encephala. Grower: San Francisco Conservatory of Flowers.

Masdevallia elephanticeps

The name for this species is derived from Latin for elephant headed and refers to the appearance of the enormous flower with its thick, forward-projecting sepaline tails resembling the pachyderm's trunk and tusks. *Masdevallia elephanticeps* was first collected by Warszewicz in 1854 in the region between Ocaña and Pamplona in the Eastern Cordillera of Colombia at elevations of 1980 to 3000 m, where the immense plants grow on the mossy branches of large trees. The distinctive, large (10 cm), bright yellow and wine-red flowers are produced at the base of the large, leathery leaves. This species should be grown under cool conditions.

Masdevallia encephala

The Greek word *encephalos* means brain and alludes to the appearance of the distinctive flower of this species. It was first collected in 1975 by J. Guevara in Colombia in the Municipality of Charalá, at an elevation of 2200 to 2600 m. "The brain," as this species is nicknamed, was first thought to be a monstrous form of some species related to *M. caudata*, but it is now recognized as a unique species abundant in several areas in the Eastern Cordillera of Colombia. The inflorescence is a single flower, borne on an erect, slender peduncle 5 to 8 cm long. The inflated sepals are deeply connate and converge at the apices, forming a small, round aperture just a few millimeters wide, surrounded by three slender tails. The side view of this unique flower is of a small, inflated head with three long whiskers, while the front view emphasizes the crazy "cheeks" and the narrow aperture formed by the inflated sepals. Quite possibly, the weird shape of the bloom prevents the pollinators from escaping too easily. The dorsal sepaline tail is yellow-green and the sepals are basically a rose-purple color. *Masdevallia encephala* grows cool to intermediate.

Masdevallia erinacea

One of the most charming miniature species, *Masdevallia erinacea* hails from Costa Rica to Ecuador in premontane rain forests and is an intermediate- to warm-growing, tufted epiphyte found at elevations of 700 to 1400 m. The flowers of this species are bristly, like a hedgehog, which is the Latin derivation for the species epithet, although some growers think the flower looks more like a space alien. It has a yellow dorsal sepal with reddish brown lateral sepals, all with downward-pointing tails. Its inflorescence is usually single flowered (although a successive second flower quite often appears after the first flower drops), 4 to 7 cm long, and it blooms spring to summer. The flowers are held just above the leaves.

Masdevallia erinacea. Grower: Brad Cotten.

Masdevallia expers

Derived from a Latin word that means without or free from, the epithet refers to the absence of sepaline tails in this species. Discovered by Father Andreetta and Mario Portillo circa 1987 in the Morona-Santiago region of southeastern Ecuador (elevation 1500 m), this tiny species appears to be endemic to this area. The descending to pendent inflorescence bears flowers successively on a few-flowered raceme. The completely tailless sepals are yellow and heavily suffused and spotted with dark red. This species is grown intermediate to cool and remains quite uncommon in collections.

Masdevallia expers. Grower: John Leathers.

Masdevallia exquisita

The species epithet is derived from the Latin word *exquisitus*, meaning choice or excellent, and refers to its striking flowers. A relatively recent discovery to the genus, *M. exquisita* was found growing epiphytically in trees along a gulch west of Coroico, Bolivia (elevation 1800 m), and was cultivated by Alexander Hirtz in Quito, Ecuador. Luer and Hirtz published the description of this species in 1993. This species is apparently endemic in forested valleys east of La Paz in north-central Bolivia. The large (15 to 20 cm), bell-shaped or shallow bowl–shaped flowers are distinguished by snow-white sepals with a brilliant, bright rosy-red suffusion on the middle third or half, and orange toward the base. The sepaline tails are long and slender, and a yellow-green color. This species is grown under cool to intermediate conditions.

Masdevallia exquisita. Grower: Brad Cotten.

Masdevallia floribunda. Grower: J. Hamilton/R. Ehlers.

Masdevallia floribunda

This is a free-flowering species—hence its name, which is derived from the Latin *floribundus*, meaning with many flowers. This fairly common species has a widespread distribution ranging from southern Mexico to Honduras, at elevations ranging from 400 to 1500 m. *Masdevallia floribunda* was probably first collected around 1840 by botanists in the state of Veracruz, Mexico. In addition, this species is also distributed over the Mexican states of Oaxaca and Chiapas, and it occurs in Guatemala, Honduras, and Belize. Living plants were first described by Lindley in 1843, and other specimens with different coloring or regions of occurrence were later described as *M. galeottiana* (purple), *M. lindeniana* (pale yellow), and *M. tuerckheimii* (Guatemalan, larger flowered, densely purple spotted). All of these have been reduced to synonymy under *M. floribunda*. The typical *M. floribunda* is characterized by peduncles that are about the same length as the leaves, with rather small (2 to 3 cm) flowers and pale yellow to white sepals with purple dots, but it is an extremely variable species. *Masdevallia floribunda* grows under intermediate to warm conditions and generally flowers from summer to fall. The plants can be grown potted or mounted, but the mounted plants must not dry out.

Masdevallia gilbertoi. Grower: Steve Beckendorf.

Masdevallia gilbertoi

This species was named in honor of Gilberto Escobar R., of Medellín, Colombia, who was the first *Masdevallia* enthusiast to cultivate this species. All plants in cultivation originate from those first cultivated by Escobar. The original site of collection by B. Tascon, in 1966, was near Anserma in the Department of Risaralda, Colombia (elevation 2000 m). One of the more stunning species of this genus, the large (10 to 13 cm) white flower with rose-red midveins has a distinctive, long, forward-pointing tail of the dorsal sepal and long, relaxed tails of the lateral sepals. The species likes moderately cool temperatures and average light and may flower profusely several times per year.

Masdevallia glandulosa. Grower: Marni Turkel.

Masdevallia glandulosa

The species epithet is derived from the Latin *glandulosus*, meaning bearing glands, and refers to the inner surface of the sepals. It was first collected in 1978 by a young Peruvian named Edgar Lopez, who found it growing epiphytically on thick, mossy trunks in a warm, wet valley of a small tributary of the Río Marañon in northern Peru (elevation 1200 m). Subsequently, it was also found in cloud forests above Zumba in the province of Zamora-Chinchipe, Ecuador. This is one of the few highly fragrant masdevallias with a sweet cinnamon or clove smell. The single, 5 to 7.5 cm, bowl-shaped flowers are borne by a slender, erect, to suberect peduncle, 4 to 5 cm long with a bract near the base. The sepals are bright rose, orange to yellow toward the base, and are conspicuously glandular-pubescent within. This species prefers intermediate (although it can tolerate warm) conditions and can bloom twice per year. During cool, damp periods the faded flowers can develop mold and should be removed to prevent cross-infection of the leaves.

Masdevallia harlequina

This species is named for Harlequin, the clown character of the *La Commedia dell'Arte*, who is usually depicted with a mask and multicolored tights. This species was quite recently discovered in the Huánuco region of Peru (without specific collection data) and cultivated at J & L Orchids of Easton, Connecticut. Luer published the species in 1997. Its has also been collected in Carpish Tunnel/Pass region of Peru, which is just up the road from the city of Huánuco at an elevation of 2800 m. This unique but delightful species is apparently quite rare and endemic to central Peru. The inflorescence is a single flower borne by a suberect to horizontal peduncle approximately 4 cm long. The dorsal sepal is pale orange, the lateral sepals are greenish to tan, and all three sepals have small patches of dark purple hairs that appear as spots. *Masdevallia harlequina* requires cool growing conditions and does not do well if grown intermediate.

Masdevallia harlequina. Grower: John Leathers.

Masdevallia hercules. Grower: John Leathers.

Masdevallia hercules

This striking species was named after Greek mythological character Hercules, famed for his strength. The name refers to the fleshy, stiff nature of the flower of this species. It is found in Ecuador and Colombia at elevations of 1300 to 2200 m. The long-lasting (up to two months), fleshy, 7 to 8 cm flower is brick-red with raised darker red veins and yellow tails. In addition, the coloring toward the base of the flower is more yellow. The plant itself is quite large, about 30 cm tall, with large, thick leaves. *Masdevallia hercules* prefers to be grown cool and has a reputation for being somewhat difficult to cultivate.

Masdevallia heteroptera

The name for this species is derived from the Greek word *heteropteron*, meaning having wings of different shapes, which refers to the difference of the dorsal versus lateral sepals. This species is thought to have been originally collected by the Belgian collec-

Masdevallia heteroptera. Grower: Ernest Katler.

tor Patín in Department of Antioquia (Medellín), Colombia, from an unknown locality, and it was formally described by Reichenbach in 1875. Subsequently, this epiphytic species has been found in cloud forests at elevations ranging from 2000 to 2650 m in the Central Cordillera of Colombia. This species is somewhat variable in its form, which may account for the number of taxonomic synonyms (*M. fissa*, *M. palmensis*, *M. restrepoidea*, *M. trinemoides*, and *Rodrigoa fasciata* and *R. heteroptera*). The dorsal sepal is greenish yellow, marked with dark purple–brown bars or dots, and the lateral sepals are oblong and deep purple and have revolute sides and subacute apices contracted into slender tails. *Masdevallia heteroptera*, like most others in the subgenus *Meleagris*, are considered difficult to grow. This species requires cool to intermediate conditions and grows more vigorously under cooler conditions.

Masdevallia hirtzii

Named in honor of Alexander Hirtz of Quito, Ecuador, who discovered the species, Father Andreetta and Hirtz simultaneously found this species growing epiphytically in a forest east of Los Encuentros, in the Cordillera del Condor region of the Zamora-Chinchipe Province, Ecuador (elevation 1550 m). The waxy, bright orange flowers, 7.6 to 10 cm, are distinguished by their arching, tubular shape with a widely expanded orifice. The petals, lip, and column are also orange. This species is grown under cool to intermediate conditions. When well grown, it can put on an abundant and attractive display of bright orange flowers and can bloom almost continuously year-round.

Masdevallia hoeijeri. Grower: Walter Teague.

Masdevallia hoeijeri

This small species is named in honor of Thomas Höeijer of the Bergius Botanical Garden Museum in Stockholm, who, with Stig Dalström, discovered the species north of Gualaquiza, Ecuador (elevation 1600 m), in 1984. *Masdevallia hoeijeri* has also been collected from the Cordillera del Condor (elevation 1500 to 1600 m), and east of the pass between Loja and Zamora (elevation 2600 m). E. Valencia also collected this species at a more distant site, at an elevation of 1600 to 1800 m in the Department of Antioquia, Colombia. The inflorescence is a solitary flower, large (15 to 20 mm) for the size of the plant, and borne by a slender, weak, suberect, short (10 to

Masdevallia hirtzii. Grower: San Francisco Conservatory of Flowers.

15 mm) peduncle. The flower features a short, greenish yellow, inflated, sepaline tube, with red-brown speckling on the veins and short yellow tails. The apex of the lip is verruculose and dark red. This species should be grown intermediate but will grow cool, and some growers find that it does very well mounted if not allowed to dry out between waterings.

Masdevallia hortensis

The Latin word *hortensis* means pertaining to the garden. This species was first discovered in a region close to the town of Jardín, Colombia, and thus it was named, in a fashion, for the locality where it was found. It was discovered by Rodrigo Escobar in 1983 in a remote, high (elevation 2600 m) area of the Western Cordillera of Colombia. The inflorescence is a congested, successively flowered raceme, borne on a slender, erect peduncle, 6 to 9 cm long, with a bract below the middle. The sepals are white, suffused with a yellow to orange-brown coloration below the middle, and are variably spotted with purple. From the front, the unique shape of the 3.5 cm flower reminds one of a bowlegged cowboy, complete with chaps. *Masdevallia hortensis* prefers to be grown cool but is somewhat difficult to maintain in cultivation.

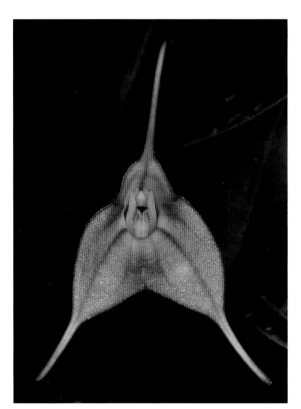

Masdevallia hymenantha. Grower: Lil Severin.

Masdevallia hymenantha

The name for this species comes from the Greek *hymen*, meaning skin or membrane, and *anthos*, meaning flower, and it refers to the thin, translucent sepals of the dried specimens sent to Reichenbach by the Matthews in 1846. This "lost" species was not seen live until 1981, when Jorge Meza collected the plants in the Department of Amazonas, Peru, between Bagua and Chachapoyas, elevation 1800 m. This species is endemic to the moist valleys of a few tributaries of the Río Marañon. The inflorescence is a solitary flower, with a curved, cylindrical sepaline tube, borne by an erect, slender peduncle, 6 to 7 cm long. The smooth sepals are light purple to hot pink with darker tails. *Masdevallia hymenantha* is grown cool to intermediate and blooms in the late fall to early winter.

Masdevallia hortensis. Grower: John Leathers.

Masdevallia ignea

The species epithet is derived from the Latin word *igneus*, meaning fire-red, and refers to the striking color of the flower of this showy species. First collected from the Eastern Cordillera of Colombia in 1879 and imported by Messrs. Low and Company, the original collector and locality are unknown. The species has been subsequently found growing luxuriantly as a terrestrial at elevations of 3000 to 3130 m in the rich humus of tall forests of the Department of Norte de Santander and in the forest below Páramo de Jurisdicciones in Colombia. After its initial discovery, it became an immediate horticultural favorite, and collectors were sent to find color variations. The colors include yellow-red, oranges, red and red-oranges, with varying degrees of pink to purple suffusion. The flower size is also quite variable, but the species is readily distinguished by the tail of the dorsal sepal that curves downward between the lateral sepals. This cool-growing species has been used extensively in hybridization and blooms in the late spring to summer.

Masdevallia ignea. Grower: John Leathers.

Masdevallia infracta

The Latin word *infractus* means sharply bent and refers to the shape of the sepaline tube of this species. *Masdevallia infracta* is a relatively frequent species, found in the mountainous areas of southern Brazil, where it occurs in various color forms and sizes. This species was one of the very earliest species identified in the genus *Masdevallia*. Some of the various color forms were originally designated as distinct species (for example, *M. albidus* and *M. aurantiacus*); other synonyms for this species include *M. aristata*, *M. forgetiana*, *M. longicaudata*, *M. tridentata*, and *M. triquetra*. *Masdevallia infracta* is characterized by a triquetrous peduncle nearly or barely as long as the leaf, which bears a congested, successively few (one to five) flowered raceme. The sepaline tube is more or less laterally compressed and suborbicular with a prominent constriction below, just distal to the mentum. The sepals may be white to yellow, variously suffused with purple, or occasionally entirely purple. *Masdevallia infracta* may be grown cool, intermediate, or warm but does best at cool to intermediate temperatures. The species blooms in the summer. *Masdevallia infracta* is frequently used in hybridizing to make more warm-tolerant hybrids.

Masdevallia infracta. Grower: Pamela Leaver.

Masdevallia iris. Grower: Marni Turkel.

Masdevallia laucheana. Grower: Lil Severin.

Masdevallia iris

The species epithet is named for the Greek goddess of the rainbow and refers to the delightful coloring of the flower of this species. This species is apparently restricted to northern Venezuela (1200 to 2250 m) and was first collected by Roberto Mejia in 1972. *Masdevallia iris* is similar to and related to *M. caudata*, but the 7.5 to 10 cm flowers are smaller, more cupped and striped, and suffused with a reddish orange color. All of the cultivated plants of this species come from Mejia's original collection. *Masdevallia iris* grows cool to intermediate.

Masdevallia laucheana

This species is named in honor of Herr Lauche of Eisgrub, Austria, who was a friend of Kränzlin. It has been in continuous cultivation since 1892, although no information on the original collector is available. Subsequently, the species has been collected in Costa Rica from a region south of San José at an elevation of 1500 m. The sepals are white and may be partially marked with purple along the veins. The dorsal sepal is connate to the lateral sepals for 6 mm to form a campanulate, sepaline tube, and the free portion is obtuse and contracts into a comparatively stout, reflexed orange tail. The free portions of the lateral sepals are contracted into decurved orange tails similar to the dorsal sepal. This species is quite similar in appearance to *M. attenuata*, however, the conical sepaline tube of *M. laucheana* is broadly dilated above the middle into a secondary mentum, whereas *M. attenuata* lacks this mentum and usually has purple stripes along the veins. Some clones of *M. laucheana* are pleasantly fragrant. This species is grown intermediate.

Masdevallia lehmannii

This medium to large, epiphytic, cool- to intermediate-growing species was named in honor of Frederich Carl Lehmann, the discoverer of the species and the German Consul at Popayán, Colombia, in the late 1800s. *Masdevallia lehmannii* was collected by Lehmann in 1876 in a dense forest on the Cordillera de Amboca in Ecuador, where it was found at 2000 to 2500 m. This species is quite similar to *M. polysticta*, with a densely, many flowered raceme up to 10 cm long. The flowers are a yellow-white to yellow-orange with an orange suffusion at the base and are spotted with red freckles. All three sepals have long, delicate yellow tails. The sepals are shortly and densely pubescent externally and more sparsely pubescent on the inner surface. The dorsal sepal is hooded, with the sepaline tail facing forward and often down between the two lateral sepaline tails. The flowers have a faint to sometimes strong unpleasant odor.

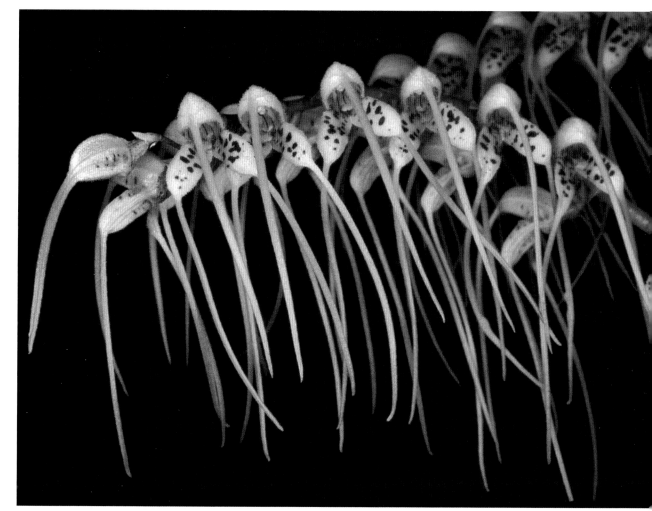

Masdevallia lehmannii. Grower unknown.

Masdevallia limax. Grower: Ron Parsons.

Masdevallia limax

The name for this species is Latin for slug, which while an accurate description of the shape of the flower is not a very attractive name for such a delightful little species. First collected in 1974 in the Tungurahua Province (elevation 2000 m) of Ecuador by Father Andreetta, it was later flowered by Benigno Malo in 1978 and described as a new species shortly afterward. It is a local but abundant species that grows in wet forests on both sides of the Central Cordillera of Ecuador. The 4 cm long, single, bright-orange tubular flower has a characteristic "pot belly," a narrow orifice, which may be somewhat lighter in color at the base of the tube and has short and lighter colored sepaline tails. This is one of the tubular species (like *M. maxilimax* and *M. mendozae*) that may be pollinated by hummingbirds. *Masdevallia limax* grows cool to intermediate.

Masdevallia livingstoneana

This species was discovered by Roezl on a trip to Panama in 1873 and was described by Reichenbach in 1874 to honor David Livingstone, the famous Scottish explorer who was rescued in Africa by the English explorer Sir Henry Morgan Stanley. The distribution of this species is quite restricted to the narrow isthmus of Panama, and today it is difficult to find in the wild. This is one of the few *Masdevallia* species that requires the hot, humid climate found at sea level in the tropics. The 2.5 cm flower is basically white with pinkish and dark wine-colored markings, with thickened sepaline tails, and all three sepals usually recurve. These plants will grow vigorously and flower well under warm, moist, but well-ventilated conditions.

Masdevallia lychniphora

Relatively few specimens of this species have been found in the wild, all within the locality of a small area of cloud forest between Chachapoyas and Pomacochas at an elevation of 2000 m in the Amazonia region of Peru. The plants grow epiphytically on the thin twigs of low forest trees. The species epithet derives from the Greek *lychnis*, which means a ruby, and *phoros*, meaning bearing, and aptly describes the bright red suffusion of the lateral sepals. The solitary, exceptionally showy flowers are borne on a nearly horizontal, short peduncle (1.2 to 2 cm long). The dorsal sepal is white to light orange with darker orange-yellow raised veins within, while the lateral sepals are bright to dark red and often have white edges. This species grows cool to intermediate and may bloom more than once per year.

Masdevallia livingstoneana. Grower: John Leathers.

Masdevallia lychniphora. Grower: San Francisco Conservatory of Flowers.

Masdevallia macrura. Grower: San Francisco Conservatory of Flowers.

Masdevallia macrura

The species name derives from the Greek *macros*, meaning long and large, and *ura*, meaning tail, and describes its long, sepaline tails. *Masdevallia macrura* was first discovered by Roezl in 1871 near Sonsón in the Central Cordillera of Colombia (2300 to 2600 m), although the living plants Roezl collected perished in the long journey to Europe, as did many thousands of plants during those early times. Shuttleworth collected plants not long after Roezl, and his were successfully established in cultivation. *Masdevallia macrura* is the largest known species of the genus *Masdevallia*, in both its vegetative and floral aspects. The flowers, which are held near to the top of or above the leaves, may measure more than 40 cm tall from the tip of the dorsal sepal to the tip of a lateral sepal and feature exquisite tapestrylike markings. The sepals are rigid, fleshy, and purple, red-brown, or yellow-brown marked with purple. The purple form is typically smaller, with a flower approximately 25 cm tall. *Masdevallia macrura* grows epiphytically and lithophytically on mossy trees and rocks in cloud forests, and although once abundant it has suffered the fate of both habitat destruction and overcollection, such that now it is uncommon. This coarse-rooted species should be grown cool and potted in somewhat coarse potting mix.

Masdevallia marthae

This species is named after Martha Posada de Robledo of Medellín, Colombia, who first discovered *M. marthae* flowering in her orchid collection in 1971. The origin of the original specimen is unknown, but it was apparently purchased among other orchids from an unknown collector. Subsequently, the species was rediscovered in 1993 on the road to a television tower at an elevation of 2400 m in the Department of Risaralda, Colombia. The striking flower of this species is characterized by an erect, ventricose sepaline tube. The sepals are yellow-green with dark brown striping along the veins, and the sepaline tails are slender and forwardly directed. This species is grown cool to intermediate but remains quite rare in cultivation.

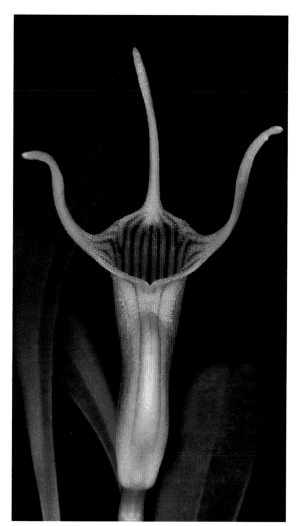

Masdevallia marthae. Grower: Ernest Katler.

Masdevallia mejiana. Grower: Ernest Katler.

Masdevallia mejiana

This species is named in honor of Alvaro Mejía of Medellín, Colombia, in whose orchid collection this species was discovered in 1970. The original collection data for this species is unknown, but it has subsequently been collected at lower elevations in the northern part of the Western Cordillera of Colombia (500 to 815 m), where it grows in the high branches of tall trees, in considerable sunlight. This profusely flowering species blooms in the dry season (between December and February) in the wild and intermittently throughout the year in cultivation. The inflorescence is characterized by a solitary (occasionally followed by a second) 10 cm white flower with faint purplish speckling and a yellow flush where the dorsal and lateral sepals fuse, and with bright yellow tails. The lateral sepals are deeply connate, forming a broad synsepal with descending yellow tails similar to the dorsal sepal. *Masdevallia mejiana* grows intermediate to warm and when in bloom emits an enticing, spicy-sweet fragrance during the day.

Masdevallia melanoxantha

The name for this species comes from the Greek *melanoxanthos*, meaning dark yellow, and refers to the color of the flower. This species was discovered by the Belgians Nicholas Funck and Louis Joseph Schlim, who collected numerous botanical specimens from Colombia and Venezuela between 1846 and 1852. It is endemic to the northern part of the Eastern Cordillera of Colombia (1400 to 2800 m) and adjacent Venezuela (1100 to 1400 m). *Masdevallia melanoxantha* has thick, coriaceous leaves, with a long (20 to 30 cm), triquetrous peduncle that bears a congested, successively several-flowered raceme up to 5 cm long. The rigid, fleshy, bilabiate flowers have a short sepaline tube, with a narrow, upright yellow or yellow-green dorsal sepal suffused with purple. The lateral sepals are burgundy-red and minutely verrucose on the inner surface. The unique shape of this flower is such that the overall appearance has been likened to a large, "goofy bird." *Masdevallia melanoxantha* is

Masdevallia melanoxantha. Grower: San Francisco Conservatory of Flowers.

grown cool to intermediate and blooms in the summer. This species may bloom repeatedly on the same spike after months of inactivity; thus, if the spike is still green, it should not be removed.

Masdevallia mendozae

This species was named in honor of Hartman Eudaldo Mendoza of Vilcabamba, Ecuador, who discovered the plant lying by a litter-covered path in a remote forested region (elevation 2200 m) of the province of Zamora-Chinchipe, Ecuador, in 1979. Later, a large colony of plants was discovered in a nearby area by Dennis D'Alessandro. This vigorous and highly floriferous species has waxy, tubular, long-lived, brilliant orange to brilliant yellow flowers. The plants are small to medium in size, epiphytic, and have slender roots. The inflorescence is solitary, showy, and more or less horizontal, borne by an erect to horizontal, slender peduncle, 3 to 6 cm long. *Masde-*

Masdevallia mendozae. Grower: San Francisco Conservatory of Flowers.

vallia mendozae is similar to *M. maxilimax* (and less so to *M. limax*), and all have bright orange sepaline tubes produced in profusion. *Masdevallia mendozae* can be distinguished by its sepaline tube without ventricose swelling, the wide aperture to the tube, its lining with fine white hairs, and its comparatively stubby sepaline tails. All three species are thought to be pollinated by moths or hummingbirds. *Masdevallia mendozae* is grown intermediate to cool and blooms in the fall to early spring.

Masdevallia minuta

In Latin, *minutus* means very small, which in the case of *M. minuta*, is an accurate description of this tiny plant. One of the earliest described species of *Masdevallia*, it was discovered by Splittgerben in Surinam in 1842, although a precise locality is not known. Lindley formally described the species from a collection by Hostmann in 1843. *Masdevallia minuta* is widely distributed in the eastern lowlands (1100 to 1300 m) of the mountainous parts of South America from the Guianas to Bolivia, although it has not been found in Ecuador, Colombia, or Brazil. The species has small, white, tubular flowers with yellow tails and likes to be grown in intermediate to warm conditions. When well bloomed, the cloudlike appearance of the abundant white flowers held above the leaves can be quite striking.

Masdevallia minuta. Grower: San Francisco Conservatory of Flowers.

Masdevallia murex

This species grows in small clumps in the wet montane forests of Ecuador and Peru at 1800 m. The name of this species is based on the similarity of the extremely verrucose apex of the lip to some species of *Murex*, a genus of marine mollusks with spiny protuberances. This species was first collected by Walter Teague in 1979 in southernmost Ecuador, growing along an old foot-trail from Amaluza to Valladolid. (Today a new gravel road has been built in this region, and unfortunately the forests are being cut and burned.) The plant flowered two years later and was published by Luer. All plants presently in cultivation are derived from the divisions of the original clone brought back by Teague. This cool to intermediate grower requires high humidity. The 3 cm flowers bloom in the summer on an ascending, 4 cm long, purple-suffused, solitary-flowered inflorescence. The flat-faced, shallow-tubed, triangular flower is held at or below leaf height. The sepals are a greenish yellow and bear purple-red veins. A final striking feature of this species is the wine-red, bristly apex of the lip.

Masdevallia murex. Grower: Brad Cotten.

Masdevallia navicularis

The species epithet is a Latin word meaning boat-shaped and refers to shape of the synsepal, but it actually resembles a pelican with its pouch opened. *Masdevallia navicularis* was first collected in 1974 by Roberto Mejia in the state of Táchira, Venezuela, where it was growing epiphytically in a cloud forest at an elevation of 2600 m. This species produces 2.5 cm flowers, somewhat smallish in proportion to the plant. It flowers successively on a gradually lengthening raceme over a period of up to a year. The sepals are purple-brown, with a yellowish dorsal sepal and virtually without ventral sepaline tails. The sepals are characterized by their thick, rigid texture that is smooth on the outside and densely warted on the inner surface. The lateral sepals form a concave, boat-shaped synsepal, and the

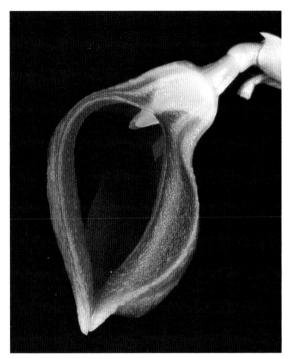

Masdevallia navicularis. Grower: Lil Severin.

narrower dorsal sepal is bent forward, covering the boat shape. The apices of all three sepals arch inward so that the points come together. This shape results in lateral "windows" to the interior of the flower. This species is grown cool to intermediate.

Masdevallia nidifica

The name of this species is derived from the Latin word *nidificus*, meaning to make a nest, which describes its caespitose habit. This is a relatively common species with a wide range of distribution—it is found in Nicaragua (at 1520 m), Costa Rica (at 1500 m), Panama (at 1100 m), Colombia (at 1200 to 2000 m), and Ecuador (at 600 to 2000 m). Some variability occurs in color, size, and shape of the petals throughout this broad range, with larger forms found on the western slopes of Pichincha, Ecuador, while smaller forms are found in Central America. The larger Ecuadoran form was collected by Consul Lehmann and described by Reichenbach in 1878. The more typical color form of the plant in cultivation is derived from the Central American populations and is known as *M. nidifica* var. *alexandrae*. The small maroon and white flowers, with long, wispy sepaline tails, bloom in the fall to winter and have a fragrance described by some as "herby." A translucent yellow color form is known as *M. nidifica* var. *ventricosa*, and a white form is known as *M. nidifica* var. *alba*. The leaves of this species can be an attractive reddish green color. *M. nidifica* does well mounted and is

Masdevallia nidifica. Grower: San Francisco Conservatory of Flowers.

grown in intermediate to warm conditions but has been seen growing well under cool conditions.

Masdevallia norops

The Greek word *norops* means bright or gleaming, which alludes to the bright yellow and orange flower of this species. This epiphytic species was first collected by Father Andreetta and Alexander Hirtz in 1976 in the province of Napo, Ecuador, elevation 1500 m, but since that time it has been found in other parts of Ecuador, including the cloud forests north of Baeza (elevation 1500 m) and above Valladolid (elevation 1900 m). Königer also collected this species in the Department of Amazonas, Peru (elevation 1500 m). This striking species has an erect, slender peduncle bearing a single spectacular flower. The sepals can be bright orange or a light yellow suffused with bright orange and are shiny, glabrous externally, and shortly pubescent within. A "channel" in the middle of each sepal follows the contour of the flower, giving the blooms an intriguing appearance. The dorsal deflexed sepal is connate to the lateral

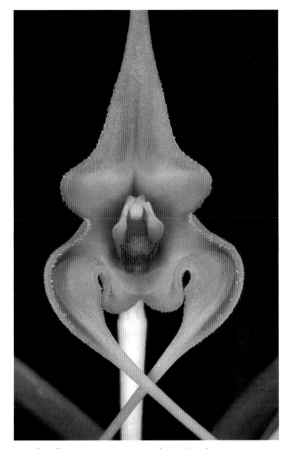

Masdevallia norops. Grower: Valerie Henderson.

Masdevallia notosibirica. Grower: Walter Teague.

sepals for 5 mm to form a broad, shallow cup, and the acute apex is contracted into an erect, yellow-green tail about 3 cm long. The unique feature of this species are the lateral sepals that curve like a sickle (falcate), with the acute apices attenuating into the tails. *Masdevallia norops* grows cool to intermediate, and though not easy to grow, it can be a very rewarding species when in bloom, generally in the winter.

Masdevallia notosibirica

This species is named for the community of Siberia, in the Department of Santa Cruz, Bolivia, where it was found by Martin Cárdenas of Cochabamba, Bolivia, in 1950. However, this species lay unidentified at Harvard University (Oakes Ames Orchid Herbarium) for 20 years until it was found by a Japanese team of botanists, led by Fumio Maekawa, in 1971, who published the species in 1973. The Greek word *notos* means southern and thus refers to the Bolivian Siberia as opposed to the Russian

Siberia. This species is endemic to a small area of cloud forest in Bolivia (2400 to 2600 m) at the southern extreme of the north slope of the Andes. It is easily recognized by its distinctive, bright pink, more or less arcuate, sepaline tube that is somewhat inflated toward the apex. The ends of the sepals form a small opening into the flower that most likely accommodates the bill of a hummingbird, and the tails of the sepals, guarding the entrance to the flower, are short and curly, like tiny pigs' tails. *Masdevallia notosibirica* is grown cool and needs to stay moist, requiring three to five waterings per week, depending on culture conditions.

Masdevallia odontocera

The species epithet comes from the Greek *odonto*, meaning tooth, and *cera*, meaning horn, and is in allusion to the tusklike tails of the lateral sepals. *Masdevallia odontocera* was first collected in 1941 by the team of J. Cuatracasas, Richard Schultes, and Elmer Smith in the cloud forests of the Eastern Cordillera of Colombia. This species grows epiphytically on the mossy trunks and branches of small trees. Solitary, showy flowers grow around the base of the plant, borne on suberect, slender peduncles, 1.5 to 4.5 cm in length. The yellow, obovate dorsal sepal points forward and has three prominent purple stripes along the veins with an upcurving, yellow tail. The light rose-purple lat-

Masdevallia odontocera. Grower: Ernest Katler.

eral sepals, with darker purplish stripes, are narrowly acute, ending in white, up-sweeping tails that are longer than the decurved tail of the dorsal sepal. Interestingly, the lateral sepals spread in opposite directions, giving this flower a unique shape. This is a fairly rare species in cultivation and is grown under cool to intermediate conditions.

Masdevallia ova-avis

This species is one of the multifloral species in the subgenus *Amanda*, but unlike most in this group, it is characterized by a cluster of flowers at the end of the inflorescence. This appearance gives this species the common name of "bird's egg" *Masdevallia*, which accurately describes the flowers that look similar to a clutch of eggs when the flowers are viewed from above. The flowers are light gray-blue, with dense, purplish speckling and orange patches toward the base of the ventral sepals. In 1974, Benigno Malo discovered this species growing epiphytically along a road from Quito to Santo Domingo, at an elevation of 2000 m. The plant is found in the dense cloud forests of Ecuador at elevations of 2000 to 2500 m, as well as on steep road embankments on the western slopes of Pinchincha in western Ecuador. *Masdevallia ova-avis* is cold- to cool-growing and prefers partial shade.

Masdevallia ova-avis. Grower: Lil Severin.

Masdevallia pachyura. Grower: Gerardus Staal.

Masdevallia pachyura

The epithet for this species is Greek for thick tail, which aptly characterizes the stout, sepaline tails of this medium-sized species. Roezl originally collected this species from an unidentified location in Ecuador, and it was published by Reichenbach in 1874. This frequent but variable epiphytic species is found on the western slopes of the Andes of south-central Ecuador (1800 to 2600 m). The simultaneous, several-flowered (four to nine) raceme is borne on a slender, suberect, 8 to 12 cm long peduncle held at or slightly above the height of the leaves. White to yellow sepals are spotted with brown to red-purple. The dorsal sepal is broadly ovate, smooth, concave, and connate to the lateral sepals for 3 to 5 mm to form a gaping sepaline cup. Thick, clublike tails are formed by contraction of the obtuse or rounded apex. The lateral sepals are spread; covered with minute, soft, fine hairs, and connate 1.5 to 2 mm to form a broadly rounded mentum beneath the column-foot. The subacute apices also contract into a thick, clavate (clublike) orange or yellow tail. This cold- to cool-growing species grows well in dappled or partial shade and blooms in the fall.

Masdevallia papillosa

Derived from the Latin *papillosus*, meaning papillae, the epithet for this species refers to minute, nipplelike projections on the sepals. *Masdevallia papillosa* was collected in 1993 by Hartman Mendoza of Vilcabamba, Ecuador, in the Zamora-Chinchipe Province, where they were found growing epiphytically in a forest east of Palanda at an elevation of 2000 m. Solitary flowers are borne on a slender, horizontal peduncle up to 3.5 cm long, and the beautiful blossoms can be larger than the leaves that bear them. The sepals are creamy on the outer third, deep rose-purple on the lower two-thirds, and prominently papillose within and smooth externally. The column, petals, and lip stand erect in the center of the sepaline cup. This small species is grown cool to intermediate, under low light.

Masdevallia papillosa. Grower: John Leathers.

Masdevallia patriciana. Grower: Brad Cotten.

Masdevallia patriciana

This species is named in honor of Patricia Cevallos de Malo, the wife of Benigno Malo, who discovered this species in 1974, growing at an undisclosed area on the slopes of the Andes (elevation 2300 m) east of Cuenca, Ecuador. The flower spike holds an exquisitely colorful little orchid with long (for its size), thread-thin yellow tails and a round sepaline tube that is purple, pink, and yellow with a prominent whitish belly. The 5 cm flowers present themselves best when grown mounted. *Masdevallia patriciana* grows best under intermediate to cool conditions and should be kept moist. It is a gem of a *Masdevallia*, well worth adding to any orchid collection.

Masdevallia patula

Patulus is a Latin word meaning outspread, which in the case of *M. patula* refers to the large, broad synsepal. This uncommon species grows epiphytically in cloud forests in the Morona-Santiago and Zamora-Chinchipe provinces of Ecuador, at altitudes of 1500 to 2500 m. It was first collected by Malo in 1975. *Masdevallia patula* has a large (10 to 12 cm), very striking flower for the size of the plant, and it booms successively on a slender, horizontal, usually descending peduncle. This species has a huge, yellowish purple synsepal and long, lateral sepaline tails that are white and quite delicate in appearance. The tall, narrow dorsal sepal has prominent purple-red stripes. It grows cool to intermediate in partial shade.

Masdevallia patula. Grower: San Francisco Conservatory of Flowers.

Masdevallia peristeria. Grower: John Leathers.

Masdevallia peristeria

This *Masdevallia* species is named for its dove-like petals; peristeria derives from the Greek word for dove or pigeon. This cold-growing epiphytic or terrestrial species is found at altitudes of 1600 to 2500 m in Colombia and Ecuador. It grows in open woodlands and along water runs near to the ground. Gustav Wallis first collected *M. peristeria* (although the locality was not given) for Messrs. Veitch, and specimens were sent to Reichenbach for identification. Reichenbach's publication of this species occurs in *The Gardeners' Chronicle* in 1874. The plant blooms in the spring and summer on a short (9 cm), terete inflorescence with a single flower. The stiff, waxy, 7.5 to 13 cm flowers have a dovelike shape visible in the column and petals and is held below the leaves. The sepals have a light yellow-tan, bright yellow, or even pinkish background coloration with dark wine-red freckles. The large, wine-red lip is also quite verrucose. This species can also have more than one flowering stem per leaf (not simultaneously), and the flowers last for many weeks. *Masdevallia peristeria* is quite easy to grow in cool conditions.

Masdevallia picturata. Grower: Marni Turkel.

Masdevallia picturata

The epithet for this species comes from the Latin *picturatus*, which means painted, and refers to the intricate spots on its flowers. One of the most widely distributed masdevallias, it has been collected in Panama, Costa Rica, Colombia, Venezuela, Guyana, Ecuador, Bolivia, and Peru. It was first collected from Venezuela somewhere near Caracas (elevation 2000 m) by Herman Wagener in 1850, but Reichenbach did not name it until 1878. *Masdevallia picturata* is usually found growing epiphytically, but it is also found growing terrestrially on clay embankments. This little species is greatly variable in size, and due to the wide variations, the species was also known earlier as *M. cryptocopis*, *M. meleagris*, and *M. ocanensis*, but these were reduced to synonyms by Luer. Plants from Central America and from Andean regions lower than 2700 m tend to be smaller and weaker and have been grouped as the subspecies *minor*. Those found growing in the cold cloud forests at elevations higher than 2700 m are more robust and have larger and more colorful flowers. The white sepals have purple spots, and the lateral sepals are bright orange at the base. The sepaline tails are quite long and hairlike, giving the flower a wispy appearance. *Masdevallia picturata* is cultivated under cool-intermediate conditions, whereas *M. picturata* ssp. *minor* prefers to be grown intermediate.

Masdevallia pileata

The epithet for this species derives from the Latin *pileatus*, meaning with a cap, and refers to the appearance of the dorsal sepal. *Masdevallia pileata* was collected in the Eastern Cordillera of Colombia (locality unknown) by Herr Hubein and was formally described by Luer and Würstle in 1982. This uncommon epiphytic species has solitary 10 cm flowers borne on an arching to horizontal, slender peduncle, 9 to 10 cm long. The sepals are white, glabrous externally, and have fine hairs on the inner surface. The white dorsal sepal is rose-purple at the base and is directed forward, like a baseball cap. The lateral sepals are white and also suffused with rose-purple at the base. The sepaline tails are yellow. This species should be grown cool.

Masdevallia pileata. Grower: John Leathers.

Masdevallia pinocchio

Masdevallia pinocchio is named after Pinocchio, the famed, long-nosed, wooden puppet of the children's story by Carlo Collodi (né Lorenzini), and the epithet refers to the tall, pointed dorsal sepal of this species. It is a rare endemic of east-central Ecuador (Valle de Quijos) at relatively low elevations (1300 to 1500 m), and it was originally collected in 1976 by Father Andreetta and Alexander Hirtz. This species is characterized by a congested, successively several-flowered raceme up to 2 cm long, borne on an erect, triquetrous peduncle 16 to 30 cm long. The unique, relatively large, (5 cm) yellow, flat flower with a reddish overlay is distinguished by the horizontally balanced, oscillating, very dark lip. *Masdevallia pinocchio* grows intermediate to cool and blooms in the late spring.

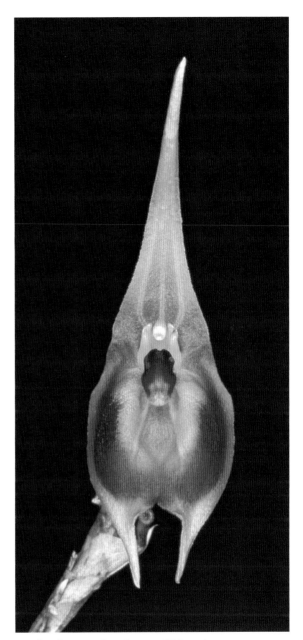

Masdevallia pinocchio. Grower: Lil Severin.

Masdevallia polysticta

The epithet for this species comes from the Greek word *poly*, meaning many, and *stictus*, meaning spotted, which describes the characteristic spotted flowers of this species. This plant is locally abundant with a widespread distribution on the western slopes of the Andes of Ecuador and adjacent northern Peru, where it occurs at elevations of 1900 to 2500 m. The first specimen was collected by Roezl from somewhere in northern Peru and described by Reichenbach in 1874. The simultaneously several-flowered raceme (up to 11 flowers) measures up to 28 cm tall, including the peduncle. The 2.5 to 4.0 cm, white to greenish or yellow-white flowers are spotted with purple, smooth on the outside, and have short to long pubescence on the sepals within. The sepaline tails are yellow, and sometimes the flowers have an orange suffusion on the inside of the ventral sepals. *Masdevallia polystica* grows cold to cool in partial shade.

Masdevallia polysticta. Grower: Lil Severin.

Masdevallia prodigiosa

This species epithet comes from the Latin *prodigiosus*, which means extraordinary or marvelous, which certainly captures the unusual but attractive features of the flower. *Masdevallia prodigiosa* was first collected in 1978 and described the next year by Königer. Once relatively common in the orchid-rich forests between Chachapoyas and Pomacochas and Pomacochas and Moyobamba in northern Peru, at elevations around 2000 m, the severe deforestation of this region threatens the native habitat of this and other orchid species, as well as other plant and animal species endemic to the area. *Masdevallia prodigiosa* thrives in cultivation under cool-intermediate conditions, flowering freely several times per year. The large (5 to 7 cm), almost translucent flowers, the color of ripe cantaloupe, are held at or above the level of the roundish leaves. This species makes a spectacular display, particularly when grown mounted.

Masdevallia prodigiosa. Grower: Ron Parsons.

Masdevallia pteroglossa

The name for this species is Greek for winged tongue and alludes to its winged lip. It was first collected by Consul Lehmann in 1883 in the Department of Cauca, Colombia, but it was not published until 1920 by Schlecter. It is known only from the Western Cordillera of Colombia (elevation 1600 to 1800 m). The inflorescence is a single flower borne by a slender, suberect peduncle, 2.5 to 4 cm long. The sepals are yellowish flecked with red, with long, slender yellow-green tails. The dorsal sepal has one and the lateral sepals two darker red stripes at the base. An added attraction to this cute species is its lip, which wiggles side to side with the slightest breeze. This species is grown cool to intermediate.

Masdevallia pteroglossa. Grower: San Francisco Conservatory of Flowers.

Masdevallia pulcherrima

The name for this species derives from the Latin *pulcherrimus*, the superlative of *pulcher*, meaning pretty, referring to the beautiful flowers. This species was collected by Father Andreetta, Alexander Hirtz, and Carl and Jane Luer in 1978 in the province of Bolivar, Ecuador, below Guaranda (at an elevation greater than 2000 m). It is a rare epiphytic species found growing in cloud forests. *Masdevallia pulcherrima* is easily recognized by the numerous, 2.5 cm, bright white, smooth flowers with prominent, large purple blotches and yellow-orange tails. The tips of the petals and the lip are also a yellow-orange color. This species is grown cool.

Masdevallia pulcherrima. Grower: John Leathers.

Masdevallia pumila

The name for this species derives from the Latin *pumilus*, meaning dwarf, and refers to the small habit of this plant. *Masdevallia pumila* was first collected in Peru by Poeppig in 1830, where it was found growing epiphytically in subandean forests near Cuchero. Subsequently it has been found to have a rather broad distribution on the eastern slopes of the Andes, at elevations of 800 to 1800 m in Colombia, Ecuador, Bolivia, and Peru. The small, whitish, long-tailed flower may be suffused with rose and is borne on a short peduncle. When well bloomed, a profusion of 5 cm flowers can encircle the base of the plant. Another distinguishing characteristic of this species are its narrow, pointed leaves, which are 6.0 to 10.5 cm long and 0.7 to 1.0 cm wide. This is a cool- to intermediate-growing species.

Masdevallia pumila. Grower: Steve Beckendorf.

Masdevallia racemosa

The species epithet comes from the Latin *racemose*, which means a cluster or bunch and refers to the inflorescence of this species, with stalked flowers along an elongated stem that continue to open in succession from below as the stem continues to grow. *Masdevallia racemosa* was first discovered by Theodore Hartweg in 1843 in the region above Popayán, in the Department of Cauca, Colombia (elevation 3000 to 3800 m), growing terrestrially in subpáramo forests in the shade of large trees. This is one of a few long-repent species (another is *M. torta*) in the genus *Masdevallia*, and although the successively flowered raceme may bear only one or two flowers at any given time, up to eighteen may eventually be produced on each inflorescence. The flower is characterized by a bright, red-orange, cylindrical sepaline tube below the middle, beyond which the broad, obtuse, nearly tailless sepals abruptly expand. The sepals are shortly pubescent within, smooth externally, and suffused with darker red-orange along the veins. This species is grown cool and will do well mounted if not allowed to dry out. It is not an easy species in cultivation and not a selection for a neophyte grower.

Masdevallia racemosa. Grower unknown.

Masdevallia reichenbachiana

This species is named in honor of Professor Heinrich Gustav Reichenbach, the renowned orchidologist, professor of botany, and director of the Botanic Gardens at Hamburg University. It was discovered in Costa Rica in 1873 by Endres, who, when he shipped living specimens to Europe, requested that it be named after Reichenbach. This species, now quite rare in the wild, occurs at elevations of 1800 to 2200 m, where it grows on mossy tree trunks and branches. The 10 cm flowers of this species are distinguished by their intense colors, which range from an orange-colored form (var. *aurantiaca*), a dark purple form, and the more common form with yellow-white sepals internally suffused with red along the sides externally. The dorsal sepaline tail frequently recurves back over the tube of the flower. This species is grown under intermediate to cool conditions and flowers in the spring and summer.

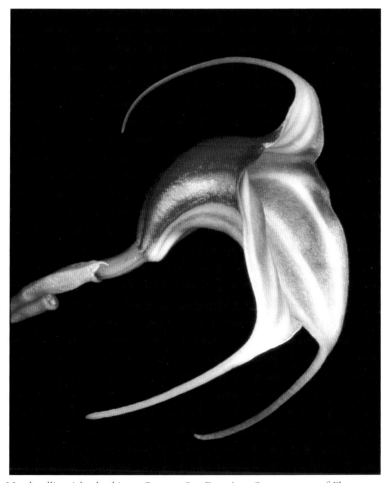

Masdevallia reichenbachiana. Grower: San Francisco Conservatory of Flowers.

Masdevallia richardsoniana

This species was named in honor of the late Don Richardson of Manhasset, New York, who was renowned for his knowledge of orchids, in particular *Masdevallia*. The first collection of this species was by D. and A. Allison in the Chanchamayo Valley of Peru (elevation 1800 m) in 1982 and was described as a new species by Luer in 1988. This small plant has colorful, 4 cm, reddish purple flowers edged in yellow-orange, borne on a slender, erect, triquetrous (although sometimes terete) peduncle. This species grows intermediate and is relatively rare in cultivation.

Masdevallia richardsoniana. Grower: Ron Parsons.

Masdevallia rimarima-alba

The rather odd name for this elegant species derives from a local Indian name *rima rima*, which means talk-talk (Rolando 1996), plus the Latin word *alba*, meaning white. The Huancas, a native civilization of the central Andes of Peru, used the leaves and roots of this orchid as a herbal medicine to improve and accelerate talking in their children. This species was known by its common name, the white uniflora, distinguishing it from the pink uniflora —the true *Masdevallia uniflora* described by Ruiz and Pavón. This species is found in the damp, scrubby vegetation above the ancient community of Huasahuasi, and it is quite likely that Ruiz and Pavón found both species during their collecting expedition to Peru circa 1778. Despite the long history of this white uniflora, it was not considered a distinct species until Luer formally described it in 1979. The sepals are white, faintly suffused with yellow toward the base, with purple veins; the petals are white; and the lip is rose. *Masdevallia rimarima-alba* is distinguished from *M. uniflora* by this coloring, a slightly larger flower, thick sepaline tails, and petals with a short, basal tooth. *Masdevallia rimarima-alba* grows epiphytically or terrestrially among small trees in the microclimate of protected ravines in the otherwise comparatively arid Huasahuasi valley, at an elevation of around 2500 m. This species is grown under cool conditions.

Masdevallia rimarima-alba. Grower: Ernest Katler.

Masdevallia rosea. Grower: Steve Beckendorf.

Masdevallia rosea 'Loma Prieta' HCC/AOS. Grower: San Francisco Conservatory of Flowers.

Masdevallia rosea

The Latin word *rosea*, meaning rose-colored, is indicated for the delicate to hot pink color of this species. First described by Lindley in 1845, this cool-growing epiphytic species is locally abundant on the eastern slopes of the Andes and ranges from southern Colombia to southern Ecuador (2200 to 3200 m). The solitary flower has a short, sepaline tube, with the free portion of the dorsal sepal abruptly contracting into a slender, orange-tinted tail. The falcate lateral sepals are connate for a few millimeters to form a small mentum, and the apices contract into fairly short, slender, orange-tinted tails. A rare white form also occurs. This species is particularly demanding of cool temperatures and blooms in the fall and winter.

Masdevallia rosea. Grower: Steve Beckendorf.

Masdevallia rubeola

From the Latin word meaning measles, the epithet refers to the dense, red-brown spotting overlaid on the tan sepals of this enchanting species. The first known collection of this species was by Roberto Vásquez in the Yungas region of Bolivia (1550 m), in 1988. It has also been collected in Peru (1500 to 2200 m) in the adjacent provinces of Junín and Pasco. This medium-sized, epiphytic species is characterized by a single, more or less downward facing, flattened flower, borne by a slender, suberect to subhorizontal peduncle 3 to 4 cm long. The sepals are smooth and diffusely dotted with red-brown "measles." The sepaline tails often reflex all the way behind the flower. This species also has the typical "wiggly lip" characteristic of the subsection *Oscillantes*. *Masdevallia rubeola* grows cool and is relatively rare in cultivation.

Masdevallia rubeola. Grower: John Leathers.

Masdevallia sanctae-inesiae. Grower unknown.

Masdevallia sanctae-inesiae

This species is named for the orchid farm Santa Ines, owned by Benigno Malo of Ecuador. It was first collected in Ecuador on the eastern slopes of the Andes in the southern part of the province of Morona-Santiago, elevation 2500 m, by Malo in 1973 and described by Luer in 1977. The 7.5 cm, cup-shaped, solitary flower has light green-yellow sepals with a suffusion of a cantaloupe-orange on the inner half of the lateral sepals. The broad, erect lip is also quite distinctive. This species grows cool to intermediate.

Masdevallia scabrilinguis

The Latin word *scabrilinguis* means with rough tongue and refers to the lip of this species, which has characteristically thick, wartlike elevations. The first known collection of the species was from the San José area of Costa Rica, by A. Skutch in 1936 (El General, elevation 915 m). *Masdevallia scabrilinguis* is also found in Panama in the province of Chiriqui. Flowers of this species are small, white, and tubular without stripes, and with yellow to orange sepaline tails. The inflorescence is usually a single

Masdevallia scabrilinguis. Grower: Brad Cotten.

flower, occasionally followed by a second, borne on a slender, erect to suberect peduncle that usually holds the flower just above the leaves. The white sepals are smooth but microscopically pubescent within. The tails of both the dorsal and lateral sepals are yellow. This species will grow happily mounted on cork or tree fern and should be cultivated under intermediate conditions, not allowing the plant to dry out. *Masdevallia scabrilinguis* can occasionally have a mass blooming.

Masdevallia schlimii

This species is named in honor of Louis Schlim, the traveling companion and half brother of Jean Linden, who discovered it growing in the Meridá region of Venezuela in 1843 (elevation 7500 m). The species occurs in western Venezuela and in the adjacent eastern region of Colombia. The loose, simultaneously (four to six) flowering raceme is borne by a 30 to 40 cm peduncle that is terete in cross section (which distinguishes it from a similar species, *M. sceptrum*, which has a triquetrous penduncle). The 12.5 cm flower is characterized by a yellow-orange dorsal sepal, which is connate with

Masdevallia schlimii. Grower: Mike Serpa.

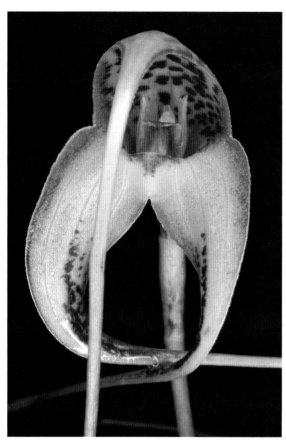

Masdevallia schmidt-mummii. Grower: Bartley Schwartz.

the lateral sepals for 5 mm to form a short, cylindrical tube. The free portion is triangular and contracts into a long, lighter colored, slender tail that may be erect or reflexed. The lateral sepals are a purple-brown color and are fused to form a broad, shallow mentum, then contracting into long, lighter colored, slender tails. The leaves of this cool- to intermediate-growing species are rigid and coriaceous.

Masdevallia schmidt-mummii

This species was named in honor of Helmuth Schmidt-Mumm of Bogotá, Colombia, who first cultivated the species, although it was not formally described until 1978. It has been collected from the Department of Santander in Colombia at elevations ranging from 1800 to 2600 m. This medium-sized, cool-growing epiphyte has very showy 4 to 6 cm solitary flowers held on slender, erect peduncles well above the top of the leaves. A single leaf may have more than one inflorescence, but not at the same time.

Masdevallia schroederiana

Masdevallia schroederiana was named by Frederich Sander in honor of Baron Schröder, who was the first to cultivate the species and to be awarded a First Class Certificate (FCC) by the Royal Horticultural Society. It is thought that Hübsch collected this species for Sanders, questionably from Peru, in 1884. Relatively recently, this species has been collected in Costa Rica, which is now thought to be the true country of origin. In Costa Rica, *M. schroederiana* was found at elevations of 1850 to 1900 m on the crest of the Cordillera de Talamanca, south of San Cristobal de Norte. This species has large (18 to 23 cm), single, showy flowers for its size and can bloom several times per year. The dorsal sepal is dark red to purple, connate to the lateral sepals to form a gaping campanulate tube, and the free portion contracts into a slender white to yellow tail. The lateral sepals have a white "mother of pearl" appearance toward the inside edge and are dark red toward the outside edge. It is grown cool to intermediate with moderate light.

Masdevallia schroederiana. Grower: Golden Gate Orchids.

Masdevallia setacea. Grower: John Leathers.

Masdevallia setacea

The epithet for this species is from the Latin *setaceus*, meaning bristled, which refers to three long tails of the sepals. The first known collection of the species was by Malo in 1975. *Masdevallia setacea* was found growing epiphytically in cloud forests on slopes east of Cuenca, Ecuador (elevation 1700 m). It has subsequently been collected in the Zamora-Chinchipe Province of Ecuador (2000 m) and the nearby province of San Martín, Peru (1600 m). This species is vegetatively similar to many of its relatives in the subsection *Caudatae* that have blackish stems. However, this elegant species is easily recognized by its relatively large (10 to 13 cm), slender, long-tailed, "goblinlike" flower that is much larger than its leaves. The inflorescence is a single flower borne on a slender, erect peduncle, 6 to 9 cm long. The species is quite variable in coloration with very light yellow forms as well as rose-purple. The yellow form can have larger flowers of 18 to 21 cm that are quite open, while the purplish forms tend to have smaller, 11 cm flowers that have recurved sepal edges. The pink to purplish color varieties often have much more reflexed sepals than the yellow varieties. The tails of both the dorsal and lateral sepals are very narrow and a green-orange color. This species is grown cool to intermediate.

Masdevallia sprucei

Reichenbach named this species in 1878 in honor of its English collector, R. Spruce, who found it growing epiphytically along the rivulet Uaiauaka, a tributary of Río Pasimoni (elevation 520 m), in the Amazonas Province of Venezuela in 1854. This species is found in wet forests at low elevations (100 to 800 m) in Amazonian Venezuela and Brazil, an area where very few other pleurothallids are found. This small species with slender roots is distinguished by the successively few-flowered raceme borne by a very slender peduncle, triquetrous in its lower portions and often becoming terete toward the apex. Well-grown plants produce a profusion of 2.5 cm yellow flowers from the base of the newer leaves. The sepals are a pale to medium yellow and microscopically pubescent within. The lateral sepals have an area of bright to dark

Masdevallia sprucei. Grower: John Leathers.

red near the base and are connate for 5 mm to form a shallow mentum. The apices of the lateral sepals are subacute and contracted into thick, yellow tails that point downward, or in some cases, toward one another. This is an intermediate- to warm-growing species.

Masdevallia staaliana

In 1994, this species was named in honor of the noted *Masdevallia* hybridizer Gerardus Staal of Palo Alto, California, who submitted this species for identification. The species originates from southwestern Ecuador (elevation 2500 to 2700 m) in the province of Azuay, where it was collected in 1993 by Alexander Hirtz. The species is characterized by its pubescent, yellowish to orangish flowers. The inflorescence, which is just slightly longer than the leaf, bears three to five simultaneous flowers. This species should be grown cool.

Masdevallia stenorrhynchos

The name for this curious-looking species derives from the Greek words *stenos* and *rhynchos*, meaning narrow and snout, respectively. It was first collected by Kalbreyer in the latter part of the 19th century but was not identified until 1922 by Kränzlin. This species has been collected only a few times from the wild; it is rare and locally distributed in the Western Cordillera of Colombia, elevation 2000 to 2100 m. *Masdevallia stenorrhynchos* is grown intermediate to cool and blooms successively up to four flowers on a triquetrous peduncle. The dorsal sepal is yellow-green with an upcurved, slender yellow tail. The lateral sepals are yellow-green, heavily suffused and spotted with purple-brown, with somewhat shorter yellow-orange tails.

Masdevallia striatella

The species epithet from the Latin *striatellus* means with little stripes and describes the appearance of the flower. *Masdevallia striatella* was first imported from Costa Rica in 1885 by James O'Brien (one of the most famous horticulturists of the late 1800s, secretary to the Royal Horticultural Society's Orchid Committee, and advisor to the editors of *The Gardeners' Chronicle*) and described by Reichenbach in 1886. This species is abundant in Costa Rica (1700 to 2400 m), although it has the distinction of also occurring, apparently, in Venezuela. The flowers are variable in size, from 1.0 to 2.5 cm, and bloom near the top of the 10 to 12 cm leaves. The apices of the purple-striped sepals are also somewhat variable—they can be contracted into short tails or gradually narrow into longer, thicker tails. The tails may be yellow, green, or purplish brown. The flowers of other clones are produced singly, although some clones also produce a

Masdevallia staaliana. Grower: Lil Severin.

Masdevallia stenorrhynchos. Grower: John Leathers.

Masdevallia striatella. Grower: Sherry Bridygham.

second flower from the same peduncle. This epiphytic species can be grown under intermediate to warm conditions and flowers in the fall and early winter. Specimen plants of *M. striatella* can produce a spectacular display of flowers. For many years this species was known by its later synonym, *M. ecaudata*.

Masdevallia strobelii

This species was named in honor of José Strobel, who first exported the species. It was found in 1958 growing on fence posts and in tree tops in open sun, in the province of Zamora-Chinchipe, Ecuador (elevation 1400 m). This very attractive, floriferous little species puts on a magnificent display of solitary flowers, although it can on occasion literally "bloom itself to death." (Some growers have been known to reduce the number of flowers before they expire to preserve the strength of the plant.) The sepals are white, intensely suffused with orange below the middle, and have small, clavate (club-shaped) glands on their inner surface. The rounded apices of the sepals contract into slender orange tails that often sweep backward. *Masdevallia strobelii* has been used extensively to generate *Masdevallia* hybrids, and several of the resulting registered hybrids have produced spectacular plants. Some *M. strobelii* heritage is in the background of many hybrids popular in cultivation today, in particular, *M.* Angel Frost. This species is best grown intermediate and will do very well either mounted or potted in sphagnum moss.

Masdevallia strobelii 'Janet' AM/AOS. Grower unknown.

Masdevallia tonduzii

This species was named in honor of Adolphe Tonduz of the *l'Institut Phytogeographique de Costa Rica*, who discovered it in 1894. It is found in the warm, moist tropical forests of the eastern lowland regions of Costa Rica and adjacent Panama, at elevations of 300 to 750 m. The single, 7 to 8 cm, fuzzy white to yellow-white flower is held just above the leaves and has yellow sepaline tails. This intermediate- to warm-growing, successively flowering species can bloom vigorously in the fall and winter. This species has a reputation for being difficult to grow, requiring high humidity, good ventilation, and care not to allow the roots or stems to rot due to overwatering.

Masdevallia tonduzii. Grower: Brad Cotten.

Masdevallia tovarensis

This species is named for the German colony of Tovar, in northern Venezuela, where it was first discovered in 1842 by Jean Linden. Although Linden initially called the species *Masdevallia candida* (which was not validly published), specimens that were sent to Reichenbach a few years later were formally named *M. tovarensis* by him. This is a very popular species and has remained so for more than a century. Despite the excessive collection of this species, *M. tovarensis* still remains locally abundant, growing in a small area of cloud forest in the coastal mountains of Venezuela. It has respectable, 5 to 8 cm, snow-white flowers and can produce two to five of them simultaneously at the apex of a stout, triquetrous peduncle 8 to 16 cm long. If undisturbed after flowering, the peduncle can develop a second set of flowers the following season. This species is easy to grow, will tolerate short periods of warm weather, and grows best under intermediate conditions, although it has been grown and flowered beautifully with cool temperatures.

Masdevallia triangularis

The name for this species is derived from Latin and refers to the triangular shape of the sepals. This species is one of the earlier discovered *Masdevallia* species, found by Linden in 1843 in the province of Mérida, Venezuela. Lindley published it in 1846. Subsequently, the species has been found in other regions of the coastal mountains of Venezuela, the mountains of western Venezuela and adjacent Colombia, as well as in southern Ecuador in the Parqué Nacionál Podocarpus. It is quite closely related to *M. instar*, and in areas where the two populations grow nearby, flowers with intermediate characteristics have been found. The inflorescence carries a solitary, 7.5 cm, widely spread, flat flower, borne by an erect, slender peduncle, 6 to 12 cm long. The sepals are smooth and yellowish orange, with minute red dots on the inner surface, faint striping on the veins, and long, thin, rigid purplish tails. This cool- to intermediate-growing species is one of the parents of the highly successful hybrid *M.* Copper Angel.

Masdevallia tovarensis. Grower: San Francisco Conservatory of Flowers.

Masdevallia triangularis 'Golden Gate'. Grower: San Francisco Conservatory of Flowers.

Masdevallia tridens

The species epithet derives from the Latin for three teeth. This description applies to the diverging sepaline tails of this species. *Masdevallia tridens* was first collected by Jameson in the province of Pichincha near Quito, Ecuador, in 1868 and published by Reichenbach in 1879. *Masdevallia tridens* has a distinctive, short, congested, ascending then horizontal raceme of relatively large, yellow flowers with a reddish lip, which overlap as they face away from the rachis in a horizontal plane. The numerous sepaline tails appear to radiate outward, completing the effect of a sunburst. A similar species (which has not been formally described) is often also called *M. tridens* and has a faint brownish spotting, but that species has a smooth exterior to the dorsal sepal, whereas the true *M. tridens* has a very pronounced, raised keel. *Masdevallia tridens* grows cold to cool.

Masdevallia tridens. Grower: San Francisco Conservatory of Flowers.

Masdevallia uniflora

This was the first *Masdevallia* species discovered about 1779 by Ruiz and Pavón (and also Dombey, whose role in this discovery is all but forgotten). This was a "lost" species for nearly two centuries, not discovered again until 1975, when Jorge Meza found it in the Department of Junin, Peru, at an elevation of 2900 m. *Masdevallia uniflora* grows epiphytically on scrub trees and terrestrially on rocks in cloud forests. This species is also somewhat scandent (that is, it climbs slowly on an ascending rhizome). The species name is derived from the Latin *uniflorus*, meaning one-flowered,

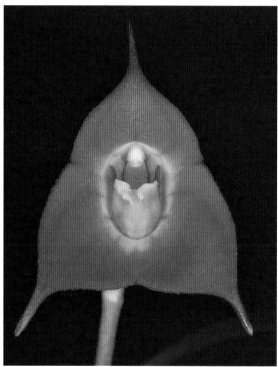

Masdevallia uniflora 'Mountain Gem'. Grower: San Francisco Conservatory of Flowers.

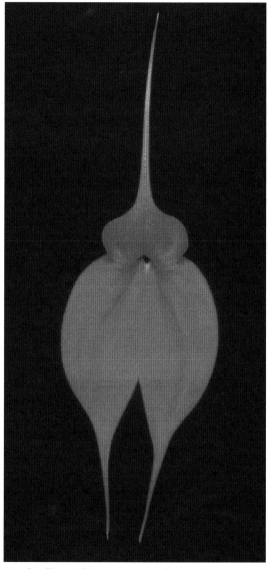

Masdevallia veitchiana. Grower: John Leathers.

and refers to the always single-flowered inflorescence. The sepals are usually a bright pink with white toward the base and have quite short, yellowish tails. *Masdevallia uniflora* is grown cool and usually blooms in the winter.

Masdevallia veitchiana

This species was named by Reichenbach in 1868 in honor of Veitch and Sons, who imported and were the first to flower this species in cultivation. The first plants were discovered by the collector Richard Pearce, who found them growing in 1867 among rocks in the high mountains of southern Peru (2000 to 3960 m). The striking, large (up to 20.3 cm), vermilion-colored flowers with an overlay of exquisite, fine purple hairs are held high above the leaves and create a high demand for the species. Veitch and Sons dispatched Walter Davis to the region to collect thousands for the European trade. This high demand has continued, although abundant supplies are available from seed now in cultivation. Thus, this species, once commonly found growing in the intense full sun among the Inca ruins at Machu Picchu and Huayna Picchu, has all but disappeared from these sites due to extensive collection. This species is known as the "King of Masdevallias," and well-grown specimen plants are stunning in their appearance and form. *Masdevallia veitchiana* also dominates much of the hybridization efforts in *Masdevallia* breeding (see Chapter 11). It requires cool growing conditions.

Masdevallia velifera

The species epithet comes from the Latin *velifer*, which means curtain or sail bearing, which refers to the broad, acutely deflexed synsepal. This curious species was first discovered in 1874 by Patin, a Belgian residing in Medellín, Colombia. The locality of collection was not disclosed, although it is believed the plant was collected near Medellín. At the beginning of the 20th century, this plant was considered to be rare in cultivation and all but disappeared from European collections. Sought in the wild for many years, this "lost species" was found again in 1985 among some unidentified species collected near Medellín (2000 to 2150 m), when some of the plants flowered in cultivation. The species should be grown cold and blooms in the late fall to early winter. It has a short, stout, single-flowered inflorescence with a 10 cm flower that is held below the leaves and has a rather foul smell.

Masdevallia velifera 'Puffin' HCC/AOS. Grower: San Francisco Conservatory of Flowers.

Masdevallia ventricularia. Grower: Marni Turkel.

Masdevallia ventricularia

The Latin word *ventriculus* means little belly, which is an accurate description of the anterior bulging of the sepaline tube of this species. *Masdevallia ventricularia* was first discovered by Dr. Jameson of Quito, Ecuador, in 1880. This species can be found in the forests of northwestern Ecuador and Colombia, at elevations of 1740 to 2200 m. The cute little species has small, single, reddish brown flowers with a whitish throat. The free parts of the sepals are triangular, with reddish vertical stripes and are terminated by a rather short tail. *Masdevallia filaria*, a very similar species, was once considered a subspecies of *M. ventricularia* but was reclassified as a separate species by Luer in 1978. This species is grown under intermediate to cool conditions and blooms in the spring to early summer.

Masdevallia welischii

This species was named in honor of David Alan Welisch of San Francisco, California, who discovered it in 1978 growing in the Vilcabamba mountains near Yanama, Peru (elevation 3000 m). *Masdevallia welischii* is closely related to *M. davisii* and *M. veitchiana*. However, *M. welischii* has distinctive bright orange sepals and small, pointy purple hairs on the dorsal sepal. Some clones of *M. welischii* are quite yellowish but contain red in the dorsal sepal and a red stripe below the lip between the lateral sepals. The inflorescence is a solitary, very attractive 5 to 6.5 cm flower that is borne on a relatively slender, ascending to suberect peduncle ranging from 12 to 18 cm in length. This is a cool-growing species and generally not tolerant of warmer temperatures. However, when well bloomed, *M. welischii* can make an impressive specimen plant.

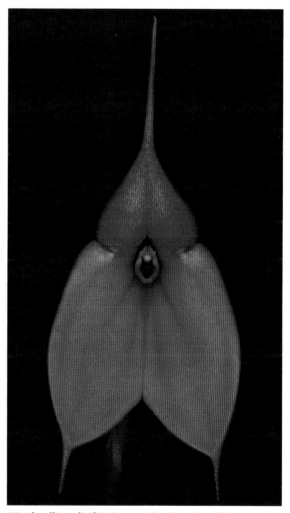

Masdevallia welischii. Grower: San Francisco Conservatory of Flowers.

Masdevallia wendlandiana. Grower: John Leathers.

Masdevallia wendlandiana

This species was named by Reichenbach, at the request of F. Sander, in honor of Herr Oberhofgärtner Hermann Wendland. This is one of the species whose reported original site of collection in the mid-1880s—namely the high mountains near Santa Rosa in the Department of Antioquia, Colombia—is probably incorrectly attributed (perhaps to disguise the original site of collection from rival collectors). This species occurs in the eastern lowland slopes (120 to 300 m) of the Andes with a quite widespread distribution (Colombia, Brazil, Ecuador, and Peru). While similar in appearance to *M. minuta*, *M. wendlandiana* is distinguished by its somewhat larger flowers and sepals suffused with purple that may also bear purple stripes. In color forms of this species, the purple pigment may be lacking or may appear only in the striping. *Masdevallia wendlandiana* is grown intermediate to warm and can flower profusely.

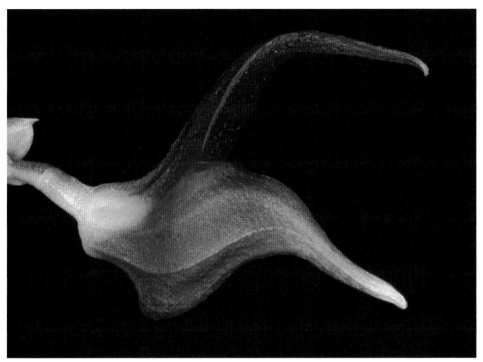

Masdevallia whiteana. Grower: San Francisco Conservatory of Flowers.

Masdevallia whiteana

This strange species is named in honor of William White of Alabama, who submitted the species for identification without collection information. Luer formally published the species in 1978, although records of this species indicate that it may have been collected as early as 1967 in the Bongará region of Peru. *Masdevallia whiteana* is a locally abundant species found in damp forests at elevations of 1500 to 2250 m in southeastern Ecuador and northern Peru. This species produces a succession of single flowers on a raceme that may be up to 10 cm long and borne on a triquetrous peduncle, 14 to 26 cm in length. The flowers are quite distinctive, and when viewed in profile they have the appearance of a gaping bird's mouth. The sepals are rigid, fleshy, and reddish purple in color. The margins of the lateral sepals are contiguous above the bases of the tails, and the dorsal sepal is larger than the synsepal. *Masdevallia whiteana* is best grown under intermediate to cool conditions.

Masdevallia ×wübbenii

Masdevallia ×wübbenii is named in honor of J. M. Wübben of the Netherlands, who was the discoverer and first to cultivate this plant. Initially described as a species, it was later decided to be a natural hybrid (as the × in front of the name denotes). This taxon is actually morphologically halfway between two species, *M. triangularis* and *M. wageneriana*, and artificial hybrids of these two species have produced plants identical to wild-collected *M. ×wübbenii*. *Masdevallia ×wübbenii* was first found in 1980, grow-

Masdevallia ×wübbenii. Grower: San Francisco Conservatory of Flowers.

ing epiphytically in forests east of Colonia Tovar, Venezuela, at an elevation of 2200 m. The flowers are characterized by yellow sepals with red flecks that are connate and form a gaping, sepaline cup. The rounded apex of the sepals abruptly contracts into slender, erect, yellow-green caudae that range from 3.5 to 5 cm long. The lip of this natural hybrid, as other species in the subsection *Oscillantes* (one of the parents, *M. wagneriana*, is in this subsection) appears to oscillate, balanced on a slender pivot. When grown well, *Masdevallia ×wübbenii* is a delightful little plant with single, showy, long-tailed flowers. It should be grown under intermediate to cool conditions.

Masdevallia xanthina

The name for this elegant species comes from the Greek *xanthos*, meaning yellow, and refers to the color of the flower. It was first collected somewhere in Colombia and cultivated by Veitch and Sons in 1880. Reichenbach noted the yellow color with eye spots at the base of the sepals—a white-flowered variation with eye spots is known as *M. xanthina* ssp. *pallida*. (This was also once described by Luer as *M. pallida* in 1978 but has since been reduced to subspecies.) This variation occurs frequently in Ecuador. The eye spots are thought to be a guide to the pollinator. The inflorescence carries a solitary 12.5 to 15.0 cm flower (which is larger than the plant), with most of the length in the sepaline tails, borne by a slender, erect to suberect peduncle, 4 to 6 cm. The sepals may be yellow, light yellow, or white, with a dark purple spot at the base of the lateral sepals. This species is found over a fairly broad range, in montane cloud forests of Colombia (2000 to 2400 m) and Ecuador (1500 to 2500 m), and is cultivated under cool to intermediate conditions.

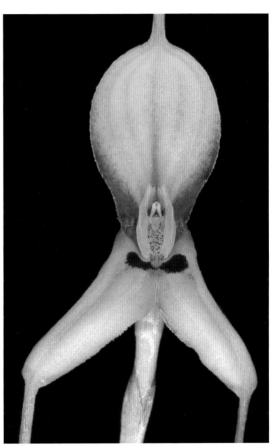

Masdevallia xanthina ssp. *pallida*. Grower: San Francisco Conservatory of Flowers.

Masdevallia yungasensis. Grower: Anna Chai.

Masdevallia yungasensis

This species is named for the Bolivian Yungas region (located north of the Cordilleras and including misty, jungle-filled valleys and gorges within the subtropical zone), where it is locally abundant. The 19th century collector, H. H. Rusby, may have made a collection of *M. yungasensis* in 1885, but it was not formally described until in 1978, after it was rediscovered by a Japanese team of botanists (Nishida, Ono, Hashimoto, and Ohga) in 1974. This species ranges from the northern declivity of the Bolivian Andes between the Yungas and the area in Santa Cruz above Siberia (Bolivia), at altitudes of 2000 to 2900 m. This delightful and vigorous species has showy flowers borne on an erect to suberect peduncle. The color of the sepals varies from white or rose with purple stripes, to yellow with brown stripes. An eastern population of the species has shorter sepaline tails, a more arcuate lip, and pubescent sepals and is known as *M. yungasensis* ssp. *calocodon*. This species can bloom several times a year and is grown cool.

CHAPTER 11

❖ ❖ ❖

Masdevallia Hybrids

Nature poses many barriers to cross-pollination of different species (such as geographic separation, different pollinators, different seasons, and different times of day that the blooms are open). Although hybrids do occur in nature, and this exchange of genetic material plays an important role in the evolution of species, nature's barriers are readily overcome in cultivation when an "unnatural" pollinator—a human—transfers the pollen of one species to the stigma of another.

The rationales to the generation of *Masdevallia* hybrids vary considerably. From a commercial perspective, a hybridizer's goal might be to generate consistent and beautiful "pot plants"—free-blooming, vigorous plants with spectacular, colorful flowers held on sturdy stems well above the leaves. Ideally, such pot plants would also be more tolerant of growing conditions, and with respect to masdevallias, more tolerant of warmth. This would broaden the potential customer base of a commercial grower. From a hobbyist's perspective, the goal might be to "see if it can be done" or to combine some unusual traits of one parent (for example, the curly tails of *M. caudivolvula* or *M. notosibirica*) with the color, flower, or fragrance from a second parent (for example, the bright orange of *M. hirtzii*, the markings of *M. chaparensis*, the stripes of *M. yungasensis*, the long tails and open cup shape of *M. caudata*, the tall and sturdy spikes and amazing colors of *M. coccinea* or *M. veitchiana*, or the fine pubescence of *M. strobelii*).

Another reason to hybridize is the phenomenon known as "hybrid vigor," in which the offspring of two species will often have qualities that surpass the parents—such as size, frequency of blooming, rate of growth, and floriferousness. Moreover, a particular hybridizer need not have the ideal growing conditions for both parents; for example, pollen from a cooler grown species is often used in a crossing with more warm-tolerant species for hybridization purposes. Many *Masdevallia* crosses pose particular problems to the hybridizer. Quantities of seed may be quite low, the frequency of germination low, and the hybrids unstable. In addition, while a number of successful "secondary hybrids" (produced when a primary hybrid is crossed with another hybrid or with another species) have occurred, many hybridizers have found that the majority of secondary hybrids are unstable and the desirable features (warm-tolerance, color, markings) often are not imparted to the offspring. Outstanding parents (for example, awarded clones or color varieties) are often used to remake "old hybrids," resulting in offspring with improved features.

The first *Masdevallia* hybrid was *Masdevallia* Chelsonii (*M. veitchiana* × *M. amabilis*), which was registered by Veitch in 1880. Many other hybrids followed, such that by 1904, more than 50 different hybrids had been registered, the majority of them using *M. veitchiana* as one of the parents. Curiously, no new hybrids were registered again until 1967, when *M.* Memoria Albert Ballentine was registered by Ballentine. Thereafter followed a literal explosion of new hybrids; as of this writing, more than 650 different grex names have been registered.

The following discussion of *Masdevallia* hybrids focuses on a number of important parents and the characteristics imparted to the hybrids. Some of the more popular or particularly outstanding hybrids are featured; however, with more than 650 hybrids from which to choose, as well as numerous unregistered hybrids, this discussion is in no way comprehensive and our apologies to those hybridizers or growers whose favorite hybrid or clone is not discussed. Moreover, because of space limitations, pictures of all of the hybrids discussed are not shown. If interested, the reader can find images of most, if not all, of the hybrids discussed on the Internet using an image search engine such as that provided by Google (www.google.com).

Masdevallia chaparensis Hybrids

These hybrids are dominated by the markings and coloration from the *M. chaparensis* parent, which can result in some delightful flowers, although they tend to be on weak stems requiring support. *Masdevallia* Chaparana (*M. chaparensis* × *M. veitchiana*) is a floriferous hybrid with delightfully shaped, spotted flowers held above the leaves on upright, sturdy inflorescences. Probably the most popular *M. chaparensis* hybrid is *M.* Sunset Jaguar (*M. chaparensis* × Copper Angel). Seedlings of this grex tend to have the markings from *M. chaparensis* but vary greatly in color from orange and yellow to coral-red and purple. Many seedlings of this grex have been awarded. *Masdevallia*

Sunset Jaguar 'Nightbreed' AM/AOS is a dark purple clone with purple spots and pink markings and a deep purple base color. 'Golden Sunset' AM/AOS, 'Red Leopard' AM/AOS, 'Psychedelic Sunset' HCC/AOS, 'Purple Sunset' HCC/CCM/AOS, and 'Mochica' HCC/AOS are other examples of awarded clones of this hybrid. *Masdevallia* Avalon Pellegrini (Chaparana × *M. triangularis*) is a cross with the same parentage as Sunset Jaguar, although the contributions of the parents are in different proportions. The shape of *M.* Wally Bernstein (*M. chaparensis* × *M. triangularis*) is strongly influenced by *M. triangularis*; seedlings of this grex tend to have long, straight tails and colors, spotting, and striping from both parents. An awarded clone of this grex is *M.* Wally Bernstein 'Purple Rain' AM/AOS. *Masdevallia* Myra (*M. uniflora* × *M. chaparensis*) exhibits the markings of the *M. chaparensis* parent but tends to inherit its background color from *M. uniflora*.

Masdevallia coccinea Hybrids

Masdevallia coccinea is one of the most attractive *Masdevallia* species, yet for many, it is one of the hardest to bloom or even grow vigorously. This cold-growing species is noted for its intolerance of warm conditions; the leaf edges will rapidly turn brown to black upon exposure to heat stress. Additionally, black spots will develop on the leaves and the flower buds will either blast or fold back, be much smaller, and/or not last long. However, it has many desirable features, including flower shape and many color variations,

Masdevallia Sunset Jaguar '61' (*M. chaparensis* × Copper Angel). Grower: John Leathers.

along a sturdy inflorescence held well above the leaves, and when happy it can be highly floriferous. Thus, it is not surprising that many primary and secondary hybrids exist with *M. coccinea* parentage. One of the older hybrids, *M.* Falcata (*M. coccinea* × *M. veitchiana*, first registered in 1899) is very attractive, featuring rich colors,

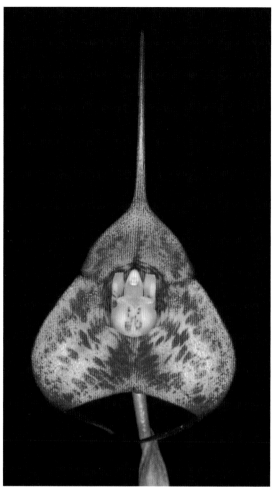

Masdevallia Myra (*M. uniflora* × *M. chaparensis*). Grower: John Leathers.

a velvety finish, and strong, erect flowers held well above the foliage.

Masdevallia Mary Staal (Angel Frost × *M. coccinea* var. *alba*) is an exquisitely beautiful hybrid. The flowers of this grex take their form from *M. coccinea* and are held on a tall, sturdy inflorescence. Important for most hobby growers, the *M.* Angel Frost parent imparts warmth tolerance to this hybrid. *Masdevallia* Mary Staal is easy to grow and bloom, and its various color variations range from white to cream to a bright, sunny yellow color; the tails and throat of the flower tend to be a darker yellow color. The clone 'Sun God' received an AM/AOS and has magnificent, bright yellow flowers that turn to orange at the caudate tips, and the texture of the flower has been described as "diamond dust." *Masdevallia* Mary Staal has been used extensively as a parent to create secondary hybrids; a notable example is *M.* Lemon Meringue (Mary Staal × *M. coccinea* var. *alba*).

Another popular *M. coccinea* hybrid is *M.* Bella Donna (*M. coccinea* × *M. datura*). *Masdevallia* Bella Donna has several awarded clones, including 'Soon Hee' HCC/AOS, 'Snow White' HCC/AOS, and the wonderful 'Sung Sook', which received an HCC and a CCM. The plant that earned the CCM, grown by Anna Chai of Belmont, California, had 178 flowers, 27 buds, and a total of 205 inflorescences. The dorsal sepals of 'Sung Sook' are a pale white blushed with rose, while the lateral sepals are white blushed with a magenta rose color; the sepaline tails blend to yellow at the tips. Another delightful primary hybrid with *M. coccinea* is *M.* Machu Picchu (*M. coccinea* × *M. ayabacana*). The flowers of this cross can be up to 16.5 cm and are a majestic purple color with a velvetlike texture. The *M. ayabacana* parent contributes warmth-tolerance to this cross. Several awarded clones of this hybrid exist, including *M.* Machu Picchu 'Crown Point' AM/AOS and 'Makawao Sunrise' AM/AOS.

Masdevallia Rose-Mary (*M. coccinea* × *M. glandulosa*) is another hybrid success story. Seedlings of this grex are vigorous, healthy plants, producing rich, pink flowers with magenta hairs, held well clear of the leaves. The flowers inherit their tubular

Masdevallia Falcata 'Gold Dollar' (*M. coccinea* × *M. veitchiana*). Grower: Tom Perlite.

Masdevallia Mary Staal (Angel Frost × *M. coccinea* var. *alba*). Grower: Brad Cotten.

shape from *M. glandulosa* and tend to have a slightly spicy, candylike fragrance. This free-blooming plant is an excellent choice for the beginner. *Masdevallia* Redwing (*M. infracta* × *M. coccinea*) is also a popular hybrid. A number of awarded clones of *M.* Redwing include 'Crimson Tapestry' AM/AOS (a brilliant crimson color, intermediate grower), 'Say' AM/AOS, and 'Purple Passion' AM/AOS. 'Purple Passion', as its name implies, has a vibrant purple hue. The grex *M.* Charisma (*M. coccinea* × *M. yungasensis*) has produced a number of awarded clones including 'Cow Hollow'

Masdevallia Mary Staal. Grower: Asuka Orchids.

Masdevallia Bella Donna 'Sung Sook' (*M. coccinea* × *M. datura*). Grower: Anna Chai.

Masdevallia Machu Picchu 'Crown Point' AM/AOS (*M. coccinea* × *M. ayabacana*). Grower: Tom Perlite.

Masdevallia Charisma (*M. coccinea* × *M. yungasensis*). Grower: Anna Chai.

AM/AOS and 'Pink Glow' AM/AOS. This cross inherits the stripes of *M. yungasensis* but retains much of the beautiful form of the *M. coccinea* parent.

Masdevallia constricta Hybrids

Masdevallia constricta (formerly known as *M. urosalpinx*) is a highly floriferous, small species with fairly large flowers for its size that hybridizes well with many other *Masdevallia* species. It imparts its free-flowering habit to its hybrids, making this a desirable species to include in the parentage of a hybrid. *Masdevallia constricta* hybrids often "straighten out" the caudae of their hybridizing partners, producing more attractive and consistent flowers. *Masdevallia constricta* also imparts its warmer growing habits when crossed with some of the more cool-growing species. *Masdevallia* Aquarius (*M. constricta* × *M. davisii*) is a pretty, white to yellow hybrid; an awarded clone is

Masdevallia Geneva Spots (White Swallow × *M. chaparensis*). Grower: Tom Perlite.

'Megan' AM/AOS, which is an electric-yellow color with a particularly pleasing flower shape. *Masdevallia* Peach Fuzz (*M. constricta* × *M. veitchiana*) is an attractive plant whose flowers seems to be made of fine velvet, in peach-yellow to bright orange, and it maintains much of the *M. constricta* flower shape. One clone, *M.* Peach Fuzz 'Golden Gate', was recently awarded a FCC/AOS. *Masdevallia* White Swallow (*M. datura* × *M. constricta*) is a new hybrid showing considerable promise; some clones of this hybrid produce beautiful white to cream tubular flowers with well-formed, straight lateral sepals darkening to yellow on the caudata. White Swallow is also highly floriferous, and several new (many of which are unregistered as yet) hybrids use this cross as one of the parents, which could show considerable promise. *Masdevallia* Geneva Spots (White Swallow × *M. chaparensis*) is a delightful hybrid featuring abundant flowers with a purple spotting on a white to mauve background. The warm-tolerant *M.* Keiko Komoda (Copper Angel × *M. constricta*) has beautiful large orange to yellow flowers with long, yellow to orange tails; this cross won an Award of Quality, and clones of this hybrid have been awarded—such as *M.* Keiko Komoda 'Free Spirit' HCC/AOS. Keiko Komoda has also been used in a number of secondary hybrids, which are also quite warm-tolerant, such as *M.* Copper Angel 'Highland' × *M.* Keiko Komoda 'Glow Worm', *M.* Windswept (Copperwing × Keiko Komoda), and *M.* Rene Komoda (Copper Angel × Keiko Komoda).

Masdevallia Peach Fuzz 'Golden Giant' FCC/AOS (*M. constricta* × *M. veitchiana*). Grower: Anna Chai.

Masdevallia decumana Hybrids

The species epithet *decumana* is derived from the Latin *decumanus*, meaning of a large size, which aptly describes the flower size compared to the rest of plant. The flowers of this species have full, widely spread lateral sepals, and this trait is often passed on to hybrids. *Masdevallia* Freckles (*M. decumana* × Angel Frost) was the first and a highly successful registered hybrid made with *M. decumana*. Blooms of this intermediate-growing cross vary in color from orange to pink, with purple specks or pure orange, as well as orange, pink, and white combinations. The flowers tend to be large, full, with broad ventral sepals and a short dorsal sepal. Clones of this cross have received at least four AMs. Other notable *M. decumana* crosses include *M.* Pixie Dust (*M. uniflora* × *M. decumana*) and *M.* Copperwing (*M. veitchiana* × *M. decumana*).

Masdevallia ignea Hybrids

Masdevallia ignea tends to impart a brilliant red color to its hybrids, although this is not always the case, since the pink color of *M.* Angel Heart (*M. ignea* × *M. infracta*) seems to be most influenced by the *M. infracta* parent. The best-known hybrid of *M. ignea* is *M.* Heathii (*M. ignea* × *M. veitchiana*), which has fairly large, brilliant yellow to yellow-orange flowers borne on tall, sturdy stems. The dorsal sepal of this cross stands upright, probably contributed by the *M. veitchiana* parent. *Masdevallia* Heathii is a very old hybrid, first registered in 1899, and the many awarded clones of this cross include 'Elena', 'Val', 'Ripper', and 'Marsh Hollow', which are well worth having in any *Masdevallia* collection. Heathii must be grown cool to thrive and flower well. A must-have secondary hybrid of *M.* Heathii is *M.* Pat Akehurst (Heathii × *M. yungasensis*), which produces a prodigious display of highly colored, striped flowers held just above the leaves on sturdy stems. Many different color forms of this cross have been produced, and some even lack the stripes contributed by the *M. yungasensis* parent. The clone *M.* Pat Akehurst 'Golden Zebra' AM/AOS has particularly large, vibrant flowers with bold red stripes.

Masdevallia Falcon Sunrise (Falcata × *M. ignea*), when crossed with either *M.* White Swallow or *M. constricta* (Falcon's Gold), has produced some new hybrids of great promise. *Masdevallia* Redshine (Falcon Sunrise × Marguerite) has produced some spectacular clones, one of which, 'Sheila', was recently awarded a FCC/AOS.

The characteristic feature of *M. ignea*—the deflexed dorsal sepal—may or may not be passed on to its hybrids. For example, *M.* Tanager (*M. ignea* × *M. ludibunda*) and *M.* Yosemite Sam (*M. odontocera* × *M. ignea*) have dorsal sepals that bend downward

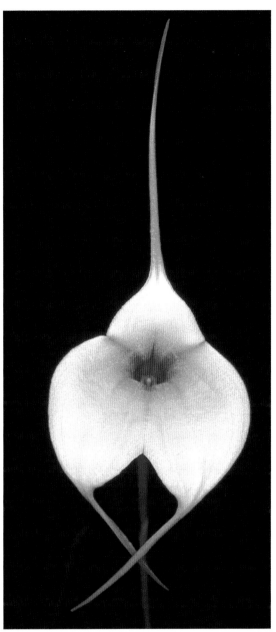

Masdevallia Pat Akehurst 'Golden Zebra' AM/AOS (Heathii × *M. yungasensis*). Grower: Tom Perlite.

Masdevallia Falcon Sunrise × White Swallow. Grower: Tom Perlite.

Masdevallia Patricia Hill (*M. ignea* × *M. welischii*).
Grower: John Leathers.

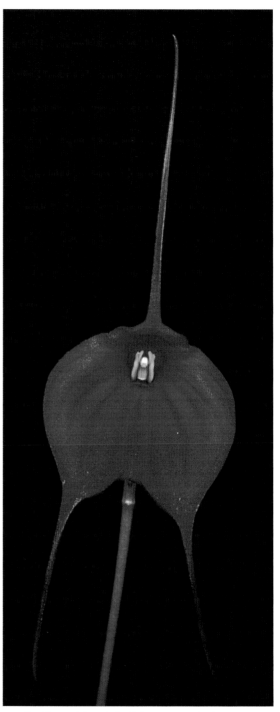

Masdevallia Redshine 'Sheila' FCC/AOS (Falcon Sunrise
× Marguerite). Grower: Tom Perlite.

across the face of the flower (although both *M. ludibunda* and *M. odontocera* also have forward- and down-facing dorsal sepals). *Masdevallia* Patricia Hill (*M. ignea* × *M. welischii*) is another attractive hybrid that features large, sturdy flowers; vibrant colors; an upright dorsal sepal; and, when well bloomed, a spectacular display. Moreover, *M.* Patricia Hill, in contrast to its parents, is quite tolerant of less than ideal conditions. *Masdevallia* Minaret (*M. yungasensis* × *M. ignea*) has the resplendent bold stripes of the *M. yungasensis* parent with the substance and blush of *M. ignea*. This wonderful hybrid has produced several spectacular clones including 'Lollipop', 'Isa', and 'Imam' CCM/AOS.

Masdevallia macrura Hybrids

Hybrids of *Masdevallia macrura* tend to have the fleshy substance and large size of this species. Several of the *M. macrura* primary and secondary hybrids have yielded highly awarded clones. *Masdevallia* Monarch (*M. veitchiana* 'Prince de Galle' × *M. macrura*) seedlings tend to have large, beautiful orange to yellow-orange flowers, held on sturdy inflorescences well above the leaves. (The *M. veitchiana* clone 'Prince de Galle' is known to have an albinistic trait that is responsible for the pure yellow hybrid clones of *M.* Mon-

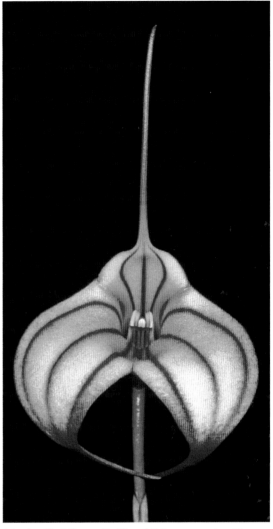

Masdevallia Minaret 'Lollipop' (*M. yungasensis* × *M. ignea*). Grower: John Leathers.

arch and other crosses made using this parent.) The *M.* Monarch clone 'Highland Gold' AM/AOS is a pure, golden yellow color without the speckling of the *M. macrura* parent. Another awarded clone of *M.* Monarch is 'Cow Hollow' AM/AOS, which is also a rich golden color. Monarch also has been used extensively as a parent and has produced some spectacular secondary hybrids. For example, *M.* Highland Monarch (Highland Fling × Monarch) has variously solid yellow to orange-colored clones, several of which have been awarded, including 'Golden Gate' AM/AOS, 'Free Spirit' AM/AOS and CCM/AOS, and 'Gina' HCC/AOS. Highland Monarch is a large, sturdy plant with numerous tall, large, almost waxy flowers that can bloom year-round, making this a desirable pot plant for the hobby grower. Other striking secondary hybrids include *M.* Dawn Monarch (Monarch × *M. triangularis*) and *M.* Harold Ripley (Monarch × Marguerite). Another popular hybrid derived from *M. macrura* is *M.* Dark Star (*M. macrura* × *M. cucullata*); at least two clones, 'Marsh Hollow' AM/AOS and 'Macabre', have been awarded.

One feature that some hybridizers have attempted to introduce into hybrids is that of successive flowering (although a limited number of successive flowering hybrids have been registered to date). A species that imparts this feature, as well as its curious lip, to its offspring is *M. pinocchio*. Two registered hybrids, *M.* Angel Nose (*M. pinocchio* × Angel Frost) and *M.* Motoi Kawatsura (*M. pinocchio* × Tuakau Candy), are rather odd-looking hybrids and probably desirable only to a few collectors.

Masdevallia tonduzii Hybrids

Masdevallia tonduzii is a popular parent used to introduce warm-tolerance into hybrids; in addition, the resulting flowers of most hybrids using *M. tonduzii* as a parent tend to be some shade of yellow. *Masdevallia* Angel Tang (*M. veitchiana* × *M. tonduzii*) is a large, warm-tolerant plant with beautiful yellow to orange flowers, often with fine purple hairs on the inner surface of the sepals. A particularly well-known warm-tolerant hybrid is *M.* Ken Dole (*M. coccinea* × *M. tonduzii*). One cross, using *M. coccinea* var. *alba*, produces beautiful white flowers with bright yellow-tipped tails; the form of the flower is somewhat intermediate between the two parents. Another popular hybrid is *M.* Maui Jewel (*M. tonduzii* × *M. glandulosa*); this vigorous hybrid is a good bloomer whose flowers tend to have a white to yellow background, yellow-tipped tails, and an inner surface covered with fine purple hairs. *Masdevallia* Shinichi Komoda (Copper Angel × *M. tonduzii*) is also a warm-tolerant and free-blooming hybrid that produces clear-yellow flowers and may bloom two times on each spike.

Masdevallia tovarensis Hybrids

Masdevallia tovarensis is an intermediate-growing species that is quite tolerant of different temperature conditions and has been shown to pass on this trait to its hybrids, although it usually does not pass on its habit of multiple simultaneous flowering. In addition, *M. tovarensis* is a rather dominant white, even subduing most of the *M. uniflora* color in translucent, white hybrid *M.* Alabaster (*M. uniflora* × *M. tovarensis*). Alabaster inherits some characteristics from *M. tovarensis*, including the simultaneous flowering habit (two flowers per stem) and wider lateral sepals; *M. uniflora* contributes only a slight flush of pink in some seedlings. *Masdevallia* McVittiae (*M. tovarensis* × *M. coccinea*) is a delightful hybrid with long flower stems and light lavender to white flowers, and it is much more warm-tolerant than *M. coccinea*. Another successful hybrid is *M.* Snowbird (*M. tovarensis* × *M. mejiana*); this cute little plant has flowers quite similar to *M. tovarensis* and flowers easily under warm conditions several times per year.

Masdevallia triangularis Hybrids

Masdevallia triangularis is a popular species used in *Masdevallia* hybrids. It tends to impart the flower form and upright inflorescence to its offspring. Several of the offspring include some of the most highly awarded *Masdevallia* crosses. For example, *M.* Copper Angel 'Highland' AM/AOS has won two quality and five cultural awards. *Masdevallia* Copper Angel 'Young Jeung' received a CCM of 93 points and had 195 flowers; in 2002, the grower of this plant, Anna Chai of Belmont, California, was awarded the Butterworth Prize, one of the highest AOS awards.

Masdevallia Copper Angel 'Young Jeung' (*M. veitchiana* × *M. triangularis*). Grower: Anna Chai. Photograph by Joung Nam Chai.

Masdevallia Dean Haas 'Gina' AM/AOS (Copper Angel × Angel Glow). Grower: Tom Perlite.

Masdevallia Highland Fling (Copper Angel × *M. veitchiana*). Grower: Anna Chai.

Masdevallia Cassiope 'Alexa' AM/AOS (*M. triangularis* × *M. coccinea*). Grower: Anna Chai.

Other clones of *M.* Copper Angel have also been awarded, including 'Mr. Mathis' AM/AOS and 'Orange Sunset' AM/AOS. The latter hybrid produces many lovely bright orange flowers, which vary somewhat in form but are borne on a tall, upright inflorescence and can bloom year-round. This prolific cool-growing hybrid is also frequently used as a parent in more complex hybrids. For example, the hybrid *M.* Dean Haas (Copper Angel × Angel Glow) has several awarded clones including 'Gina' AM/AOS, 'Straight Tails' AM/AOS, and 'Rachel' AM/AOS. *Masdevallia* Sunset Jaguar (Copper Angel × *M. chaparensis*), as discussed above, is also a highly awarded secondary hybrid. Other well-known hybrids include *M.* Copper Frost (Copper Angel × Angel Frost), *M.* Fandango (Copper Angel × Monarch), *M.* Highland Fling (Copper Angel × *M. veitchiana*), and *M.* Copper Queen (Copper Angel × *M. macrura*). *Masdevallia* Cassiope (*M. triangularis* × *M. coccinea*) is a hybrid with the coloring and form of *M. triangularis*, but it has the larger flowers of *M. coccinea*. One of the clones, *M.* Cassiope 'Alexa', has won both AM/AOS and CCM awards.

Masdevallia uniflora Hybrids

Masdevallia uniflora usually imparts a strong purplish color to its offspring. This species also makes a good parent, since the offspring frequently inherit the erect inflorescence that blooms well above the leaves. *Masdevallia* Magdalena (*M. coccinea* × *M. uniflora*) is an exquisite hybrid with pink to purple flowers held on sturdy stems well above the plant. *Masdevallia* Juno (*M. uniflora* × *M. corniculata*) seedlings are highly floriferous and tend to have triangular, plump, deep purple flowers held on strong, upright stems; the clone 'Hillsview' was awarded a HCC/AOS in 1996. The flower of *M.* Pixie Dust (*M. uniflora* × *M. decumana*) is a delicate pink sprinkled with a purple glitter; this hybrid tends to be more warm-tolerant than the *M. uniflora* parent. Secondary hybrids using Pixie Dust as one of the parents have produced several awarded clones, including *M.* Lynette 'Sunrise' HCC/AOS (Pixie Dust × *M.*

Masdevallia Magdalena (*M. coccinea* × *M. uniflora*). Grower: Tom Perlite.

Masdevallia Harlequin (*M. yungasensis* × *M. uniflora*). Grower unknown.

caudata) and *M.* Tequila Rose 'Yummy Rasperry' HCC/AOS. *Masdevallia* Theresa Hill (*M. odontocera* × *M. uniflora*) takes its form from the *M. odontocera* parent, and the awarded clone 'Paolini Ferrusi' AM/AOS inherits its beautiful, intense fuchsia color from the *M. uniflora* parent. The hybrid *M.* Raymondo de los Andes (*M. macrura* × *M. uniflora*) has also produced some large, spectacular bluish purple flowers, the clone 'Violet Jewel' receiving a HCC/AOS. *Masdevallia* Harlequin (*M. yungasensis* × *M. uniflora*) is a delightful, free-flowering little hybrid with coloring similar to a peppermint candy. One of the better intergeneric crosses, *Dracuvallia* Blue Boy (*M. uniflora* × *Dracula chimaera*) has received an AD. The flowers of this cross are an iridescent blue to lavender-pink color, and the flowers are held on an upright inflorescence.

Masdevallia veitchiana Hybrids

Masdevallia veitchiana has been used as a parent to produce more hybrids than any other species in this genus because it imparts many desirable features to its offspring: large, brilliantly colored flowers; fine purple hairs; exceptionally attractive flower shape (which is quite dominant); prolific, free-flowering habit; and long, sturdy stems. Moreover, it produces large seed pods with abundant seeds. *Masdevallia veitchiana* can bloom year-round under good growing conditions and will impart this trait to many of its hybrids, often even when the other parent is a very restrictive, once-per-year bloomer. Also of importance is the large stigmatic cavity, which makes the species easy to pollinate. The one negative influence (at least to some hybridizers) is that the orange color of *M. veitchiana* dominates nearly all of its offspring, although considerable variation occurs in the shades of orange that are produced. The first hybrid (in fact, the first hybrid of any *Masdevallia*) was *M.* Chelsonii (*M. veitchiana* × *M. amabilis*), which was registered by Veitch in 1880. This hybrid was described by Florence H. Woolward in her 1898 book, *The Genus Masdevallia*, to have "an orange-red (color), more or less closely set with minute, crimson hairs." A number of the

Masdevallia Gairiana 'Laurie' (*M. davisii* × *M. veitchiana*). Grower: John Leathers.

early hybrids are still popular; some clones of the original 100-year-old hybrids exist and many have been remade. These include *M.* Falcata (*M. veitchiana* × *M. coccinea*), *M.* Gairiana (*M. davisii* × *M. veitchiana*), *M.* Heathii (*M. veitchiana* × *M. ignea*), and *M.* Kimballiana (*M. caudata* × *M. veitchiana*).

Interestingly, although 15 hybrids were registered with *M. veitchiana* as a parent by 1903, no further introductions occurred until 1979, when *M.* Prince Charming (*M. angulata* × *M. veitchiana*) was registered by Rod McLellan. A quick perusal of Appendix I reveals the explosion of *Masdevallia* hybrids that has occurred in the last 30 years and moreover demonstrates that *M. veitchiana* is a common parent or "grandparent" of many of the new hybrids. Most hybridizers will first cross a new *Masdevallia*

Masdevallia Angel Frost (*M. strobelii* × *M. veitchiana*). Grower: John Leathers.

Masdevallia Angel Frost 'Blanca'. Grower: Tom Perlite.

species with *M. veitchiana*; consequently, many attractive primary and secondary hybrids are available with *M. veitchiana* parentage. One of the more popular modern-day hybrids, registered by J & L Orchids in 1982, is *M.* Angel Frost (*M. strobelii* × *M. veitchiana*). Many clones of this hybrid exist, some with "white frost" (hairs) (such as Angel Frost 'Highland') and others with "purple frost" (such as Angel Frost 'Frosty Sunset'). The flower color tends to be a beautiful tangerine orange, although the clone 'Blanca' has a very light, almost white flower with dark orange sepaline tails. Angel Frost has been extensively hybridized as well and is the parent of a number of well-known and highly successful hybrids, including *M.* Mary Staal (*M. coccinea* var. *alba* × Angel Frost), *M.* Angel Glow (Angel Frost × Marguerite), *M.* Copper Frost (Copper Angel × Angel Frost), and *M.* Inca Prince (which is a back-cross of Angel Frost × *M. veitchiana*). *Masdevallia* Whiskers (*M. glandulosa* × *M. veitchiana*) is an interesting hybrid with an even distribution of glandular hairs over its surface; in this hybrid, the "whiskers" are

Masdevallia Kimballiana (*M. caudata* × *M. veitchiana*) held by the grower, Anna Chai, of Belmont, California.

Masdevallia Joy Edstrom 'Sheila' AM/AOS (*M. veitchiana* × *M. racemosa*). Grower: Tom Perlite.

contributed by both parents: *M. glandulosa* has big, globular hairs (and a very nice fragrance that tends to be lost in the hybrids), in contrast to the fine hairs of *M. veitchiana*. The hybrid *M. Kimballiana* (*M. caudata* × *M. veitchiana*) has produced a number of desirable clones, including 'Woody', 'James', and 'Sang Pill'. A number of recent unregistered hybrids use Kimballiana as a parent, and no doubt some new, exciting seedlings are forthcoming.

Another notable hybrid that received an Award of Quality is *M.* Southern Sun (*M. hirtzii* × *M. veitchiana*). Several clones of this parent have also received awards, including the super-productive and striking 'Solar Flare' HCC/AOS. This hybrid has well-shaped, bright-orange flowers. *Masdevallia* Marguerite (*M. veitchiana* × *M. infracta*) also produces large, upright, open flowers with long sepaline tails; this hybrid has been used as a parent to produce some additional interesting secondary hybrids such as *M.* Morning Glory (Marguerite × *M. chaparensis*). One seedling of Morning Glory has a wonderful purple background with the markings of *M. chaparensis*; however, it has the strong, upright stems and larger flower contributed by the Marguerite parentage. An unusual cross (one of the few successful hybrids made with *M. racemosa* as a parent) is *M.* Joy Edstrom (*M. veitchiana* × *M. racemosa*). This hybrid, in contrast to its parents, is quite warm-tolerant and easy to grow. *Masdevallia veitchiana* has also been used in some intergeneric crosses, and one of the more attractive dracuvallias is *Dracuvallia* Ellie Bernstein (*M. veitchiana* × *Dracula robledorum*). This hybrid has light orange to reddish upright flowers.

Masdevallia yungasensis Hybrids

Hybrids using *Masdevallia yungasensis* as one of the parents tend to inherit the striped veins characteristic of this species, although the flowers tend to be held on somewhat weak stems and require support. *Masdevallia* Taukau Candy (*M. yungasensis* × *M. triangularis*) has produced some striking seedlings, including the clone 'Sunrise', which received an AM/AOS as well as a CCM/AOS. This clone has the wonderful stripes of the *M. yungasensis* parent and the long, colorful tails and orange color of *M. triangu-*

laris. Another popular hybrid is *M.* Harlequin (*M. yungasensis* × *M. uniflora*); seedlings of this cross are various shades of pink to purple from *M. uniflora* with the striping from the *M. yungasensis* parent. Secondary hybrids using Harlequin as one of the parents have produced some spectacular plants, including clones of some unregistered crosses of *M.* Bella Donna × *M.* Harlequin ('Morning Glory' and 'Sweet Candy' both received HCC/AOS), and *M.* Myck Santos (Harlequin × Night Stripes). Another recent but popular secondary hybrid is *M.* Pat Akehurst (*M. yungasensis* × Heathii); this hybrid is quite variable, with many different colors, striping, and shapes in the seedlings. The seedlings tend to be highly floriferous and may bloom several times per year. One awarded clone is Pat Akehurst 'Luscious', which has pastel orange to white flowers with attractive purple stripes and orange tails.

Today a seemingly endless variety of *Masdevallia* hybrids have been created, and many new ones appear every year. *Masdevallia* hybrids, in contrast to many of the species of the genus, are relatively easy to grow and tolerant of "less-than-ideal" *Masdevallia* growing conditions. For the beginning orchid hobbyist interested in growing masdevallias, hybrids may be an excellent introduction to the enjoyment of these "gems of the first water."

APPENDIX I

❖ ❖ ❖

Registered *Masdevallia* Hybrids

NAME	PARENTAGE	HYBRIDIZER	REGIS-TRATION YEAR
Aardvark	(*M. pachyura* × *M. velifera*)	G. Staal	1993
Absaroka Thunder	(*M. ignea* × *M. pteroglossa*)	S. Hastings	1998
Acis	(*M. abbreviata* × *M. veitchiana*)	Hincks	1890
Aconcagua	(Copper Angel × *M. ayabacana*)	Hoosier Orchid Co. (Glicenstein/Hoosier)	2003
Ada's Delight	(Mary Staal × Kimballiana)	A. Kelly (C. Halls)	2000
Adelina	(*M. velifera* × *M. deformis*)	E. Dreise	1992
Adieu	(Copper Angel × *M. strobelii*)	J. Leathers	1994
Adrie Sijm	(*M. rosea* × *M. chaparensis*)	G. Staal	1993
Adrienne	(Heathii × Shuttryana)	N. Butler (T. & T. Gillbanks)	2002
Afterglow	(Angel Frost × *M. amabilis*)	R. Thomson	1991
Ahlenberger Vollmond	(*M. strobelii* × *M. schroederiana*)	P. Teipel	2001
Ajax	(Chelsonii × *M. peristeria*)	Veitch	1896
Akira Kawatsura	(Tuakau Candy × Heathii)	T. Kawatsura	1998
Alabaster	(*M. tovarensis* × *M. uniflora*)	M. Turkel	1991
Alceste	(Asmodia × *M. veitchiana*)	Veitch	1901
Alicia	(*M. glandulosa* × *M. guttulata*)	E. Dreise	1990
Alma's Golden Triangle	(Steven Male × Xanthino-Veitchiana)	Flowers/Sea	1995
Alpha Sunrise	(Falcata × Bella Donna)	R. Macdonald	2002
Alyssa Maria	(*M. datura* × *M. veitchiana*)	E. Dreise	1992
Amber	(*M. coriacea* × Kimballiana)	T. Hill	1990
Amesiana	(*M. tovarensis* × *M. veitchiana*)	Sander	1890
Amethyst	(*M. uniflora* × *M. glandulosa*)	T. Hill	1990
Amy	(*M. deceptrix* × *M. decumana*)	E. Lorincz	2002

NAME	PARENTAGE	HYBRIDIZER	REGIS-TRATION YEAR
Andean Adventure	(Cotacachi × *M. decumana*)	D. P. Weise	2002
Andean Glow	(Autumn Glow × Copperwing)	Orchid Zone	1997
Andean Prince	(*M. welischii* × *M. panguiënsis*)	Orchid Zone	1997
Andean Princess	(*M. coccinea* × *M. panguiënsis*)	Orchid Zone	1997
Andromeda	(*M. fragrans* × *M. schroederiana*)	D. Richardson	1976
Angel Blush	(Angel Frost × Harlequin)	R. Thomson	1991
Angel Candy	(Sunny Angel × Tuakau Candy)	Mostly Masdevallias (J. Schwind)	2000
Angel Fire	(*M. triangularis* × *M. ayabacana*)	J & L	1989
Angel Frost	(*M. veitchiana* × *M. strobelii*)	J & L	1982
Angel Fuzz	(Peach Fuzz × Copper Angel)	Hoosier (Glicenstein/Hoosier)	2002
Angel Glow	(Angel Frost × Marguerite)	J & L	1986
Angel Gold	(Sunny Angel × Goldie)	M. Ferrusi	2004
Angel Heart	(*M. ignea* × *M. infracta*)	J & L	1991
Angel Nose	(Angel Frost × *M. pinocchio*)	G. Staal	1993
Angel Tang	(*M. veitchiana* × *M. tonduzii*)	J & L	1986
Angel Trumpet	(Orange Ice × Moonflower)	Hoosier Orchid Co. (Glicenstein/Hoosier)	2003
Angel Wings	(Angel Frost × *M. wurdackii*)	J & L	1989
Angelita	(Angel Frost × *M. sanctae-inesiae*)	J & L	1988
Angle Dangle	(Harlequin × *M. angulata*)	R. Thomson	1994
Anita's Doll	(*M. discolor* × *M. wurdackii*)	Hoosier Orchid Co.	1997
Ann Jesup	(*M. veitchiana* × *M. uniflora*)	G. Staal	1992
Anna-Britt	(*M. veitchiana* × *M. lenae*)	J. Sönnemark	1997
Anna Chai	(*M. veitchiana* × *M. norops*)	G. Staal (R. Thomson)	2003
Anna-Claire	(*M. angulifera* × *M. constricta*)	J. Page	1993
Anne Leggett	(*M. coccinea* × *M. macrura*)	G. Staal	1993
Annemarie	(*M. mejiana* × Kimballiana)	E. Dreise	1990
Annette Hall	(Copper Angel × Manco Inca)	L. O'Shaughnessy (Orchid Zone)	2003
Antizana	(Angel Frost × *M. yungasensis*)	Ray Thomson	1995
Apricot Moon	(*M. welischii* × *M. datura*)	P. Nicholas	1999
Aquarius	(*M. constricta* × *M. davisii*)	P. Chin	1991
Arabesque	(Fuzzy Navel × *M. ampullacea*)	J. Page	1997
Asmodia	(Chelsonii × *M. reichenbachiana*)	Veitch	1894
Auburn Hero	(*M. veitchiana* × *M. hercules*)	J & L	1995
Autumn Glow	(Falcata × *M. davisii*)	Orchid Zone	1996
Autumn Leaves	(Kimball's Kissin' Cousin × *M. veitchiana*)	Orchid Zone	1993
Avalon Pellegrini	(Chaparana × *M. triangularis*)	G. Staal	1995
Ayako Kawatsura	(Copper Angel × *M. schroederiana*)	T. Kawatsura	1995
Ayers Rock	(*M. triangularis* × *M. panguiënsis*)	J. Page	1997
Baby Ben	(*M. striatella* × *M. decumana*)	Hoosier Orchid Co.	1997
Baby Dragon	(*M. veitchiana* × *M. livingstoneana*)	Hoosier Orchid Co.	1998
Baby Glow	(Angel Glow × Baby Dragon)	Hoosier (Glicenstein/Hoosier)	2004
Barbarella	(*M. tovarensis* × *M. cinnamomea*)	R. Thomson	1993
Barbarosa	(*M. coccinea* × *M. ephippium*)	R. Thomson	1994
Baron Vargas	(Red Baron × *M. vargasii*)	Hoodview	1991
Bella Donna	(*M. coccinea* × *M. datura*)	J. Leathers	1992

NAME	PARENTAGE	HYBRIDIZER	REGIS-TRATION YEAR
Belumana	(*M. strobelii* × *M. decumana*)	M. Ferrusi	1992
Ben Berliner	(*M. ignea* × *M. xanthina*)	M. Turkel	1993
Bermuda Triangle	(Sunspot × *M. triangularis*)	Hoosier Orchid Co. (Glicenstein/Hoosier)	2003
Betsy Growell	(Grouse × *M. triangularis*)	Hoosier Orchid Co. (Glicenstein/Hoosier)	2003
Bibelot	(*M. citrinella* × *M. mendozae*)	M. Turkel	1992
Bill Bergstrom	(Copper Angel × *M. decumana*)	G. Staal	1995
Bill Jacobs	(Kimballiana × *M. constricta*)	P. Kane	1995
Black Raspberry	(Velveteen Angel × *M. calura*)	Hoosier Orchid Co. (Glicenstein/Hoosier)	2003
Black Widow	(*M. ayabacana* × *M. cucullata*)	J & L	1995
Blanch	(Stella × *M. instar*)	Hillsview	1998
Blood Orange	(Kimball's Kissin' Cousin × *M. discoidea*)	Hoosier Orchid Co. (Glicenstein/Hoosier)	2003
Blue Angel	(Kimballiana × *M. coccinea*)	Orchid Zone	1993
Blush	(Angel Frost × *M. monogona*)	H. Meng	1998
Blushing Belle	(*M. uniflora* × Angel Frost)	J & L	1989
Bob Hoffman	(*M. welischii* × Angel Frost)	G. Staal	1991
Bob Kohn	(*M. yungasensis* × *M. velifera*)	G. Staal	1995
Bobcat	(Sunset Jaguar × *M. lamprotyria*)	Mountain	1994
Bocking Hybrid	(*M. cucullata* × *M. veitchiana*)	Courtauld	1899
Bolivia Beauty	(Carousel × *M. exquisita*)	Clackamas	2001
Bright Angel	(Stella × *M. coccinea*)	Orchid Zone	1993
Bright Eye	(Misfit × *M. exquisita*)	Hoosier Orchid Co. (Glicenstein/Hoosier)	2003
Bright Spice	(John Leathers × *M. triangularis*)	D. Butler	2000
Bright Spot	(Chaparana × Parlatoreana)	B. M. Duncan (originator unknown)	2002
Brilor	(Pinchincha × Sunny Angel)	Milligan	2000
Bronze Leopard	(Chaparana × Proud Prince)	Orchid Zone	1998
Bucciquin	(*M. buccinator* × Harlequin)	H. Rohrl	1996
Butternut	(*M. stenorrhynchos* × Angel Frost)	J & L	1987
Calabasa	(Genie × *M. veitchiana*)	B. Schwarz	1991
Calliope	(Angel Frost × *M. notosibirica*)	J & L	1991
Camand Flame	(Dean Haas × *M. constricta*)	M. Bamber (T. Perlite)	2001
Cameo	(Confetti × *M. exquisita*)	Hoosier Orchid Co. (Glicenstein/Hoosier)	2004
Canary	(Peach Fuzz × *M. triangularis*)	Hoosier Orchid Co.	1997
Candy Cane	(Bella Donna × Harlequin)	M. Ferrusi (Warrnambool Orchids)	2003
Candy Floss	(Harlequin × *M. wageneriana*)	J. Page	1992
Cape Triangle	(Copper Angel × *M. angulifera*)	Duckitt	1997
Capel Apricot	(Angel Frost × Night Shade)	W. Howey (P. Altmann)	2002
Caralisa	(*M. echo* × *M. angulata*)	M. Connell	1993
Carl Djerassi	(*M. coccinea* × *M. davisii*)	G. Staal	1993

NAME	PARENTAGE	HYBRIDIZER	REGIS-TRATION YEAR
Carmita	(*M. welischii* × Mary Staal)	R. Thomson	1996
Carol Tarlow	(*M. notosibirica* × *M. coccinea*)	G. Staal	1993
Carousel	(Harlequin × *M. coccinea*)	R. Hull	1991
Cassiope	(*M. coccinea* × *M. triangularis*)	Hincks	1892
Caudato-Estradae	(*M. caudata* × *M. estradae*)	Veitch	1889
Celestial Stripes	(*M. yungasensis* × *M. pinocchio*)	L. O'Shaughnessy (G. Staal)	2002
Celia	(*M. ephippium* × Kimballiana)	Albright	1987
Celine Dion	(*M. coccinea* × *M. welischii*)	Highland Tropicals	1993
Celtic Frost	(Angel Frost × *M. glandulosa*)	Beall Pink	1993
Chameleon	(*M. chaparensis* × Harlequin)	P. Nicholas	1999
Chaparana	(*M. chaparensis* × *M. veitchiana*)	Katler	1988
Charisma	(*M. coccinea* × *M. yungasensis*)	Montessa	1990
Charlotte	(*M. mejiana* × *M. misasii*)	E. Dreise	1991
Chelsonii	(*M. amabilis* × *M. veitchiana*)	Veitch	1880
Cherry Ripe	(Redwing × *M. schroederiana*)	W. Baker	2000
Cherry Swirl	(*M. rimarima-alba* × *M. setacea*)	L. Moskovitz	1994
Cherub	(*M. deformis* × *M. strobelii*)	J & L	1991
Cheryl Shohan	(Xanthino-Veitchiana × Redwing)	Okika (Akatsuka Orch. Gdns.)	2001
Chickadee	(*M. caloptera* × *M. instar*)	Hoosier Orchid Co.	1991
Chimborazo	(*M. coccinea* × *M. rimarima-alba*)	R. Thomson	1992
Chisnall's Treasure	(Redwing × *M. barlaena*)	Chisnall's	1995
Christina van Kesteren	(*M. scabrilinguis* × *M. veitchiana*)	G. Staal	1993
Cinnamon Gold	(*M. davisii* × *M. decumana*)	Orchid Zone	1993
Cinnamon Twist	(*M. ayabacana* × *M. goliath*)	Golden Gate	1997
Cinque	(Angel Frost × *M. infracta*)	R. Sintchak	1991
Circe	(*M. schroederiana* × *M. veitchiana*)	Veitch	1898
Circus Lights	(*M. bottae* × *M. patriciana*)	M. Turkel	1992
Claret Chalice	(*M. uniflora* × *M. maculata*)	Beall Pink	1986
Claude	(*M. oscitans* × *M. veitchiana*)	Hoosier Orchid Co. (Glicenstein/Hoosier)	2003
Clea Bland	(*M. veitchiana* × *M. paivaëana*)	D. Bland	1993
Clyde Des Sains	(Angel Frost × *M. racemosa*)	P. Chin	1991
Coconut Ice	(*M. barlaena* × *M. datura*)	D. F. Butler (originator unknown)	2003
Colossal Chap	(Chaparana × *M. colossus*)	R. F. Hamilton	1995
Concord	(*M. coccinea* × *M. angulata*)	T. Hill	1990
Confetti	(*M. strobelii* × *M. glandulosa*)	J & L	1988
Conni Ferrusi	(Pixie Dust × *M. decumana*)	M. Ferrusi	1998
Cool Lady	(*M. ignea* × Kimballiana)	Ixchel	1988
Copper Angel	(*M. veitchiana* × *M. triangularis*)	J & L	1982
Copper Frost	(Copper Angel × Angel Frost)	J & L	1986
Copper Genie	(Copper Angel × Genie)	B. Schwarz	1991
Copper Queen	(Copper Angel × *M. macrura*)	J & L	1992
Copper Sun	(Rising Sun × Copperwing)	Orchid Zone	1997
Copperwing	(*M. veitchiana* × *M. decumana*)	Orchid Zone	1993
Coquette	(Harlequin × Minaret)	Chieri Orchids	1995
Coral Belles	(Copper Angel × *M. pachyura*)	J & L	1991

NAME	PARENTAGE	HYBRIDIZER	REGIS-TRATION YEAR
Cornet	(*M. ignea* × *M. mendozae*)	M. Turkel	1992
Cotacachi	(Bocking Hybrid × Harlequin)	R. Thomson	1994
Cotillion	(*M. hymenantha* × *M. coccinea*)	J & L	1995
Cotopaxi	(Harlequin × Gretchen Motter)	R. Thomson	1992
Courtauldiana	(*M. caudata* × *M. rosea*)	N. C. Cookson	1889
Crown Prince	(Myra × *M. caudata*)	P. & V. Ling (P. Altmann)	2002
Cupbearer	(*M. veitchiana* × *M. selenites*)	Hoosier Orchid Co.	1992
Curlei	(*M. macrura* × *M. tovarensis*)	Curle	1896
Curly Burton	(*M. triangularis* × *M. hirtzii*)	N. Burton (W. Burton)	2001
Curly George	(*M. notosibirica* × *M. caudivolvula*)	W. Burton	1997
Cuzco Gold	(*M. veitchiana* × *M. instar*)	T. Hill	1991
Cynthia	(*M. veitchiana* × *M. gilbertoi*)	G. Staal	1991
Cynthia Hindley	(Davina × *M. glandulosa*)	A. Barty	2001
Daidaleia	(Whiskers × *M. decumana*)	H. Rohrll	1998
Dainty Miss	(Angelita × *M. schroederiana*)	M. Light	1995
Dan Harvey	(*M. coccinea* × *M. floribunda*)	P. Pettit	1991
Dandy Dancer	(Redwood × *M. sanctae-inesiae*)	P. L. Jackson	2003
Dark Star	(*M. macrura* × *M. cucullata*)	L & R	1994
Darling Beauty	(Confetti × *M. veitchiana*)	Duckitt	1998
Darya-i-nur	(*M. datura* × Fraseri)	P. Chin	1997
Davina	(*M. amabilis* × *M. triangularis*)	A. Barty	1992
Dawn Monarch	(Monarch × *M. triangularis*)	Orchid Zone	1996
Dean Haas	(Copper Angel × Angel Glow)	Highland Tropicals	1992
Decade	(Urubamba × *M. decumana*)	R. Hill	2003
Deimos	(*M. barlaena* × *M. nidifica*)	T. Hill	1989
Delma Hart	(Minaret × Night Shade)	G. Hart (originator unknown)	1999
Delta Star	(*M. instar* × *M. triangularis*)	G. Staal	2002
Desert Sunset	(*M. veitchiana* × *M. setacea*)	J. Page	1994
Diana	(*M. wageneriana* × *M. caudata*)	D. Richardson	1977
Dina	(*M. coriacea* × *M. infracta*)	A. & C. Tarlow	1976
Doctor Joe Walker	(*M. peristeria* × Prince Charming)	J. L. Walker	1995
Doctor Who	(*M. veitchiana* × *M. colossus*)	M. J. Lee	1994
Don Dragoni	(*M. veitchiana* × *M. rodolfoi*)	P. Chin	1991
Don's Angel	(*M. veitchiana* × *M. rolfeana*)	J & L	1982
Don's Dream	(Marguerite × *M. yungasensis*)	O. Neils	1991
Doris	(*M. racemosa* × *M. triangularis*)	Hincks	1894
Double Take	(*M. coccinea* × Charisma)	Orchid Zone	1997
Dragon Fire	(*M. panguiënsis* × *M. veitchiana*)	J & L	1995
Dragon Gem	(*M. ignea* × *M. ayabacana*)	A. Mysiewicz	1991
Dragon Tongue	(*M. ignea* × *M. macrura*)	A. Mysiewicz	1991
Dusty Pink	(Pixie Dust × *M. coccinea*)	G. Staal	2002
Earl Bishop	(Fraseri × Marguerite)	Allen Clark	1997
Ecocho	(*M. coccinea* × *M. echo*)	L & R	1994
Edith May	(Inca Prince × *M. coccinea*)	A. Barty	1996
Edith's Dilemma	(*M. replicata* × *M. veitchiana*)	A. Barty	1993
El Dorado	(*M. datura* × *M. uniflora*)	D. P. Weise	2002

NAME	PARENTAGE	HYBRIDIZER	REGIS-TRATION YEAR
Elegance	(Angel Blush × Ann Jesup)	P. L. Jackson	2003
Elfriedchen	(*M. strobelii* × *M. constricta*)	E. Dreise	1990
Elgar	(*M. angulata* × *M. aenigma*)	M. Whitmore (originator unknown)	2002
Elisabeth	(*M. sernae* × *M. veitchiana*)	E. Dreise	1991
Eloise Harper	(Bella Donna × *M. caudata*)	G. Fuller (Paradise, NZ)	2003
Else Teipel	(*M. tovarensis* × *M. constricta*)	P. Teipel	2003
Elven Gem	(*M. welischii* × *M. infracta*)	Orchid Zone	1994
Elven Magic	(*M. davisii* × *M. infracta*)	Orchid Zone	1992
Elven Peaches	(Copper Angel × Elven Poppies)	Orchid Zone	1997
Elven Poppies	(*M. davisii* × Kimball's Kissin' Cousin)	Orchid Zone	1993
Elven Song	(*M. coccinea* × Fairy Princess)	Orchid Zone	1996
Elvenking	(Elven Poppies × Monarch)	Orchid Zone	1998
Emma	(*M. wurdackii* × *M. kuhniorum*)	E. Dreise	1992
Emperor	(*M. velifera* × *M. veitchiana*)	G. Staal	1993
Enchantment	(*M. chaparensis* × *M. decumana*)	G. Staal	1997
Estradae-Xanthina	(*M. estradae* × *M. xanthina*)	(originator unknown)	19th century
Eunice	(Cuzco Gold × *M. peristeria*)	R. Macdonald	1998
Eva's Mostacita	(*M. buccinator* × *M. trochilus*)	Orquideas Eva	1998
Evil Heart	(*M. rimarima-alba* × *M. yungasensis*)	J. Leathers	1994
Fairy Princess	(*M. infracta* × *M. caudata*)	Orchid Zone	1993
Fairytale Gold	(Fancy Pants × *M. triangularis*)	Orchid Zone	1997
Falcata	(*M. coccinea* × *M. veitchiana*)	Lawrence	1899
Falcata's Angel	(Falcata × Hoosier Angel)	T. & T. Gillbanks	2002
Falcon	(Falcata × *M. triangularis*)	J & L	1989
Falcon Sunrise	(Falcata × *M. ignea*)	Orchid Zone	1997
Falcon's Gold	(Falcon Sunrise × *M. constricta*)	Golden Gate	2003
Fancy Free	(Fancy Pants × Rising Sun)	Orchid Zone	1998
Fancy Pants	(*M. ignea* × Copper Angel)	Orchid Zone	1992
Fandango	(Copper Angel × Monarch)	Orchid Zone	1998
Fanfare	(Genie × *M. mendozae*)	M. Aldridge	1993
Fantasia	(*M. coccinea* × *M. princeps*)	Orchid Zone	1998
Fire and Ice	(*M. floribunda* × *M. exquisita*)	Hoosier Orchid Co. (Glicenstein/Hoosier)	2003
Firebrand	(*M. triangularis* × *M. barlaena*)	New Plymouth	1993
Firecracker	(Swallow × *M. welischii*)	Orchid Zone	1994
Firespots	(Chaparana × Firecracker)	K. Muir (T. Root)	2003
Firestorm	(Pollyana × *M. veitchiana*)	J. Page	1994
Flaming Arrow	(Copperwing × *M. panguiënsis*)	L. O'Shaughnessy	2002
Flash Point	(*M. sprucei* × *M. ignea*)	J & L	2001
Florida	(*M. tonduzii* × *M. barlaena*)	H. Morgan	1991
Flying Colors	(*M. welischii* × Copper Angel)	Highland Tropicals	1992
Fool's Gold	(Angel Frost × Genie)	Highland Tropicals	1992
Forever Young	(*M. infracta* × *M. exquisita*)	D. P. Weise	2002
Fox Glove	(*M. macrura* × *M. notosibirica*)	Ann Jesup (G. Staal)	1999

NAME	PARENTAGE	HYBRIDIZER	REGIS-TRATION YEAR
Fracas	(*M. caesia* × *M. infracta*)	New Plymouth	1993
Framar	(Marguerite × *M. infracta*)	H. Rohrl	1996
Fraseri	(*M. coccinea* × *M. ignea*)	Fraser	1882
Fraseri-Ludibunda	(Fraseri × *M. estradae*)	(originator unknown)	1882
Freckles	(Angel Frost × *M. decumana*)	J & L	1988
Free Spirit	(*M. striatella* × Hirasaki)	L. O'Shaughnessy	2002
Friar Tuck	(*M. oscitans* × *M. hirtzii*)	Hoosier Orchid Co. (Glicenstein/Hoosier)	2003
Frosty Man	(Celtic Frost × *M. decumana*)	M. Ferrusi	1998
Fuchsia Dawn	(*M. coccinea* × Pixie Shadow)	Orchid Zone	1996
Fuzzy Navel	(Angel Frost × *M. constricta*)	Hoodview	1991
Gairiana	(*M. davisii* × *M. veitchiana*)	Veitch	1884
Galaxy	(*M. triangularis* × Kimballiana)	J. Page	1996
Ganymede	(*M. veitchiana* × *M. civilis*)	Hoosier Orchid Co.	1991
Geleniana	(*M. caudata* × *M. xanthina*)	Sander	1887
Gemini	(*M. tovarensis* × *M. limax*)	J. Page	1992
Geneva Royale	(Magdalena × Marguerite)	Golden Gate	2003
Geneva Spots	(*M. chaparensis* × White Swallow)	Golden Gate	2001
Genie	(*M. angulata* × *M. coriacea*)	R. McLellan Co.	1981
Gertrude Puttock	(Copper Angel × *M. coccinea*)	S. Gettel	1990
Glaphyrantha	(*M. barlaena* × *M. infracta*)	Veitch	1886
Glow Worm	(*M. veitchiana* × *M. limax*)	J & L	1986
Gocong Vn	(Stella × *M. maculata*)	Nguyen Orchids	1998
Gold Purse	(*M. veitchiana* × *M. notosibirica*)	G. Staal	1992
Goldbug	(*M. davisii* × *M. sanctae-inesiae*)	Orchid Zone	1997
Golden Angel	(Kimballiana × Copper Angel)	Golden Gate	2000
Golden Bantam	(Goldbug × Goldie Hoosier)	Glicenstein/Hoosier	2002
Golden Blocks	(Kimballiana × *M. welischii*)	G. Staal	1993
Golden Falcon	(*M. norops* × *M. macrura*)	L. Moskovitz	1994
Golden Girl	(Copper Angel × *M. uniflora*)	Baker & Chantry	1995
Golden Krieks	(*M. infracta* × *M. chaparensis*)	G. Staal	2002
Golden Monarch	(Golden Angel × Monarch)	Golden Gate	2000
Golden Sun	(Canary × Angel Tang)	Hoosier Orchid Co. (Glicenstein/Hoosier)	2003
Golden Sunrise	(Dean Haas × Falcon Sunrise)	Golden Gate	2003
Golden Tiger	(*M. veitchiana* × *M. yungasensis*)	Golden Gate	1991
Golden Trident	(*M. falcago* × *M. yungasensis*)	Hoosier Orchid Co.	1992
Golden Wings	(*M. davisii* × Kimballiana)	Orchid Zone	1993
Goldfinch	(*M. constricta* × *M. triangularis*)	Hoosier Orchid Co.	1996
Goldie	(*M. tonduzii* × Paradise Sunset)	B. C. Berliner	1996
Gollum	(Kimball's Kissin' Cousin × *M. oreas*)	Hoosier Orchid Co. (Glicenstein/Hoosier)	2003
Grace Arms	(*M. ignea* × Minaret)	G. Fuller	1993
Grand Sun	(Monarch × Kimballiana)	Clackamas (Orchid Zone)	2001
Gremlin	(*M. angulata* × *M. strobelii*)	J & L	1986
Gretchen Motter	(Falcata × *M. maculata*)	Beall	1987

NAME	PARENTAGE	HYBRIDIZER	REGIS-TRATION YEAR
Grouse	(*M. prodigiosa* × *M. peristeria*)	Hoosier Orchid Co.	1993
Guillemot	(Angel Frost × *M. rolfeana*)	Hoosier Orchid Co.	2001
Gwendoline	(*M. davisii* × Maryann)	A. Barty	2003
Hampshire Prolific	(Copper Angel × *M. floribunda*)	Klehm Growers	1996
Hana Nguyen	(Ruby Slippers × *M. constricta*)	Nguyen Orchids (I. Komoda)	2002
Hani	(*M. coccinea* × *M. chaparensis*)	E. Katler	1992
Harlequin	(*M. yungasensis* × *M. uniflora*)	Beall Pink	1987
Harlequinette	(Harlequin × *M. floribunda*)	R. Thomson	1991
Harold Ripley	(Marguerite × Monarch)	Highland Tropicals	1995
Harvest Moon	(Sunbeam × *M. davisii*)	J & L	1991
Heathii	(*M. ignea* × *M. veitchiana*)	Heath	1899
Hebe	(*M. coriacea* × *M. veitchiana*)	Hincks	1889
Heidi	(*M. wageneriana* × *M. triangularis*)	E. Dreise	1991
Helix	(Hugh Rogers × *M. veitchiana*)	W. A. Baker	1998
Helma	(*M. decumana* × *M. tovarensis*)	E. Dreise	1992
Hennie Spijker	(*M. veitchiana* × *M. deformis*)	G. Staal	1992
Henrica Jansen	(*M. veitchiana* × *M. welischii*)	G. Staal	1992
Henrietta	(*M. caudata* × *M. ignea*)	Ames	1893
Herra	(Aquarius × *M. pulcherrima*)	Hoosier Orchid Co. (Glicenstein/Hoosier)	2003
Highland Fling	(Copper Angel × *M. veitchiana*)	Highland Tropicals	1992
Highland Monarch	(Highland Fling × Monarch)	M. Adams (B. Schwartz)	2001
Hincksiae	(*M. caudata* × Gairiana)	Hincks	1902
Hincksiana	(*M. ignea* × *M. tovarensis*)	Hincks	1887
Hirasaki	(*M. datura* × *M. notosibirica*)	N. Busher (originator unknown)	2002
Hitomi	(*M. uniflora* × *M. rolfeana*)	Nobuhara	1987
Hobgoblin	(Angel Frost × *M. erinacea*)	P. Nicholas	1994
Holographic	(Angelita × *M. floribunda*)	M. Light	2002
Hoosier Angel	(*M. floribunda* × *M. veitchiana*)	Hoosier Orchid Co.	1991
Hoosier Belle	(*M. guayanensis* × *M. echo*)	Hoosier Orchid Co.	1991
Hoosier Premier	(*M. veitchiana* × *M. pachyura*)	Hoosier Orchid Co.	1991
Hoosier Velvet	(Velveteen Angel × Urubama)	Hoosier Orchid Co. (Glicenstein/Hoosier)	2003
Hortensia	(*M. decumana* × Freckles)	P. Chin	1997
Hot Flashes	(Little Hottie × *M. ayabacana*)	Mountain Orchids	2002
Hot Stuff	(*M. odontocera* × *M. venusta*)	Mountain Orchids	2003
Hugh Rogers	(*M. amabilis* × *M. yungasensis*)	M. Rathbone	1993
Ibáñez-Behar	(Falcata × *M. floribunda*)	H. Ibáñez	1996
Igneo-Chelsonii	(Chelsonii × *M. ignea*)	(originator unknown)	1880
Igneo-Estradae	(*M. estradae* × *M. ignea*)	Lawrence	1902
Ilia Lin	(*M. wageneriana* × *M. barlaena*)	M. Ferrusi	1992
Imogen	(*M. schlimii* × *M. veitchiana*)	Veitch	1898
Imperial Flame	(Heathii × *M. macrura*)	Crownpoint	1992
Inca Gold	(Urubamba × *M. constricta*)	Hoodview	1991
Inca Jewel	(*M. coccinea* × Urubamba)	Hoodview	1994
Inca Prince	(*M. veitchiana* × Angel Frost)	R. Thomson	1994

NAME	PARENTAGE	HYBRIDIZER	REGIS-TRATION YEAR
Inca Snow	(*M. coccinea* × *M. constricta*)	Hoodview	1992
Inca Warrior	(*M. cucullata* × Heathii)	Hoodview	1994
Indian Corn	(*M. floribunda* × *M. mendozae*)	F. Feysa	1995
Indian Summer	(Prince Charming × *M. triangularis*)	J & L	1992
Isabella	(*M. paivaëana* × *M. exquisita*)	Hoosier Orchid Co. (Glicenstein/Hoosier)	2003
Jack and Wendy	(Falcata × Cassiope)	A. Millet	2003
Jack O'Lantern	(Kimballiana × Fraseri)	R. Hull	1995
Jan Letts	(Angel Frost × *M. setacea*)	L & R	1994
Janet Halcrow	(*M. davisii* × *M. trochilus*)	A. Barty	1997
Janice Hanson	(Angel Frost × *M. caudata*)	Baker & Chantry	1996
Jatsea	(Andromeda × *M. oscitans*)	Hoosier Orchid Co. (Glicenstein/Hoosier)	2004
Javelin	(*M. pachyura* × *M. schroederiana*)	G. Staal	1993
Jazz Time	(Angel Frost × *M. caudivolvula*)	L & R	1994
Jeannette	(*M. amabilis* × *M. coccinea*)	G. Fuller	2000
Jerry Sedenko	(Freckles × Hortensia)	T. Hill	2001
Jessie Winn	(*M. davisii* × *M. tovarensis*)	Winn	1893
Jewel	(*M. uniflora* × *M. princeps*)	Orchid Zone	1998
Jim Harper	(*M. veitchiana* × Rubicon)	G. Fuller (Paradise, NZ)	2002
Jim Nybakken	(Bella Donna × Sunset Jaguar)	Sunset	2002
Jiminy Cricket	(*M. oreas* × *M. vieriana*)	Hoosier Orchid Co.	2002
John Leathers	(*M. chaparensis* × *M. yungasensis*)	B. Cobbledick	1992
Joy Edstrom	(*M. veitchiana* × *M. racemosa*)	A. Koomanoff	1991
Judy	(*M. kuhniorum* × *M. veitchiana*)	E. Dreise	1993
June Winn	(Redwing × *M. decumana*)	J & L	1995
Jungle Red	(*M. glandulosa* × *M. ignea*)	Maduro's Trop. Fl.	2000
Juno	(*M. uniflora* × *M. corniculata*)	T. Hill	1987
Kabouter	(*M. strobelii* × *M. macrura*)	G. Staal	1992
Kaleidoscope	(Cassiope × Copperwing)	M. Ferrusi	2002
Kara's Delight	(*M. instar* × Copper Angel)	N. Hewinson	1998
Karen	(*M. veitchiana* × *M. torta*)	Santa Barbara Orchid Estate	1992
Karen Eleanor	(Lemon Glow × *M. veitchiana*)	P. & G. Fox (originator unknown)	2002
Karen Muir	(Angel Frost × Heathii)	Highland Tropicals	1995
Katie	(*M. amabilis* × *M. glandulosa*)	A. Barty	1996
Keiko Komoda	(Copper Angel × *M. constricta*)	I. Komoda	1995
Ken Dole	(*M. coccinea* × *M. tonduzii*)	G. Staal	1992
Kentucky Star	(*M. wurdackii* × *M. instar*)	C. Chowning	1997
Kiah	(*M. strobelii* × *M. hymenantha*)	P. Grech	1996
Kimball Collins	(Kimballiana × *M. collina*)	Hoodview	1991
Kimballiana	(*M. caudata* × *M. veitchiana*)	Sander	1899
Kimball's Kissin' Cousin	(*M. tricallosa* × *M. veitchiana*)	Hoosier Orchid Co.	1992
Kimball's Sun	(Sun Dancer × Kimballiana)	C. Halls	2001
Kimbuctoo	(*M. buccinator* × Kimballiana)	H. Rohrl	1996
King of Kings	(Copper Queen × Falcata)	P. L. Jackson	2003
Kinglet	(*M. sprucei* × *M. exquisita*)	Hoosier Orchid Co.	2002

NAME	PARENTAGE	HYBRIDIZER	REGIS-TRATION YEAR
Latacunga	(*M. infracta* × Chaparana)	R. Thomson	1992
Latin Sun	(Sun Dancer × Latacunga)	G. Hart (originator unknown)	2003
Lavaflow	(*M. caesia* × *M. caudata*)	New Plymouth	1993
Lavender Ice	(Redwing × *M. glandulosa*)	I. Komoda	2001
Lawrence Van Nguyen	(Copper Angel × *M. titan*)	Nguyen Orchids (I. Komoda)	2002
Leda	(*M. arminii* × *M. estradae*)	Hincks	1895
Lemon Drop	(Sunny Angel × *M. floribunda*)	J & L	1991
Lemon Glow	(Angel Frost × *M. instar*)	R. Thomson	1991
Lemon Meringue	(Mary Staal × *M. coccinea*)	C. & R. Coles	1994
Lemon Pie	(Sunspot × *M. exquisita*)	Hoosier Orchid Co. (Glicenstein/Hoosier)	2003
Lemon Rein	(Lemon Glow × Rein Staal)	A. & G. Peden (originator unknown)	2003
Leopard Spots	(*M. caudata* × *M. peristeria*)	Hoodview	1991
Lil	(*M. infracta* × *M. aenigma*)	L. Severin	1995
Lilac Rose	(*M. lilacina* × *M. rosea*)	Mountain Orchids	2002
Linda	(Davina × *M. caudata*)	A. Barty	1998
Lindsey Yuen	(Copper Angel × *M. wendlandiana*)	I. Komoda	1996
Little Dragon	(*M. veitchiana* × *M. calura*)	Orchid Zone	1992
Little Hottie	(*M. ignea* × *M. hymenantha*)	Mountain Orchids	2002
Little Leopard	(Sunset Jaguar × *M. floribunda*)	Mountain Orchids	1993
Lollipop	(*M. triangularis* × *M. uniflora*)	J. Page	1996
Louise	(Stella × *M. infracta*)	J & L	1991
Louise Klein	(*M. weberbaueri* × *M. infracta*)	Florafest	1991
Lucianne Phillips	(Prince Charming × *M. hirtzii*)	G. Staal	2002
Lucky Dip	(Southern Sun × *M. glandulosa*)	J. Page	1997
Lucky Stripe	(*M. yungasensis* × *M. infracta*)	J & L	1997
Lyn Sherlock	(Bella Donna × *M. coccinea*)	Paradise	2000
Lynette	(Pixie Dust × *M. caudata*)	J. Page	1996
Mabel	(*M. amabilis* × *M. attenuata*)	A. Barty	1995
Machu Delight	(Machu Picchu × *M. constricta*)	L. Vogelpoel	1996
Machu Picchu	(*M. ayabacana* × *M. coccinea*)	Beall Pink	1986
Magdalena	(*M. coccinea* × *M. uniflora*)	J & L	1991
Magic Moment	(Snowbird × *M. yungasensis*)	L & R	1994
Malcolm	(*M. livingstoneana* × *M. patriciana*)	M. Light	2002
Malcom Adams	(Redwing × Shuttryana)	M. Ferrusi	2003
Manabu Saito	(Mary Staal × Sunset Jaguar)	G. Staal	1995
Manco Inca	(Urubamba × *M. veitchiana*)	L. Sanford (T. Hill)	2002
Mandy	(Monarch × *M. chaparensis*)	S. Male (Highland Tropicals)	2000
Marball	(Marguerite × Kimballiana)	H. Rohl	1997
Mardi Gras	(Copper Angel × *M. glandulosa*)	J & L	1991
Margaret Brown	(Peppermint Rock × *M. andreettana*)	F. Feysa	1996
Marguerite	(*M. veitchiana* × *M. infracta*)	J & L	1982
Marilyn Lee	(*M. velifera* × *M. scabrilinguis*)	M. J. Lee	1998
Marilyn Light	(Angel Frost × *M. velifera*)	G. Staal	1997
Marimba	(*M. peristeria* × *M. veitchiana*)	Santa Barbara Orchid Estate	1988

NAME	PARENTAGE	HYBRIDIZER	REGISTRATION YEAR
Mario Ferrusi	(*M. decumana* × *M. hercules*)	G. Staal	1997
Mariomaska	(*M. chaparensis* × *M. datura*)	G. Staal	1994
Marmalade	(*M. barlaena* × *M. strobelii*)	W. Crawford	1995
Martha Staal	(*veitchiana* × *M. lata*)	G. Staal	1992
Mary Ames	(Gairiana × *M. ignea*)	(originator unknown)	1884
Mary Dragoni	(*M. schroederiana* × *M. coccinea*)	D. Dragoni	1988
Mary Staal	(*M. coccinea* × Angel Frost)	G. Staal	1991
Mary Sugiyama	(Angel Frost × *M. tonduzii*)	I. Komoda	1996
Maryann	(Kimballiana × *M. sanctae-inesiae*)	T. Hill	1991
Matthew	(Angel Frost × *M. deceptrix*)	E. Lorincz	2001
Maui Angel	(Copper Angel × *M. tricallosa*)	I. Komoda	1998
Maui Angelita	(Angel Frost × *M. attenuata*)	Tropical Orchid Farm	1998
Maui Jewel	(*M. tonduzii* × *M. glandulosa*)	I. Komoda	1997
Maui Sunrise	(*M. triangularis* × Orange Delight)	I. Komoda	1998
Maui Sunset	(Orange Delight × Marguerite)	I. Komoda	1998
McVittiae	(*M. coccinea* × *M. tovarensis*)	Thompson	1892
Meadowlark	(Sunny Angel × *M. triangularis*)	Hoosier Orchid Co. (W. Rhodehamel)	2003
Measuresiana	(*M. amabilis* × *M. tovarensis*)	Sander	1890
Mejifrost	(Angel Frost × *M. mejiana*)	L & R	1994
Mellow Yellow	(Copper Angel × *M. wurdackii*)	J. Page	1994
Melting Sunset	(*M. ignea* × *M. trochilus*)	L & R	1994
Memoria Albert Ballentine	(*M. guttulata* × *M. weberbaueri*)	Ballentine	1967
Memoria Alex Arms	(*M. veitchiana* × *M. caesia*)	G. Fuller	1992
Memoria Henry Scardefield	(*M. veitchiana* × *M. corniculata*)	J & L	1991
Memoria Peter Stebbing	(Antizana × *M. triangularis*)	S. Stebbing (C. Halls)	2001
Midas Touch	(Copper Queen × Falcata)	P. L. Jackson	2003
Midnight Plum	(*M. coccinea* × *M. discoidea*)	Orchid Zone	1998
Midnight Ruby	(*M. calura* × *M. oscitans*)	Hoosier Orchid Co.	2002
Milky Way	(*M. coccinea* × *M. hirtzii*)	J. Page	1994
Milo	(*M. peristeria* × *M. decumana*)	M. Ferrusi	2004
Mime	(Circe × Harlequin)	R. Hull	1997
Minaret	(*M. yungasensis* × *M. ignea*)	Pettit	1990
Mini Sun	(Cynthia × *M. hirtzii*)	J. Page	1994
Misfit	(*M. paivaëana* × *M. attenuata*)	Hoosier Orchid Co.	1991
Monarch	(*M. macrura* × *M. veitchiana*)	O. Neils	1991
Mona's Pride	(Claret Chalice × *M. weberbaueri*)	I. Klein	1994
Monica Rae Kortz	(*M. sororcula* × *M. ignea*)	G. Staal	1995
Moon Goddess	(Circe × *M. collina*)	Hoodview	1993
Morning Dew	(*M. ignea* × *M. datura*)	G. Staal	2002
Morning Glory	(*M. chaparensis* × Marguerite)	Orchid Zone	1998
Motoi Kawatsura	(Tuakau Candy × *M. pinocchio*)	T. Kawatsura	1998
Mount Feathertop	(Bella Donna × *M. datura*)	C. Halls	2000
Mountain Nymph	(*M. decumana* × *M. lamprotyria*)	Mountain Orchids	1994
Myck Santos	(Harlequin × Night Stripes)	J. Venturina	1997
Myra	(*M. uniflora* × *M. chaparensis*)	Cobbledick	1990

NAME	PARENTAGE	HYBRIDIZER	REGIS-TRATION YEAR
Nancy	(*M. mejiana* × *M. strobelii*)	E. Dreise	1994
Nemo	(Angel Frost × *M. deformis*)	J & L	1991
Night Goddess	(Juno × *M. collina*)	Hoodview	1993
Night Light	(Angel Frost × *M. aenigma*)	Highland Tropicals	1992
Night Shade	(Angel Frost × *M. datura*)	J. Leathers	1994
Night Stripes	(*M. yungasensis* × *M. datura*)	J. Leathers	1994
Nol van Oudgaarden	(*M. chaparensis* × *M. colossus*)	G. Staal	1993
Northern Angel	(Southern Sun × Angel Glow)	M. Ferrusi	2002
Northern Envy	(Southern Sun × *M. welischii*)	M. Ferrusi	2002
Northern Flash	(Southern Sun × *M. ignea*)	M. Ferrusi	2002
Northern Lights	(Rising Sun × *M. norops*)	Orchid Zone	1997
Northern Sun	(*M. veitchiana* × Southern Sun)	M. Ferrusi	1998
Nova	(*M. echo* × *M. navicularis*)	Hoosier Orchid Co. (Glicenstein/Hoosier)	2003
Noveau	(Tanager × *M. vieriana*)	Hoosier Orchid Co. (Glicenstein/Hoosier)	2003
Nuthatch	(*M. pachyura* × *M. exquisita*)	Hoosier Orchid Co. (Glicenstein/Hoosier)	2004
Okemos Sprite	(Sunny Angel × Swallow)	M. Ferrusi	2004
Opalescent	(Measuresiana × *M. uniflora*)	G. Fuller	2000
Orange Blossom	(Elven Poppies × Fancy Pants)	Orchid Zone	1997
Orange Bounty	(Hortensia × *M. hirtzii*)	M. Ferrusi	2002
Orange Delight	(Angel Frost × *M. hirtzii*)	I. Komoda	1997
Orange Grove	(*M. veitchiana* × *M. trochilus*)	L & R	1994
Orange Ice	(*M. strobelii* × *M. mendozae*)	Hoosier Orchid Co.	1992
Orange Sherbet	(*M. strobelii* × *M. reichenbachiana*)	Hoosier Orchid Co.	1998
Oriole	(*M. veitchiana* × *M. reichenbachiana*)	Hoosier Orchid Co.	1991
Otago Gold	(Lemon Glow × Heathii)	G. & J. Letts	1996
Otavalo	(*M. instar* × *M. coccinea*)	R. Thomson	1992
Othello	(*M. infracta* × *M. collina*)	Hoodview	1991
Owen Neils	(Copper Angel × *M. sanctae-inesiae*)	Highland Tropicals	1992
Pagoda	(Redwing × Kimball's Kissin' Cousin)	Hoosier Orchid Co. (Glicenstein/Hoosier)	2003
Panama Nazarene	(Sunset Jaguar × *M. triangularis*)	Maduro's Trop. Fl.	2000
Panama Orange	(Staalight × *M. glandulosa*)	Maduro's Trop. Fl.	2000
Panama Peppermint	(*M. amabilis* × *M. lineolata*)	Maduro's Trop. Fl.	2000
Panama Pink	(*M. glandulosa* × *M. decumana*)	Maduro's Trop. Fl.	2000
Panama Red	(Fuzzy Navel × *M. welischii*)	Maduro's Trop. Fl.	2000
Panama Ruby	(*M. uniflora* × *M. collina*)	Hoodview	1991
Papa's Sweetie Pie	(*M. lamprotyria* × *M. exquisita*)	Hoosier Orchid Co. (H. Meng)	2004
Paradise Sunset	(*M. triangularis* × *M. ignea*)	P. O. N.	1987
Parakeet	(*M. ignea* × *M. caloptera*)	Hoosier Orchid Co.	1991
Parlatoreana	(*M. barlaena* × *M. veitchiana*)	(originator unknown)	1886
Partizan	(Parlatoreana × Antizana)	C. Halls	2001
Party Dress	(*M. patriciana* × *M. lychniphora*)	M. Light	2002

NAME	PARENTAGE	HYBRIDIZER	REGIS-TRATION YEAR
Party Time	(Mardi Gras × *M. floribunda*)	Hoosier Orchid Co. (Glicenstein/Hoosier)	2002
Pat Allwood	(*M. davisii* × *M. mendozae*)	A. Barty	2000
Patricia Fyfe	(Night Shade × *M. hirtzii*)	A. Barty	2003
Patricia Hill	(*M. ignea* × *M. welischii*)	J. Leathers	1994
Pat's Memory	(Stella × *M. veitchiana*)	B. & C.	1990
Peach Daiquiri	(Peach Fuzz × Marguerite)	Hoosier Orchid Co. (Glicenstein/Hoosier)	2003
Peach Fuzz	(*M. constricta* × *M. veitchiana*)	O. Neils	1990
Peach Melba	(Peach Fuzz × Angel Tang)	Hoosier Orchid Co. (Glicenstein/Hoosier)	2003
Peachie	(*M. floribunda* × *M. triangularis*)	D&M Crawford	1992
Pelican	(*M. angulata* × *M. trochilus*)	Hoosier Orchid Co.	1992
Peppermint	(*M. strobelii* × *M. yungasensis*)	J & L	1987
Peppermint Glow	(*M. infracta* × Harlequin)	R. Thomson	1991
Peppermint Rock	(Minaret × *M. caudata*)	New Plymouth	1993
Peppermint Surprise	(*M. striatella* × *M. glandulosa*)	Hoosier Orchid Co.	1996
Periacea	(*M. coriacea* × *M. peristeria*)	L. B. Kuhn	1975
Peris Kimball	(Kimballiana × *M. peristeria*)	Hoodview	1991
Perky Peggy	(*M. pachyura* × *M. ignea*)	Sea Breeze	1987
Peter Raven	(*M. decumana* × *M. triangularis*)	O. Neils	1996
Peter Watts	(*M. veitchiana* × *M. elephanticeps*)	P. Watts	1992
Petite Princess	(Fairy Princess × Hani)	Orchid Zone	1998
Phipfrac	(*M. infracta* × *M. trochilus*)	New Plymouth	1993
Phoebe	(Aquarius × Peach Fuzz)	Hoosier Orchid Co. (Glicenstein/Hoosier)	2003
Pichincha	(Copper Angel × *M. yungasensis*)	R. Thomson	1993
Pilarcitos	(*M. ignea* × *M. scabrilinguis*)	H. Rohl	1996
Pin Stripes	(*M. yungasensis* × Ann Jesup)	L. O'Shaugnessy (G. Staal)	2002
Pink Blizzard	(*M. coccinea* × Stormy Weather)	Hoosier Orchid Co. (Glicenstein/Hoosier)	2003
Pink Fairy	(*M. coccinea* × *M. lamprotyria*)	R. Hull	2000
Pink Ice	(*M. uniflora* × *M. setacea*)	L & R	1994
Pink Mandarin	(Tanager × Hoosier Belle)	Hoosier Orchid Co. (Glicenstein/Hoosier)	2002
Pink Mist	(*M. strobelii* × *M. coccinea*)	J & L	1989
Pink Parfait	(*M. uniflora* × *M. caudata*)	J & L	1991
Pink Pearl	(*M. xanthina* × *M. uniflora*)	R. Hull	1996
Pink Rainbow	(*M. asterotricha* × *M. glandulosa*)	Hoosier Orchid Co. (Glicenstein/Hosier)	2003
Pink Zebra	(*M. coccinea* × Minaret)	Hoosier Orchid Co. (Glicenstein/Hoosier)	2003
Pinwheel	(*M. yungasensis* × *M. caudata*)	J & L	1995
Pipit	(Canary × *M. sprucei*)	Hoosier Orchid Co. (W. Rhodehamel)	2003

NAME	PARENTAGE	HYBRIDIZER	REGIS-TRATION YEAR
Pixie Angel	(*M. caloptera* × Kimballiana)	Orchid Zone	1994
Pixie Bloomers	(Fancy Pants × *M. decumana*)	Orchid Zone	1998
Pixie Caramel	(*M. schroederiana* × *M. macrura*)	Orchid Zone	1998
Pixie Copper	(Rising Sun × Falcata)	Orchid Zone	1997
Pixie Dust	(*M. uniflora* × *M. decumana*)	J & L	1991
Pixie Gem	(*M. coccinea* × Amethyst)	Orchid Zone	1997
Pixie Gold	(*M. davisii* × *M. caudata*)	Orchid Zone	1993
Pixie Lavender	(Bright Angel × *M. decumana*)	Orchid Zone	1997
Pixie Leopard	(Chaparana × *M. decumana*)	Orchid Zone	1997
Pixie Pearl	(Redwing × *M. constricta*)	Orchid Zone	1998
Pixie Shadow	(*M. infracta* × *M. schroederiana*)	Orchid Zone	1994
Pixie Toy	(Maryann × Copper Angel)	Orchid Zone	1996
Pixie Treasure	(Autumn Glow × *M. floribunda*)	Orchid Zone	1996
Pixie Violets	(*M. coccinea* × *M. decumana*)	Orchid Zone	1996
Plum Wine	(*M. floribunda* × *M. glandulosa*)	D. & M. Crawford	1997
Pluto	(*M. coccinea* × Gairiana)	Hincks	1899
Polish Petunia	(*M. hirtzii* × *M. foetens*)	Hoosier Orchid Co. (W. Klikunas)	2000
Pollyana	(*M. triangularis* × *M. infracta*)	J & L	1983
Pomona Purple	(Harlequin × Juno)	R. Thomson	1995
Pony Tails	(*M. glandulosa* × *M. macrura*)	L. O'Shaugnessy (G. Staal)	2002
Pot of Gold	(*M. strobelii* × *M. hirtzii*)	J. Page	1997
Pretty Woman	(*M. caudata* × *M. setacea*)	J & L	1995
Prince Charming	(*M. veitchiana* × *M. angulata*)	R. McLellan Co.	1979
Prodigy	(*M. veitchiana* × *M. prodigiosa*)	Hoosier Orchid Co.	1991
Proud Prince	(Prince Charming × *M. veitchiana*)	R. Plows	1991
Pumpkin Pie	(Freckles × Copper Angel)	J. Leathers	1995
Purple Condor	(*M. caudata* × *M. decumana*)	Sunset Orchids	2001
Purple Heart	(*M. coccinea* × *M. elephanticeps*)	Santa Barbara Orchid Estate	1985
Pygmalion	(*M. uniflora* × *M. racemosa*)	T. Hill	1991
Pywacket	(Copper Angel × *M. schlimii*)	Hoosier Orchid Co. (Glicenstein/Hoosier)	2003
Quail	(Kimballiana × *M. floribunda*)	T. Hill	1991
Radiance	(Auburn Hero × Hortensia)	M. Ferrusi	2002
Rainbow Tiger	(Blanch × Harlequin)	Hillsview	1998
Raymondo de los Andes	(*M. uniflora* × *M. macrura*)	G. Staal	1997
Rebecca	(*M. amabilis* × *M. ignea*)	Ames	1893
Red Baron	(*M. coccinea* × *M. maculata*)	Beall Pink	1984
Red Gum	(*M. veitchiana* × *M. maculata*)	W. Reis	1992
Red Lion	(*M. velifera* × *M. coccinea*)	G. Staal	1992
Red Lys	(Angel Heart × Minaret)	A. Millet	2002
Red Panther	(*M. welischii* × *M. chaparensis*)	G. Staal	1992
Red Sail	(*M. ignea* × *M. echo*)	L & R	1994
Red Sun	(*M. welischii* × Urubamba)	W. Miles	1997
Red Velvet	(*M. yungasensis* × *M. coriacea*)	A & P Orchids	1998
Redpoll	(*M. barlaena* × *M. auropurpurea*)	Hoosier	1992
Redshine	(Falcon Sunrise × Marguerite)	Golden Gate	2002

NAME	PARENTAGE	HYBRIDIZER	REGIS-TRATION YEAR
Redwing	(*M. infracta* × *M. coccinea*)	Santa Barbara Orchid Estate	1985
Redwood	(*M. veitchiana* × Kimballiana)	W. Reis	1992
Reggae	(Harlequin × *M. ignea*)	Chieri Orchids	1992
Rein Staal	(*M. veitchiana* × *M. wurdackii*)	G. Staal	1991
Rhys's Freckles	(Kimballiana × Hortensia)	M. Ferrusi	1997
Rice Queen	(*M. coccinea* × *M. xanthina*)	P. Chin	1993
Rio Sunrise	(Redwing × *M. strobelii*)	Hillsview	1998
Rising Sun	(*M. veitchiana* × *M. rimarima-alba*)	Orchid Zone	1993
Rodensue	(*M. constricta* × *M. floribunda*)	Venger's	1995
Ron Hawley	(*M. uniflora* × *M. strobelii*)	Hawley/Levi	1986
Rosamund	(Kimballiana × *M. vargasii*)	E. Dreise	1991
Rose-Mary	(*M. coccinea* × *M. glandulosa*)	G. Staal	1992
Rubicon	(*M. coccinea* × Heathii)	Mayhead	1988
Ruby Rose	(*M. veitchiana* × *M. pyxis*)	R. Thomson	1992
Ruby Slippers	(*M. coccinea* × *M. calura*)	T. Hill	1994
Rushtonii	(*M. ignea* × *M. racemosa*)	(originator unknown)	19th century
Sa Rang	(Charisma × *M. uniflora*)	A. S. Chai (Golden Gate)	2002
Sandy Bay	(Sunny Angel × *M. coccinea*)	P. Nicholas	1998
Sassy Miss	(*M. veitchiana* × *M. misasii*)	J. Page	1992
Satin Rose	(Blue Angel × *M. coccinea*)	Orchid Zone	1997
Selfridgeana	(*M. arminii* × *M. ignea*)	Sander	19th century
Senga	(Stella × *M. glandulosa*)	A. Barty	1997
Seraphim	(Angel Frost × *M. strobelii*)	T. Hill	1991
Shinichi Komada	(Copper Angel × *M. tonduzii*)	I. Komoda	1995
Shirley's First	(*M. auropurpurea* × *M. veitchiana*)	S. Sidnam	1990
Shizuko Kawatsura	(Tuakau Candy × Copper Candy)	T. Kawatsura	1998
Shooting Stars	(*M. caloptera* × *M. veitchiana*)	Orchid Zone	1993
Shuttryana	(*M. caudata* × *M. coccinea*)	Lawrence	1892
Sidney	(*M. coccinea* × *M. patriciana*)	M. Turkel	1993
Snow Angel	(Bright Angel × Charisma)	Orchid Zone	1997
Snow Gum	(*M. lineolata* × Fuzzy Navel)	P. Nicholas	1998
Snow Magic	(Hani × *M. coccinea*)	Orchid Zone	1998
Snow White	(*M. tovarensis* × Angel Frost)	T. Goshima	2000
Snowberry	(*M. coccinea* × *M. caloptera*)	Orchid Zone	1997
Snowbird	(*M. tovarensis* × *M. mejiana*)	J & L	1982
Snowflake	(Snowbird × *M. nivea*)	Hoosier Orchid Co. (Glicenstein/Hoosier)	2003
Snowkist	(*M. coccinea* × Maryann)	Orchid Zone	1996
Snowy Egret	(Snowbird × *M. coccinea*)	Hoosier Orchid Co. (Glicenstein/Hoosier)	2003
Solar Flare	(*M. veitchiana* × Falcata)	Cal-Orchid (Beall)	2001
Soufflé	(Angel Tang × *M. tonduzii*)	B. C. Berliner	1997
Southern Aurora	(Falcata × Harlequin)	P. Nash	1991
Southern Belle	(Charisma × Coconut Ice)	D. F. Butler (P. Altmann)	2003

NAME	PARENTAGE	HYBRIDIZER	REGIS- TRATION YEAR
Southern Moonlight	(Confetti × Kimballiana)	J. Page	1997
Southern Star	(Susan × Anna-Claire)	J. Page	2000
Southern Sun	(*M. veitchiana* × *M. hirtzii*)	J. Page	1992
Sparrow	(*M. guayanensis* × *M. caloptera*)	Hoosier Orchid Co.	1991
Speckles	(*M. davisii* × *M. stenorrhynchos*)	R. F. Hamilton	1995
Spiderling	(Copper Angel × *M. venezuelana*)	H. Jesup	1995
Spiderman	(Copper Angel × *M. lehmannii*)	J & L	1992
Spooky	(*M. caudata* × *M. angulata*)	R. McLellan Co.	1980
Spring Peeper	(*M. wurdackii* × *M. caudata*)	F. Feysa	1995
Sprinkles	(Steven Male × *M. decumana*)	G. Staal	1998
Staalight	(Harlequin × *M. constricta*)	R. Thomson	1991
Starburst	(*M. instar* × *M. striatella*)	Hoosier Orchid Co.	1991
Stardust	(*M. decumana* × *M. datura*)	G. Staal	2002
Starfire	(Dark Star × *M. coccinea*)	Orchid Zone	1998
Starlet	(*M. caloptera* × *M. infracta*)	Orchid Zone	1993
Stella	(*M. coccinea* × *M. estradae*)	Hincks	1890
Steve Vance	(Copper Angel × *M. princeps*)	I. Komoda	1999
Steven Male	(*M. sanctae-inesiae* × *M. veitchiana*)	Highland Tropicals	1992
Stormy Weather	(*M. chaparensis* × Myra)	Hoosier Orchid Co. (T. Hill)	2003
Strawberry Cheesecake	(*M. coccinea* × *M. sprucei*)	Hoosier Orchid Co. (Glicenstein/Hoosier)	2003
Sugar Baby	(*M. veitchiana* × *M. floribunda*)	J & L	1988
Sugar Frost	(Sugar Baby × Angel Frost)	R. Thomson	1994
Sun and Snow	(Angel Frost × Confetti)	J. Page	1997
Sun Bittern	(Kimball's Kissin' Cousin × *M. decumana*)	Hoosier Orchid Co. (Glicenstein/Hoosier)	2003
Sun Dancer	(Sunny Angel × *M. veitchiana*)	P. Nicholas	1993
Sun Ray	(*M. coccinea* × *M. wurdackii*)	G. Staal	1993
Sunbeam	(*M. triangularis* × *M. strobelii*)	J & L	1989
Sunbird	(Aquarius × Canary)	Hoosier Orchid Co. (Glicenstein/Hoosier)	2003
Sunburst	(Angel Glow × *M. caloptera*)	J. Page	1993
Sunny Angel	(*M. triangularis* × Angel Frost)	J & L	1986
Sunny Marguerite	(Sunny Angel × Marguerite)	Hoosier Orchid Co. (Glicenstein/Hoosier)	2003
Sunrise Candy	(Tuakau Candy × Bella Donna)	M. Ferrusi	2004
Sunrise Spice	(Cassiope × *M. decumana*)	O. Neils	1993
Sunset Gold	(Monarch × *M. tonduzii*)	K. Muir (T. Root)	2003
Sunset Jaguar	(*M. chaparensis* × Copper Angel)	S. Gettel	1990
Sunset Leopard	(Sunset Jaguar × *M. decumana*)	Sunset Orchids	2001
Sunspot	(*M. sanctae-inesiae* × *M. tonduzii*)	Hoosier Orchid Co.	1998
Susan	(Gremlin × *M. veitchiana*)	N. P. P. R.	1990
Suzy Bedford	(*M. schroederiana* × *M. caudata*)	Ixchel	1988
Swallow	(Falcata × *M. infracta*)	Golden Gate	1991
Sweet Anna	(Angel Frost × Anna-Claire)	D. Butler	2000
Taffeta	(*M. glandulosa* × *M. setacea*)	J & L	1991

NAME	PARENTAGE	HYBRIDIZER	REGIS-TRATION YEAR
Tahitian Dancer	(Copper Angel × *M. maculata*)	Hoosier Orchid Co. (Glicenstein/Hoosier)	2003
Tanabilis	(*M. amabilis* × Tanager)	Hoosier Orchid Co. (Glicenstein/Hoosier)	2003
Tanager	(*M. ludibunda* × *M. ignea*)	Hoosier Orchid Co.	1991
Tangerine Dragon	(*M. mendozae* × *M. veitchiana*)	Hoosier Orchid Co.	1992
Tangerine Frost	(Angel Frost × Monarch)	Orchid Zone	1997
Tanja	(*M. mendozae* × *M. decumana*)	E. Dreise	1991
Tashi	(*M. angulata* × *M. decumana*)	M. Ferrusi	2004
Tasmanian Devil	(Angel Frost × *M. floribunda*)	F. Feysa	1995
Tawny Star	(Copper Angel × Dark Star)	Orchid Zone	1998
Ted Khoe	(*M. constricta* × *M. welischii*)	P. Chin	1991
Teipel's Amethyst	(Veilchen × *M. constricta*)	P. Teipel	2003
Teipel's Falcogland	(Falcon's Gold × *M. glandulosa*)	P. Teipel	2003
Tequila Rose	(Pixie Dust × Amethyst)	M. Ferrusi	2002
Teresita	(Heathii × *M. floribunda*)	T. Hill	1989
Theresa Hill	(*M. uniflora* × *M. odontocera*)	M. Ferrusi	1996
Thumbelina	(*M. instar* × *M. uniflora*)	Highland Tropicals	1992
Tiedye	(*M. chaparensis* × *M. rhodehameliana*)	Hoosier Orchid Co. (E. Michel)	2003
Tiger Butter	(Golden Tiger × *M. davisii*)	Orchid Zone	1997
Tiger Kiss	(Golden Tiger × Monarch)	Orchid Zone	1998
Tiger Rose	(Red Baron × *M. yungasensis*)	J & L	1995
Tigertale	(Golden Tiger × Kimballiana)	Orchid Zone	1997
Tinker Belles	(*M. datura* × *M. erinacea*)	L. O'Shaugnessy (G. Staal)	2002
Titania	(*M. macrura* × *M. hirtzii*)	J. Page	1996
Titi Staal	(*M. tovarensis* × *M. notosibirica*)	G. Staal	1992
Todd Kelley	(*M. veitchiana* × *M. nidifica*)	Baker & Chantry	1993
Toltec Gold	(*M. davisii* × *M. macrura*)	Orchid Zone	1993
Tom Nasser	(Marguerite × *M. veitchiana*)	B. Schwarz	1991
Topaz	(Marguerite × *M. constricta*)	J. Page	1997
Towering Inferno	(Falcata × *M. coccinea*)	Beall Pink	1993
Toyoki Kawatsura	(Tuakau Candy × *M. exquisita*)	T. Kawatsura	1998
Tuakau Goldstrike	(*M. davisii* × *M. triangularis*)	L & R	1994
Tungurahua	(*M. veitchiana* × *M. aenigma*)	R. Thomson	1995
Tuxedo	(*M. patriciana* × *M. hirtzii*)	M. Light	2002
Twilight	(Claret Chalice × *M. decumana*)	Chieri Orchids	1992
Twinkle Bells	(*M. datura* × *M. exquisita*)	M. Ferrusi	2004
Twinkle Toes	(Claret Chalice × *M. datura*)	P. Nicholas	1994
Twinky	(*M. coccinea* × *M. citrinella*)	M. Turkel	1992
Urubamba	(*M. ayabacana* × *M. veitchiana*)	Beall Pink	1986
Ute	(*M. mejiana* × *M. veitchiana*)	E. Dreise	1992
Veitchen	(Falcata × *M. schroederiana*)	P. Teipel	2003
Veitchiano-Estradae	(*M. estradae* × *M. veitchiana*)	Hincks	1893
Veitchiano-Fragrans	(*M. fragrans* × *M. veitchiana*)	R. I. Measures	1904
Veitchiano-Wageneriana	(*M. veitchiana* × *M. wageneriana*)	Sander	1898
Velvet Glow	(Falcata × *M. panguiënsis*)	J & L	1992

NAME	PARENTAGE	HYBRIDIZER	REGIS-TRATION YEAR
Velvet Tangerine	(Copperwing × Southern Sun)	M. Ferrusi	2002
Velveteen Angel	(*M. uniflora* × *M. panguiënsis*)	J & L	1991
Velveteen Cowboy	(*M. coccinea* × *M. navicularis*)	Hoosier Orchid Co. (Glicenstein/Hoosier)	2003
Vin Rouge	(*M. infracta* × *M. rolfeana*)	Chieri Orchids	1992
Violet Frost	(Angel Frost × *M. davisii*)	L & R	1994
Violet Fuzz	(Angel Frost × *M. trochilus*)	L & R	1994
Violet Gems	(*M. uniflora* × Wally Bernstein)	M. Ferrusi	2002
Violetta	(*M. amabilis* × *M. striatella*)	L & R	1994
Wally Bernstein	(*M. chaparensis* × *M. triangularis*)	G. Staal	1995
Watercolor Dreamer	(Blue Angel × Hani)	Orchid Zone	1996
Whimsy	(*M. veitchiana* × *M. caudivolvula*)	L & R	1994
Whirligig	(*M. caudivolvula* × *M. caesia*)	Highland Tropicals	1992
Whiskers	(*M. veitchiana* × *M. glandulosa*)	J & L	1991
White Swallow	(*M. constricta* × *M. datura*)	P. Chin	1993
Willy's	(*M. veitchiana* × *M. attenuata*)	W. Scharft (originator unknown)	2003
Windswept	(Copperwing × Keiko Komoda)	L. O'Shaughnessy (I. Komoda)	2001
Winged Leopard	(Copperwing × *M. macrura*)	M. Ferrusi	2002
Winifred	(*M. veitchiana* × Davina)	A. Barty	1998
Winter Blush	(Angel Frost × *M. chaparensis*)	P. Chin	1991
Wössner Feuer	(Dean Haas × *M. veitchiana*)	F. Glanz	2002
Xanthino-Veitchiana	(*M. veitchiana* × *M. xanthina*)	Lawrence	1902
Yellow Bird	(Xanthino-Veitchiana × *M. reichenbachiana*)	H. Rohrl	1998
Yellow Storm	(Copper Angel × Rein Staal)	A & P Orchids	1998
Yma Sumac	(*M. oscitans* × Urabamba)	Hoosier Orchid Co. (Glicenstein/Hoosier)	2004
Yosemite Sam	(*M. odontocera* × *M. ignea*)	Mountain Orchids	1995
Yutaka Kawatsura	(*M. gilbertoi* × *M. schroederiana*)	T. Kawatsura	1995
Zwaluw	(*M. heteroptera* × *M. veitchiana*)	G. Staal	1993

APPENDIX II

❖ ❖ ❖

Species and Culture

SPECIES	COUNTRIES	GROWING CONDITIONS
Masdevallia abbreviata Rchb.f.	Ecuador, Peru	Cool to intermediate
Masdevallia acaroi Luer and Hirtz	Ecuador	Cool
Masdevallia acrochordonia Rchb.f.	Ecuador	Cool to intermediate
Masdevallia adamsii Luer	Belize	Intermediate
Masdevallia adrianae Luer	Ecuador	Cool to intermediate
Masdevallia aenigma Luer and Escobar	Colombia	Cool to intermediate
Masdevallia agaster Luer	Ecuador	Intermediate
Masdevallia aguirrei Luer and Escobar	Colombia	Unknown*
Masdevallia albella Luer and Teague	Ecuador, Peru	Cool
Masdevallia alexandri Luer	Ecuador	Cool
Masdevallia alismifolia Kränzl.	Colombia	Cool
Masdevallia ×alvaroi Luer and Escobar	Colombia	Intermediate
Masdevallia amabilis Rchb.f. and Warsc.	Peru	Cool
Masdevallia amaluzae Luer and Malo	Ecuador	Intermediate
Masdevallia amanda Rchb.f. and Warsc.	Colombia, Ecuador, Venezuela	Cool
Masdevallia ametroglossa Luer and Hirtz	Ecuador	Cool to intermediate
Masdevallia amoena Luer	Ecuador	Cool to intermediate
Masdevallia amplexa Luer	Peru	Intermediate
Masdevallia ampullacea Luer and Andreetta	Ecuador	Intermediate
Masdevallia anachaeta Rchb.f.	Colombia, Ecuador, Peru, Bolivia	Cool to intermediate
Masdevallia anceps Luer and Hirtz	Ecuador	Cool to intermediate
Masdevallia andreettana Luer	Ecuador	Cool to intermediate
Masdevallia anemone Luer	Ecuador	Unknown*
Masdevallia anfracta Königer and J. J. Portilla	Ecuador	Warm

* Species known only by herbarium specimen or original cultivated specimen that has since been lost.

SPECIES	COUNTRIES	GROWING CONDITIONS
Masdevallia angulata Rchb.f	Colombia, Ecuador	Cool to intermediate
Masdevallia angulifera Rchb.f. ex Kränzl.	Colombia	Cool to intermediate
Masdevallia anisomorpha Garay	Colombia	Cool
Masdevallia antonii Königer	Peru	Cool
Masdevallia aphanes Königer	Ecuador, Peru	Cool to intermediate
Masdevallia apparitio Luer and Escobar	Colombia	Cool
Masdevallia arangoi Luer and Escobar	Colombia	Cool
Masdevallia ariasii Luer	Peru	Intermediate
Masdevallia arminii Linden and Rchb.f.	Colombia	Cool
Masdevallia assurgens Luer and Escobar	Colombia	Cool
Masdevallia asterotricha Königer	Peru	Cool to intermediate
Masdevallia atahualpa Luer	Peru	Cool
Masdevallia attenuata Rchb.f.	Costa Rica, Panama	Intermediate
Masdevallia audax Königer	Peru	Cool
Masdevallia aurea Luer	Ecuador	Cool to intermediate
Masdevallia aurorae Luer and M. W. Chase	Peru	Cool to intermediate
Masdevallia ayabacana Luer	Peru	Intermediate to warm
Masdevallia bangii Schltr.	Colombia, Ecuador, Peru	Intermediate
Masdevallia barlaena Rchb.f.	Peru	Cool
Masdevallia barrowii Luer	Ecuador	Cool
Masdevallia belua Königer and D. D'Alessandro	Ecuador	Cool to intermediate
Masdevallia bennettii Luer	Peru	Intermediate to warm
Masdevallia berthae Königer	Ecuador	Cool
Masdevallia bicolor Poepp. and Endl.	Bolivia, Colombia, Ecuador, Peru, Venezuela	Cool to intermediate
Masdevallia bicornis Luer	Ecuador	Cool to intermediate
Masdevallia boliviensis Schltr.	Bolivia	Cool
Masdevallia bonplandii Rchb. f.	Colombia, Ecuador, Peru	Cool
Masdevallia bottae Luer and Andreetta	Ecuador	Intermediate
Masdevallia bourdetteana Luer	Ecuador	Cool
Masdevallia brachyantha Schltr.	Bolivia	Cool to intermediate
Masdevallia brachyura Lehm. and Kränzl.	Ecuador	Intermediate
Masdevallia brenneri Luer	Ecuador	Cool to intermediate
Masdevallia brockmuelleri Luer	Colombia	Cool
Masdevallia bryophila Luer	Peru	Intermediate (?)
Masdevallia buccinator Rchb.f. and Warsc.	Colombia	Cool
Masdevallia bucculenta Luer and Hirtz	Ecuador	Cool to intermediate
Masdevallia bulbophyllopsis Kränzl.	Ecuador	Cool
Masdevallia burianii Luer and Dalström	Bolivia	Cool
Masdevallia cacodes Luer and Escobar	Ecuador	Cool to intermediate
Masdevallia caesia Roezl	Colombia	Cool
Masdevallia calagrasalis Luer	Ecuador	Cool to intermediate
Masdevallia calocalix Luer	Ecuador	Cool to intermediate (?)
Masdevallia caloptera Rchb.f.	Peru	Cool to intermediate
Masdevallia calosiphon Luer	Peru	Cool

(?) Limited information on culture conditions. The conditions are "suggested" based on collection information.

SPECIES	COUNTRIES	GROWING CONDITIONS
Masdevallia calura Rchb.f.	Costa Rica	Cool to intermediate
Masdevallia campyloglossa Rchb.f.	Colombia, Ecuador, Peru	Intermediate
Masdevallia cardiantha Königer	Peru	Intermediate
Masdevallia carmenensis Luer and Malo	Ecuador	Cool
Masdevallia carpishica Luer and Cloes	Peru	Cool
Masdevallia carruthersiana Lehm. and Kränzl.	Ecuador	Cool to intermediate
Masdevallia castor Luer and Cloes	Peru	Cool (?)
Masdevallia catapheres Königer	Peru	Cool
Masdevallia caudata Lindl.	Colombia, Venezuela	Cool to intermediate
Masdevallia caudivolvula Kränzl.	Colombia	Cool
Masdevallia cerastes Luer and Escobar	Colombia	Cool
Masdevallia chaestostoma Luer	Ecuador	Cool
Masdevallia chaparensis Hashimoto	Bolivia	Cool
Masdevallia chasei Luer	Costa Rica	Intermediate
Masdevallia chimboënsis Kränzl.	Colombia	Intermediate
Masdevallia chontalensis Rchb.f.	Costa Rica, Panama	Intermediate
Masdevallia chuspipatae Luer and Teague	Bolivia	Cool to intermediate
Masdevallia cinnamomea Rchb.f.	Peru	Cool
Masdevallia citrinella Luer and Malo	Ecuador	Cool to intermediate
Masdevallia civilis Rchb.f. and Warsc.	Peru	Cool
Masdevallia clandestina Luer and Escobar	Colombia	Cool
Masdevallia cleistogama Luer	Peru	Cool (?)
Masdevallia cloesii Luer	Peru	Cool
Masdevallia cocapatae Luer, Teague, and Vásquez	Bolivia	Cool to intermediate
Masdevallia coccinea Linden ex Lindl.	Colombia	Cool
Masdevallia collantesii D. E. Benn and Christenson	Peru	Cool to intermediate (?)
Masdevallia collina L. O. Williams	Panama	Intermediate to warm
Masdevallia colossus Luer	Ecuador, Peru	Cool
Masdevallia concinna Königer	Peru	Cool to intermediate
Masdevallia condorensis Luer and Hirtz	Ecuador	Intermediate
Masdevallia constricta Peopp. and Endl.	Ecuador, Peru	Intermediate
Masdevallia corazonica Schltr.	Ecuador	Cool to intermediate
Masdevallia cordeliana Luer	Peru	Cool (?)
Masdevallia corderoana Lehm. and Kränzl.	Ecuador	Cool
Masdevallia coriacea Lindl.	Colombia, Ecuador, Peru	Cool to intermediate
Masdevallia corniculata Rchb.f.	Colombia, Ecuador	Cool to intermediate
Masdevallia cosmia Königer and Sijm	Peru	Cool (?)
Masdevallia cranion Luer	Peru	Cool
Masdevallia crassicaudis Luer and J. J. Portilla	Ecuador	Intermediate
Masdevallia crescenticola Lehm. and Kränzl.	Colombia, Ecuador	Warm
Masdevallia cretata Luer	Ecuador	Cool (?)
Masdevallia cucullata Lindl.	Colombia, Ecuador	Cool to intermediate
Masdevallia cuprea Lindl.	French Guiana, Guyana, Suriname, Venezuela	Intermediate to warm
Masdevallia cupularis Rchb.f.	Costa Rica	Cool

(?) Limited information on culture conditions. The conditions are "suggested" based on collection information.

SPECIES	COUNTRIES	GROWING CONDITIONS
Masdevallia curtipes Barb. Rodr.	Brazil	Intermediate to warm (?)
Masdevallia cyclotega Königer	Peru	Cool
Masdevallia cylix Luer and Malo	Ecuador	Cool
Masdevallia dalessandroi Luer	Ecuador	Intermediate
Masdevallia dalstroemii Luer	Ecuador	Cool
Masdevallia datura Luer and Vásquez	Bolivia	Cool to intermediate
Masdevallia davisii Rchb.f.	Peru	Cool
Masdevallia deceptrix Luer and Würstle	Venezuela	Intermediate
Masdevallia decumana Königer	Ecuador, Peru	Cool to intermediate
Masdevallia deformis Kränzl	Ecuador	Cool to intermediate
Masdevallia delhierroi Luer and Hirtz	Colombia	Cool
Masdevallia delphina Luer	Ecuador	Cool to intermediate
Masdevallia demissa Rchb.f.	Costa Rica	Warm
Masdevallia deniseana Luer and J. J. Portilla	Ecuador	Intermediate
Masdevallia densiflora Luer	Unknown, possibly Colombia	Unknown*
Masdevallia descendens Luer and Andreetta	Ecuador	Intermediate
Masdevallia dimorphotricha Luer and Hirtz	Ecuador	Cool to intermediate
Masdevallia discoidea Luer and Würstle	Brazil	Intermediate to warm
Masdevallia discolor Luer and Escobar	Colombia	Cool to intermediate
Masdevallia don-quijote Luer and Andreetta	Ecuador	Intermediate to warm
Masdevallia dorisiae Luer	Ecuador	Cool to intermediate
Masdevallia draconis Luer and Andreetta	Ecuador	Intermediate
Masdevallia dreisei Luer	Ecuador	Cool (?)
Masdevallia dryada Luer and Escobar	Colombia	Cool
Masdevallia dudleyi Luer	Peru	Cool
Masdevallia dunstervillei Luer	Venezuela	Unknown*
Masdevallia dura Luer	Ecuador	Cool
Masdevallia dynastes Luer	Ecuador	Cool to intermediate
Masdevallia eburnea Luer and Maduro	Panama	Intermediate to warm (?)
Masdevallia echo Luer	Peru	Intermediate
Masdevallia ejiriana Luer and J. J. Portilla	Ecuador	Cool
Masdevallia elachys Luer	Bolivia	Cool
Masdevallia elegans Luer and Escobar	Peru	Cool
Masdevallia elephanticeps Rchb.f. and Warsc.	Colombia	Cool
Masdevallia empusa Luer	Ecuador, Peru	Intermediate
Masdevallia enallax Königer	Unknown	Cool (?)
Masdevallia encephala Luer and Escobar	Colombia	Cool to intermediate
Masdevallia ensata Rchb.f.	Venezuela	Cool to intermediate
Masdevallia erinacea Rchb.f.	Colombia, Costa Rica, Ecuador, Panama	Intermediate to warm
Masdevallia estradae Rchb. f.	Colombia	Cool
Masdevallia eucharis Luer	Ecuador	Cool
Masdevallia eumeces Luer	Peru	Intermediate
Masdevallia eumeliae Luer	Peru	Cool

(?) Limited information on culture conditions. The conditions are "suggested" based on collection information.
* Species known only by herbarium specimen or original cultivated specimen that has since been lost.

SPECIES	COUNTRIES	GROWING CONDITIONS
Masdevallia eurynogaster Luer and Andreetta	Ecuador	Intermediate
Masdevallia excelsior Luer and Andreetta	Ecuador	Cool to intermediate
Masdevallia expansa Rchb.f.	Colombia	Cool
Masdevallia expers Luer and Andreetta	Ecuador	Cool to intermediate
Masdevallia exquisita Luer and Escobar	Bolivia	Cool to intermediate
Masdevallia falcago Rchb.f.	Colombia	Intermediate
Masdevallia figueroae Luer	Peru	Cool
Masdevallia filaria Luer and Escobar	Colombia	Cool to intermediate
Masdevallia flaveola Rchb.f.	Costa Rica, Panama	Intermediate
Masdevallia floribunda Lindl.	Costa Rica, Guatemala, El Salvador, Honduras, Mexico, Nicaragua, Belize	Intermediate to warm
Masdevallia foetens Luer and Escobar	Colombia	Cool to intermediate
Masdevallia formosa Luer and Cloes	Peru	Intermediate (?)
Masdevallia forsterae Luer	Unknown	Cool (?)
Masdevallia fractiflexa Lehm. and Kränzl.	Ecuador	Cool
Masdevallia fragrans Woolward	Colombia	Cool
Masdevallia frilehmannii Luer and Vásquez	Bolivia	Intermediate (?)
Masdevallia fuchsii Luer	Peru	Cool to intermediate
Masdevallia fulvescens Rolfe	Costa Rica	Cool to intermediate
Masdevallia garciae Luer	Venezuela	Intermediate
Masdevallia gargantua Rchb.f.	Colombia	Cool
Masdevallia geminiflora Ortiz	Colombia, Ecuador	Cool to intermediate
Masdevallia gilbertoi Luer and Escobar	Colombia	Cool
Masdevallia glandulosa Königer	Ecuador, Peru	Intermediate
Masdevallia glomerosa Luer and Andreetta	Ecuador	Cool to intermediate
Masdevallia gloriae Luer and Maduro	Panama	Cool
Masdevallia gnoma Sweet	Ecuador	Intermediate
Masdevallia goliath Luer and Andreetta	Ecuador	Cool to intermediate to warm
Masdevallia graminea Luer	Ecuador	Cool
Masdevallia guayanensis Lindl. ex Benth.	Guyana, Venezuela	Intermediate
Masdevallia guerrieroi Luer and Andreetta	Ecuador	Intermediate to warm
Masdevallia gutierrezii Luer	Bolivia	Intermediate to warm
Masdevallia guttulata Rchb.f.	Ecuador	Intermediate to warm
Masdevallia harlequina Luer	Peru	Cool
Masdevallia hartmanii Luer	Ecuador	Cool to intermediate
Masdevallia heideri Königer	Bolivia	Cool
Masdevallia helenae Luer	Bolivia	Cool to intermediate
Masdevallia helgae Luer and J. J. Portilla	Ecuador	Cool to intermediate
Masdevallia henniae Luer and Dalström	Ecuador	Intermediate
Masdevallia hercules Luer and Andreetta	Colombia, Ecuador	Cool
Masdevallia herradurae Lehm. and Kränzl.	Colombia	Intermediate to warm
Masdevallia heteroptera Rchb.f.	Colombia	Cool to intermediate
Masdevallia hians Rchb.f.	Colombia	Cool
Masdevallia hieroglyphica Rchb.f.	Colombia	Cool

(?) Limited information on culture conditions. The conditions are "suggested" based on collection information.

SPECIES	COUNTRIES	GROWING CONDITIONS
Masdevallia hirtzii Luer and Andreetta	Ecuador	Cool to intermediate
Masdevallia hoeijeri Luer and Hirtz	Colombia, Ecuador	Cool to intermediate
Masdevallia hortensis Luer and Escobar	Colombia	Cool
Masdevallia hubeinii Luer and Würstle	Colombia	Cool
Masdevallia hydrae Luer	Ecuador	Cool
Masdevallia hylodes Luer and Escobar	Colombia	Cool
Masdevallia hymenantha Rchb.f.	Peru	Cool to intermediate
Masdevallia hystrix Luer and Hirtz	Ecuador	Cool
Masdevallia icterina Köni{g}er	Peru	Cool
Masdevallia idea Luer and Arias	Peru	Cool
Masdevallia ignea Rchb.f.	Colombia	Cool
Masdevallia immensa Luer	Peru	Cool
Masdevallia impostor Luer and Escobar	Colombia, Ecuador, Venezuela	Intermediate
Masdevallia indecora Luer and Escobar	Colombia	Cool
Masdevallia infracta Lindl.	Bolivia, Brazil	Cool to intermediate to warm (does best cool to intermediate)
Masdevallia ingridiana Luer and J. J. Portilla	Ecuador	Cool to intermediate (?)
Masdevallia instar Luer and Andreetta	Ecuador, Peru	Cool
Masdevallia ionocharis Rchb.f.	Peru	Cool
Masdevallia irapana Sweet	Venezuela	Intermediate (?)
Masdevallia iris Luer and Escobar	Venezuela	Cool to intermediate
Masdevallia ishikoi Luer	Bolivia	Cool to intermediate
Masdevallia isos Luer	Bolivia	Cool to intermediate (?)
Masdevallia jarae Luer	Peru	Cool
Masdevallia josei Luer	Ecuador	Cool (?)
Masdevallia juan-albertoi Luer and Arias	Peru	Cool
Masdevallia karineae Nauray ex Luer	Peru	Cool
Masdevallia klabochiorum Rchb.f.	Colombia, Ecuador, Peru	Cool to intermediate
Masdevallia kuhniorum Luer	Peru	Intermediate
Masdevallia kyphonantha Sweet	Venezuela	Intermediate
Masdevallia laevis Lindl.	Colombia, Ecuador	Cool
Masdevallia lamprotyria Königer	Peru	Cool to intermediate
Masdevallia lankesteriana Luer	Costa Rica	Intermediate to warm
Masdevallia lansbergii (Rchb.f.) Schltr.	Venezuela	Intermediate to warm (?)
Masdevallia lappifera Luer and Hirtz	Ecuador	Cool to intermediate (?)
Masdevallia lata Rchb.f.	Costa Rica, Panama	Warm
Masdevallia laucheana Kränzl.	Costa Rica	Intermediate
Masdevallia lehmannii Rchb.f	Ecuador	Cool to intermediate
Masdevallia lenae Luer and Hirtz	Ecuador	Cool to intermediate
Masdevallia leonardoi Luer	Ecuador	Cool (?)
Masdevallia leonii D. E. Benn and Christenson	Peru	Unknown*
Masdevallia leontoglossa Rchb.f.	Colombia	Cool
Masdevallia leptoura Luer	Colombia, Ecuador, Peru	Cool

(?) Limited information on culture conditions. The conditions are "suggested" based on collection information.
* Species known only by herbarium specimen or original cultivated specimen that has since been lost.

SPECIES	COUNTRIES	GROWING CONDITIONS
Masdevallia leucantha Lehm. and Kränzl.	Ecuador	Intermediate
Masdevallia lewisii Luer and Vásquez	Bolivia	Cool
Masdevallia ×ligiae Luer and Escobar	Colombia	Cool
Masdevallia lilacina Königer	Peru	Intermediate
Masdevallia lilianae Luer	Ecuador, Peru	Cool to intermediate
Masdevallia limax Luer	Ecuador	Cool to intermediate
Masdevallia lineolata Königer	Peru	Cool
Masdevallia lintriculata Königer	Ecuador	Intermediate
Masdevallia livingstoneana Roezl and Rchb.f.	Colombia, Costa Rica, Panama	Warm
Masdevallia loui Luer and Dalström	Ecuador	Cool to intermediate (?)
Masdevallia lucernula Königer	Peru	Cool to intermediate
Masdevallia ludibunda Rchb.f.	Colombia	Intermediate to warm
Masdevallia ludibundella Luer and Escobar	Colombia	Cool (?)
Masdevallia luziae-mariae Luer and Vásquez	Bolivia	Intermediate (?)
Masdevallia lychniphora Königer	Peru	Cool to intermediate
Masdevallia macrogenia (Arango) Luer and Escobar	Colombia	Intermediate
Masdevallia macroglossa Rchb.f.	Colombia, Venezuela	Cool
Masdevallia macropus Lehm. and Kränzl.	Ecuador	Cool
Masdevallia macrura Rchb.f.	Colombia, Venezuela	Cool
Masdevallia maculata Klotzsch and H. Karsten	Venezuela	Intermediate
Masdevallia maduroi Luer	Panama	Intermediate (?)
Masdevallia mallii Luer	Ecuador	Cool to intermediate (?)
Masdevallia maloi Luer	Ecuador	Cool to intermediate
Masdevallia manaloi Luer and Arias	Peru	Cool
Masdevallia manchinazae Luer and Andreetta	Ecuador	Intermediate
Masdevallia mandarina (Luer and Escobar) Luer	Colombia, Ecuador	Cool
Masdevallia manta Königer	Ecuador	Cool to intermediate (?)
Masdevallia marginella Rchb.f.	Costa Rica	Cool to intermediate
Masdevallia marizae Luer	Peru	Cool
Masdevallia marthae Luer and Escobar	Colombia	Cool to intermediate
Masdevallia martineae Luer	Bolivia	Cool to intermediate
Masdevallia martiniana Luer	Ecuador	Warm
Masdevallia mascarata Luer and Vásquez	Bolivia	Intermediate to warm
Masdevallia mastodon Rchb.f.	Colombia	Cool
Masdevallia mataxa Königer and H. Mend.	Ecuador	Intermediate
Masdevallia maxilimax Luer	Ecuador	Intermediate
Masdevallia mayaycu Luer and Hirtz	Ecuador	Intermediate
Masdevallia medinae Luer and J. J. Portilla	Ecuador	Intermediate
Masdevallia medusa Luer and Escobar	Colombia	Cool
Masdevallia mejiana Garay	Colombia	Intermediate to warm
Masdevallia melanoglossa Luer	Ecuador	Cool
Masdevallia melanopus Rchb.f.	Peru	Cool to intermediate
Masdevallia melanoxantha Linden and Rchb.f.	Colombia, Venezuela	Cool to intermediate
Masdevallia meleagris Lindl.	Colombia	Cool
Masdevallia menatoi Luer and Vásquez	Bolivia	Cool to intermediate

(?) Limited information on culture conditions. The conditions are "suggested" based on collection information.

SPECIES	COUNTRIES	GROWING CONDITIONS
Masdevallia mendozae Luer	Ecuador	Cool to intermediate
Masdevallia mentosa Luer	Ecuador	Intermediate
Masdevallia merinoi Luer and J. J. Portilla	Ecuador	Intermediate
Masdevallia mezae Luer	Peru	Cool to intermediate
Masdevallia microptera Luer and Würstle	Peru	Cool (?)
Masdevallia microsiphon Luer	Ecuador	Intermediate
Masdevallia midas Luer	Ecuador	Cool
Masdevallia minuta Lindl.	Bolivia, Brazil, Colombia, Ecuador, French Guiana, Guyana, Peru, Suriname, Venezuela	Intermediate to warm
Masdevallia misasii Braas	Colombia	Cool
Masdevallia molossoides Kränzl.	Costa Rica, Nicaragua, Panama	Intermediate
Masdevallia molossus Rchb.f.	Colombia	Cool
Masdevallia monogona Königer	Peru	Cool to intermediate
Masdevallia mooreana Rchb.f.	Colombia	Cool to intermediate
Masdevallia morochoi Luer and Andreetta	Ecuador	Cool to intermediate
Masdevallia murex Luer	Ecuador	Cool to intermediate
Masdevallia mutica Luer and Escobar	Colombia	Cool
Masdevallia ×mystica Luer	Colombia	Cool to intermediate
Masdevallia naranjapatae Luer	Ecuador	Intermediate to warm
Masdevallia navicularis Garay and Dunst.	Venezuela	Cool to intermediate
Masdevallia nebulina Luer	Bolivia	Cool
Masdevallia newmaniana Luer and Teague	Ecuador	Intermediate
Masdevallia nicaraguae Luer	Nicaragua	Intermediate to warm
Masdevallia nidifica Rchb.f.	Colombia, Costa Rica, Ecuador, Panama	Cool to intermediate to warm
Masdevallia niesseniae Luer	Colombia	Cool (?)
Masdevallia nikoleana Luer and J. J. Portilla	Ecuador, Peru	Cool (?)
Masdevallia nitens Luer	Bolivia	Cool
Masdevallia nivea Luer and Escobar	Colombia	Cool
Masdevallia norae Luer	Brazil, Colombia, Venezuela	Warm
Masdevallia norops Luer and Andreetta	Ecuador	Cool to intermediate
Masdevallia notosibirica Maekawa and Hashimoto	Bolivia	Cool
Masdevallia obscurans Luer	Brazil	Intermediate to warm (?)
Masdevallia odontocera Luer and Escobar	Colombia	Cool to intermediate
Masdevallia odontopetala Luer	Ecuador	Cool to intermediate
Masdevallia omorenoi Luer and Vásquez	Bolivia	Intermediate (?)
Masdevallia ophioglossa Rchb.f.	Ecuador	Cool to intermediate
Masdevallia oreas Luer and Vásquez	Bolivia	Cool
Masdevallia ortalis Luer	Peru	Cool to intermediate
Masdevallia oscarii Luer and Escobar	Colombia	Cool
Masdevallia oscitans Luer	Brazil	Intermediate to warm
Masdevallia os-draconis Luer and Escobar	Colombia	Intermediate to warm
Masdevallia os-viperae Luer and Andreetta	Ecuador, Peru	Intermediate (?)
Masdevallia ova-avis Rchb.f.	Ecuador	Cool

(?) Limited information on culture conditions. The conditions are "suggested" based on collection information.

SPECIES	COUNTRIES	GROWING CONDITIONS
Masdevallia pachyantha Rchb.f.	Colombia	Cool
Masdevallia pachysepala (Rchb.f.) Luer	Colombia, Venezuela	Cool (?)
Masdevallia pachyura Rchb.f.	Ecuador	Cool
Masdevallia paivaëana Rchb.f.	Bolivia	Cool
Masdevallia pandurilabia C. Schweinf.	Peru	Cool
Masdevallia panguiënsis Luer and Andreetta	Ecuador	Intermediate to warm
Masdevallia pantomima Luer and Hirtz	Ecuador	Cool
Masdevallia papillosa Luer	Ecuador	Cool to intermediate
Masdevallia paquishae Luer and Hirtz	Ecuador, Peru	Cool to intermediate
Masdevallia pardina Rchb.f.	Colombia, Ecuador	Cool
Masdevallia parvula Schltr.	Bolivia, Colombia, Ecuador, Peru	Cool
Masdevallia pastinata Luer	Colombia	Cool (?)
Masdevallia patchicutzae Luer and Hirtz	Ecuador	Cool to intermediate
Masdevallia patriciana Luer	Ecuador	Cool to intermediate
Masdevallia patula Luer and Malo	Ecuador	Cool to intermediate
Masdevallia peristeria Rchb.f.	Colombia, Ecuador	Cool
Masdevallia pernix Königer	Peru	Cool
Masdevallia persicina Luer	Ecuador	Intermediate
Masdevallia pescadoënsis Luer and Escobar	Colombia	Intermediate
Masdevallia phacopsis Luer and Dalström	Bolivia	Cool
Masdevallia phasmatodes Königer	Peru	Cool
Masdevallia phlogina Luer	Peru	Cool
Masdevallia phoenix Luer	Peru	Intermediate
Masdevallia picea Luer	Peru	Cool
Masdevallia picta Luer	Peru	Cool
Masdevallia picturata Rchb.f.	Bolivia, Colombia, Costa Rica, Ecuador, Panama, Peru, Venezuela	Cool to intermediate
Masdevallia pileata Luer and Würstle	Colombia	Cool
Masdevallia pinocchio Luer and Andreetta	Ecuador	Cool to intermediate
Masdevallia planadensis Luer and Escobar	Colombia, Ecuador	Cool
Masdevallia plantaginea (Poepp. and Endl.) Cogn.	Ecuador, Peru	Intermediate
Masdevallia platyglossa Rchb. f.	Colombia, Ecuador	Intermediate
Masdevallia pleurothalloides Luer	Panama	Intermediate (?)
Masdevallia plynophora Luer	Peru	Cool to intermediate
Masdevallia ×*polita* Luer and Sijm	Unknown	Cool to intermediate
Masdevallia pollux Luer and Cloes	Ecuador, Peru	Cool
Masdevallia polychroma Luer	Ecuador	Cool (?)
Masdevallia polysticta Rchb.f.	Ecuador, Peru	Cool to intermediate
Masdevallia popowiana Königer and J. G. Wein	Peru	Cool
Masdevallia porphyrea Luer	Ecuador	Cool to intermediate
Masdevallia portillae Luer and Andreetta	Ecuador	Cool to intermediate
Masdevallia posadae Luer and Escobar	Colombia, Peru	Intermediate to warm
Masdevallia pozoi Königer	Ecuador, Peru	Cool to intermediate
Masdevallia princeps Luer	Peru	Cool to intermediate
Masdevallia prodigiosa Königer	Peru	Cool to intermediate

(?) Limited information on culture conditions. The conditions are "suggested" based on collection information.

| --- | --- | --- |
Masdevallia prolixa Luer	Peru	Cool
Masdevallia prosartema Königer	Peru	Cool
Masdevallia pteroglossa Schltr.	Colombia	Cool to intermediate
Masdevallia pterygiophora Luer and Escobar	Colombia	Cool (?)
Masdevallia pulcherrima Luer and Andreetta	Ecuador	Cool
Masdevallia pumila Poepp and Endl.	Bolivia, Colombia, Ecuador, Peru	Cool to intermediate
Masdevallia purpurella Luer and Escobar	Colombia	Cool to intermediate
Masdevallia pygmaea Kränzl.	Colombia, Costa Rica, Ecuador	Intermediate
Masdevallia pyknosepala Luer and Cloes	Peru	Intermediate (?)
Masdevallia pyxis Luer	Peru	Cool
Masdevallia quasimodo Luer and Teague	Bolivia	Cool
Masdevallia racemosa Lindl.	Colombia	Cool
Masdevallia rafaeliana Luer	Costa Rica, Panama	Cool to intermediate
Masdevallia receptrix Luer and Vásquez	Bolivia	Cool (?)
Masdevallia rechingeriana Kränzl.	Venezuela	Intermediate
Masdevallia recurvata Luer and Dalström	Peru	Cool
Masdevallia regina Luer	Peru	Intermediate
Masdevallia reichenbachiana Endres ex Rchb.f.	Costa Rica	Cool to intermediate
Masdevallia renzii Luer	Colombia	Cool
Masdevallia repanda Luer and Hirtz	Ecuador	Cool
Masdevallia replicata Königer	Peru	Cool
Masdevallia revoluta Königer	Ecuador	Intermediate to warm
Masdevallia rex Luer and Hirtz	Ecuador	Intermediate to warm
Masdevallia rhinophora Luer and Escobar	Colombia	Cool
Masdevallia rhodehameliana Luer	Peru	Cool to intermediate
Masdevallia richardsoniana Luer	Peru	Intermediate
Masdevallia ricii Luer and Vásquez	Bolivia	Cool to intermediate
Masdevallia rigens Luer	Peru	Intermediate to warm
Masdevallia rimarima-alba Luer	Peru	Cool
Masdevallia robusta Luer	Ecuador	Cool to intermediate (?)
Masdevallia rodolfoi (Braas) Luer	Peru	Cool to intermediate
Masdevallia rolandorum Luer and Sijm	Peru	Intermediate to warm (?)
Masdevallia rolfeana Kränzl.	Costa Rica	Cool to intermediate
Masdevallia rosea Lindl.	Ecuador	Cool
Masdevallia roseola Luer	Ecuador	Intermediate
Masdevallia rubeola Luer and Vásquez	Bolivia, Peru	Cool
Masdevallia rubiginosa Königer	Ecuador, Peru	Cool to intermediate
Masdevallia rufescens Königer	Ecuador, Peru	Cool to intermediate
Masdevallia saltatrix Rchb.f.	Colombia	Cool
Masdevallia sanchezii Luer and Andreetta	Ecuador	Intermediate to warm
Masdevallia sanctae-fidei Kränzl.	Colombia, Venezuela	Cool to intermediate
Masdevallia sanctae-inesiae Luer and Malo	Ecuador	Cool to intermediate
Masdevallia sanctae-rosae Kränzl.	Colombia	Cool
Masdevallia sanguinea Luer and Andreetta	Ecuador	Intermediate
Masdevallia scabrilinguis Luer	Costa Rica, Panama	Intermediate

(?) Limited information on culture conditions. The conditions are "suggested" based on collection information.

SPECIES	COUNTRIES	GROWING CONDITIONS
Masdevallia scalpellifera Luer	Ecuador	Cool (?)
Masdevallia scandens Rolfe	Bolivia	Cool
Masdevallia sceptrum Rchb.f.	Colombia, Venezuela	Cool
Masdevallia schizantha Kränzl.	Colombia	Cool
Masdevallia schizopetala Kränzl.	Bolivia, Colombia, Costa Rica, Panama	Intermediate
Masdevallia schizostigma Luer	Peru	Cool to intermediate (?)
Masdevallia schlimii Linden ex Lindl.	Colombia, Venezuela	Cool
Masdevallia schmidt-mummii Luer and Escobar	Colombia	Cool
Masdevallia schoonenii Luer	Peru	Cool
Masdevallia schroederiana Sander ex Veitch	Costa Rica	Cool to intermediate
Masdevallia schudelii Luer	Ecuador	Cool to intermediate
Masdevallia scitula Königer	Peru	Cool
Masdevallia scobina Luer and Escobar	Colombia	Cool
Masdevallia scopaea Luer and Vásquez	Bolivia	Cool to intermediate
Masdevallia segrex Luer and Hirtz	Ecuador	Cool to intermediate
Masdevallia segurae Luer and Escobar	Colombia	Cool
Masdevallia selenites Königer	Peru	Cool
Masdevallia semiteres Luer and Escobar	Peru	Cool
Masdevallia serendipita Luer and Teague	Bolivia	Intermediate
Masdevallia sernae Luer and Escobar	Colombia, Ecuador	Intermediate to warm
Masdevallia sertula Luer and Andreetta	Ecuador	Cool
Masdevallia setacea Luer	Ecuador, Peru	Cool to intermediate
Masdevallia setipes Schltr.	Bolivia	Cool
Masdevallia siphonantha Luer	Colombia	Cool
Masdevallia smallmaniana Luer	Ecuador	Cool (?)
Masdevallia soennemarkii Luer and Dalström	Bolivia	Cool
Masdevallia solomonii Luer and Vásquez	Bolivia	Cool
Masdevallia spilantha Königer	Peru	Cool
Masdevallia sprucei Rchb.f.	Brazil, Venezuela	Intermediate to warm
Masdevallia staaliana Luer and Hirtz	Ecuador	Cool
Masdevallia stenorrhynchos Kränzl.	Colombia	Cool to intermediate
Masdevallia stigii Luer and Jost	Ecuador	Cool
Masdevallia stirpis Luer	Venezuela	Intermediate
Masdevallia strattoniana Luer	Ecuador	Cool to intermediate
Masdevallia striatella Rchb.f.	Costa Rica	Intermediate to warm
Masdevallia strobelii Sweet and Garay	Ecuador	Intermediate
Masdevallia ×*strumella* Luer	Colombia	Cool
Masdevallia strumifera Rchb.f.	Colombia, Peru, Venezuela	Cool
Masdevallia strumosa Ortiz and Calderón	Colombia	Cool
Masdevallia stumpflei Braas	Peru	Cool
Masdevallia suinii Luer and Hirtz	Ecuador	Cool (?)
Masdevallia sulphurella Königer	Peru	Cool to intermediate
Masdevallia sumapazensis Ortiz	Colombia	Cool
Masdevallia ×*synthesis* Luer	Venezuela	Intermediate

(?) Limited information on culture conditions. The conditions are "suggested" based on collection information.

SPECIES	COUNTRIES	GROWING CONDITIONS
Masdevallia tentaculata Luer	Ecuador	Cool
Masdevallia terborchii Luer	Peru	Cool
Masdevallia theleüra Luer	Ecuador	Intermediate
Masdevallia thienii Dodson	Colombia, Costa Rica, Ecuador, Panama	Intermediate
Masdevallia tinekeae Luer and Vásquez	Bolivia	Cool
Masdevallia titan Luer	Peru	Intermediate
Masdevallia tokachiorum Luer	Panama	Intermediate to warm
Masdevallia tonduzii Woolward	Costa Rica, Panama	Intermediate to warm
Masdevallia torta Rchb.f.	Colombia	Cool to intermediate
Masdevallia tovarensis Rchb.f.	Venezuela	Cool to intermediate
Masdevallia trautmanniana Luer and J. J. Portilla	Ecuador	Cool
Masdevallia triangularis Lindl.	Colombia, Ecuador, Venezuela	Cool to intermediate
Masdevallia tricallosa Königer	Peru	Cool to intermediate
Masdevallia tricycla Luer	Ecuador	Cool (?)
Masdevallia tridens Rchb.f.	Ecuador	Cool
Masdevallia trifurcata Luer	Ecuador	Intermediate
Masdevallia trigonopetala Kränzl.	Colombia, Ecuador	Intermediate
Masdevallia trochilus Linden and André	Colombia, Ecuador, Peru	Cool to intermediate
Masdevallia truncata Luer	Ecuador	Cool (?)
Masdevallia tsubotae Luer	Colombia	Cool (?)
Masdevallia tubata Schltr.	Bolivia	Cool
Masdevallia tubuliflora Ames	Belize, Costa Rica, Guatemala, Honduras, Nicaragua	Warm
Masdevallia tubulosa Lindl.	Colombia, Ecuador, Peru, Venezuela	Cool to intermediate
Masdevallia uncifera Rchb.f.	Colombia, Ecuador	Cool
Masdevallia uniflora Ruiz and Pavón	Peru	Cool
Masdevallia urceolaris Kränzl.	Colombia	Cool
Masdevallia ustulata Luer	Colombia, Ecuador, Peru	Cool
Masdevallia utriculata Luer	Panama	Intermediate (?)
Masdevallia valenciae Luer and Escobar	Colombia	Cool
Masdevallia vargasii C. Schweinf.	Bolivia, Brazil, Colombia, Ecuador, Peru	Intermediate
Masdevallia vasquezii Luer	Bolivia	Cool
Masdevallia veitchiana Rchb.f.	Peru	Cool
Masdevallia velella Luer	Colombia	Intermediate (?)
Masdevallia velifera Rchb.f.	Colombia	Cool
Masdevallia venatoria Luer and Malo	Ecuador	Cool to intermediate
Masdevallia venezuelana Sweet	Venezuela	Intermediate
Masdevallia ventricosa Schltr.	Ecuador	Cool
Masdevallia ventricularia Rchb.f.	Colombia, Ecuador	Cool to intermediate
Masdevallia venus Luer and Hirtz	Ecuador	Cool
Masdevallia venusta Schltr.	Peru	Cool
Masdevallia verecunda Luer	Venezuela	Intermediate (?)
Masdevallia vexillifera Luer	Peru	Cool

(?) Limited information on culture conditions. The conditions are "suggested" based on collection information.

SPECIES	COUNTRIES	GROWING CONDITIONS
Masdevallia vidua Luer and Andreetta	Ecuador	Cool to intermediate
Masdevallia vieriana Luer and Escobar	Colombia	Warm
Masdevallia virens Luer and Andreetta	Ecuador	Intermediate
Masdevallia virgo-cuencae Luer and Andreetta	Ecuador	Cool to intermediate
Masdevallia vittatula Luer and Escobar	Colombia, Ecuador	Cool
Masdevallia vomeris Luer	Peru	Cool
Masdevallia wageneriana Linden ex Lindl.	Venezuela	Cool to intermediate
Masdevallia walteri Luer	Costa Rica	Cool to intermediate
Masdevallia weberbaueri Schltr.	Ecuador, Peru	Intermediate
Masdevallia welischii Luer	Peru	Cool
Masdevallia wendlandiana Rchb.f.	Bolivia, Brazil, Colombia, Ecuador, Peru	Intermediate to warm
Masdevallia whiteana Luer	Ecuador, Peru	Cool to intermediate
Masdevallia ×wübbenii Luer	Venezuela	Cool to intermediate
Masdevallia wuelfinghoffiana Luer and J. J. Portilla	Ecuador	Cool
Masdevallia wuerstlei Luer	Colombia	Cool
Masdevallia wurdackii C. Schweinf.	Peru	Cool to intermediate
Masdevallia xanthina Rchb.f.	Colombia, Ecuador	Cool to intermediate
Masdevallia xanthodactyla Rchb.f.	Ecuador, Peru	Cool
Masdevallia ximenae Luer and Hirtz	Ecuador	Intermediate
Masdevallia xylina Rchb.f.	Colombia	Cool
Masdevallia yungasensis Hashimoto	Bolivia	Cool
Masdevallia yungasensis ssp. *calocodon* (Luer & Vásquez) Luer	Bolivia	Cool
Masdevallia zahlbruckneri Kränzl.	Ecuador	Intermediate to warm
Masdevallia zamorensis Luer and J. J. Portilla	Ecuador	Intermediate
Masdevallia zapatae Luer and Escobar	Colombia	Intermediate
Masdevallia zebracea Luer	Peru	Cool to intermediate (?)
Masdevallia zongoënsis Luer and Hirtz	Bolivia	Cool
Masdevallia zumbae Luer	Ecuador	Intermediate
Masdevallia zumbuehlerae Luer	Ecuador	Cool (?)
Masdevallia zygia Luer and Malo	Ecuador	Cool

(?) Limited information on culture conditions. The conditions are "suggested" based on collection information.

GLOSSARY

❖ ❖ ❖

actinomorphic: radially symmetrical

acuminate: narrowing to a sharp point with an angle less than 45 degrees

acute: apical angle between 45 and 90 degrees

adherent: dissimilar parts touching but not joined

adnate: dissimilar parts joined

aggregate: close together, clustered

alate: having a straight wing

alba: white form of a flower; usually an albino

albino: a pigmentless white phenotype

alliance: a group of similar genera—for example, the Pleurothallid Alliance

AM: Award of Merit by the American Orchid Society, granted to flowers scoring 80 to 89 points out of 100

annulus: an obscure ring that surrounds the ramicaul at the emergence of the inflorescence

anterior: front

anther: the terminal part of a stamen consisting of two lobes, each containing two sacs in which the pollen matures

anther cap: the covering of the pollen masses on the column of the flower

AOS: American Orchid Society

aphyllous: without leaves

apical: at or near the tip

apiculate: acute tip

appressed: closely against, angle of divergence less than 15 degrees

approximate: close together, but not joined

aristate: with a long, narrow, bristlelike projection

articulate: jointed

aseptic: free from disease organisms

asexual: without involving sex, such as in vegetative propagation

attenuated: narrowing to a point

auricles: earlike appendages

axil: angle between upper surface of leaf and stem where they join

backbulb: an old, often leafless, sympodial pseudobulb that is alive and can be used to propagate a new plant

basal: at the base of a plant part

bicuspidate: having two prongs

bifoliate: having two leaves on a single pseudobulb

bigeneric: involving two distinct genera in the parentage of a hybrid

bilateral: having two vertical planes

bilobed: having two lobes

blade: the expanded portion of a leaf above the petiole

bract: a sheathlike structure on the peduncle or rhizome

bud: a flower before it begins to enlarge; also a tiny new growth or leaf

caespitose: with abbreviated rhizomes, the ramicauls approximate or produced in clumps or tufts

calli: plural of callus

callus (callous): a hard protuberance or thickening, usually on orchid lips

capitate: enlarged or globose at the apex, like a head

capsule: the seed pod of an orchid, which often containing thousands, even millions, of seeds

carina, carinae (plural): a raised ridge

carinate: shaped like the keel of a boat, with a raised ridge

caudae: tail

caudicle: a slender, stalklike appendage of the pollinium or pollen mass

CBR: Certificate of Botanical Recognition; an AOS award given only once to an orchid species when it is first displayed in bloom

CCM: Certificate of Cultural Merit; an AOS award presented to the grower of a well-flowered and healthy specimen

cellular glandular: with prominent glandular or capitate cells, with a cobblestone appearance

central growing point: on a monopodial orchid, the point from which the upright vegetative growth continually grows

channeled: grooved longitudinally

CHM: Certificate of Horticultural Merit; an AOS award given to a species of outstanding interest to growers

cilia: minute but conspicuous hairs

ciliate: with minute hairs

CITES: Convention on International Trade in Endangered Species; the multinational agreement that lists plant and animal species that are considered endangered and the rules by which their trade is governed

clavate: club-shaped; for example, the clavate hairs of *Masdevallia strobelii*

cleft: channeled or sulcate, with a longitudinal groove

cleistogamous: a flower that self-fertilizes

clonal name: a name given to an individual orchid plant (and its vegetative propagations), often awarded

clone: all the vegetative manifestations of a single orchid plant grown originally from a single seed; designated within single quotes

cluster: a group of flowers or leaves in close proximity to one another

cm: centimeter; metric unit of measure equal to about 0.39 inch

colchicine: a chemical compound applied to cells to inhibit mitosis and used to induce tetraploids in plants raised in flasks

cold temperature: for orchids, a minimum winter nighttime temperature of 4°C (40°F), with daytime temperatures of 10 to 16°C (50 to 60°F)

column: the fused sexual organs, stamen and anthers, of an orchid flower; probably the most unique feature of the orchid family

column-foot: the extension at the base of the orchid column to which the lip is attached

community pot: a single container in which many tiny orchid seedlings are planted together, later to be individually repotted

congested: the inflorescence densely flowered, or flowers closely spaced

connate: having similar parts joined

cool temperature: for orchids, a minimum winter nighttime temperature of 7°C (45°F), with daytime temperatures of 10 to 17°C (50 to 63°F)

coriacea: leathery

cornute: horn-shaped

costate: with longitudinal raised ridges; ribbed

crested: with irregular, longitudinal lamellae

crispate: finely wavy along the edge

cross: the progeny resulting from transferring pollen from one plant to the flower of another; the act itself

crown: the central part of the rosette of leaves in a monopodial orchid such as *Phalaenopsis*, from which new growth arises

cucullate: hooded

cuneate: wedge-shaped

cultivar: an individual plant and its vegetative propagations in cultivation; a horticultural variety

deciduous: plants that lose all their leaves annually at the end of a growing period

declined: bent down or forward

deflexed: bent down abruptly

dentata: with margins that have sharp teeth

dentate: tooth

denticulate: finely dentate

diffuse: spread out

diploid: having a normal number of two sets of chromosomes; also known as 2N

dioecious: having male and female sexual parts on separate flowers or plants

disc: the upper surface of the central portion of the lip

discoid: disc-shaped

division: creating new plants from old by cutting the rhizome of an orchid into pieces containing pseudobulbs and rhizome or by cutting off the top half of a stem

DNA: Deoxyribose Nucleic Acid; the genetic material used to determine the genetic relationship between individuals or species

dormancy: a rest period during which no vegetative growth occurs; often follows a growth period and/or the loss of leaves or other growths; usually cooler temperatures and less water are required during dormancy

dorsal: on the upper side

dorsal sepal: the uppermost sepal of a flower

elliptical: shaped like an ellipse, widest at the middle

endemic: native to a particular region

entire: with smooth or unlobed margins

epichile: the terminal portion of a divided lip; literally, on lip

epiphytic: a plant that grows on another plant for support (not a parasite); nutrients are not taken from the supporting host but are derived instead from rain, air, and available debris

equitant: having all the leaves arranged flat in one plane—such as an iris, for example

falcate: sickle or knife-shaped

family: the usual major subdivision of an order or suborder, commonly consisting of a group of related genera, ending with *acae*, as in *Orchidaceae*

FCC: First Class Certificate; the highest quality flower award of the AOS given to flowers scoring 90 or more points on a scale of 100 points

filamentous: slender, like a hair or thread

filiform: slender, like a hair or thread

fissa: cleft

flask: a container used for the laboratory germination of orchid seeds or for growing other laboratory-micropropagated orchid seedlings

floral bract: the bract subtending a pedicel

floriferous: a plant that flowers freely

flower spike: flower inflorescence bearing a solitary bloom atop a single stalk or in racemes or panicles

foot-candle: a measure used to determine intensity of light; the illumination produced by a candle at a distance of 1 foot

fractiflex: zig-zag

fringed: furnished with hairlike appendages on the edges

generic: of or pertaining to a genus, as in a generic name such as *Masdevallia*

genus: a group of organisms (species) classified together because of similar traits and an assumed common ancestry

glabrous: smooth, hairless

grex: the group of progeny of a specific hybrid cross; the name given to the group

growths: new shoots that emerge—pseudobulb, rhizome, leaf, stem, inflorescence, or root

gynoecium: the female ovule-bearing part of a flower (composed of ovary, style, and stigma)

HCC: Highly Commended Certificate; granted to a flower scoring 75 to 79 points on a scale of 100. The majority of awarded orchids receive this award, which implies that although the flower being judged is outstanding, there is room for improvement.

herbarium: a collection of pressed, dried, and mounted specimens of plants; the institute housing such a collection

hirsute: covered with long, rather coarse or stiff hairs

holotype: the specimen upon which the taxon is based

hybrid: progeny from the union of two different species, or of a species and a hybrid, or of two hybrids hypochile: the basal part of a divided lip; literally, under lip

incurved: curving inward or upward

inflorescence: the flowering stem of the orchid

intergeneric: a hybridization between two or more genera

intermediate temperature: for orchids, a minimum winter nighttime temperature of 10°C (50°F), with daytime temperatures of 13 to 20°C (55 to 68°F)

JC: Judges Commendation; award given by the AOS for special plant and/or flower characteristics

keel: a central dorsal ridge, like the keel of a boat

keiki: an adventitious plantlet that develops from an orchid's flower inflorescence or cane; like a pseudobulb

labellum: lip; the modified third petal of the flower that often acts as the landing platform for pollinators

lamella: a tall carina or keel; a platelike thickening or callus

lamellate: with a lamella or lamellae

lamina: the blade of a leaf, sepal, or petal

lateral sepal: the two lowermost sepals that extend to the sides

lax: loose; flowers distantly spaced

lip: the orchid labellum

lithophytic: any plant that grows and lives attached to a rock; literally, rock plant habit

lobe: any division or segment of an organ, such as a leaf or petal

m: meter; metric unit of measure equivalent to about 3 ft. 3.3 in.

maculate: spotted

medium, media (plural): the potting material or mix of materials used inside an orchid pot

mericlone: an exact copy of an original orchid plant made via meristem propagation in a lab

meristem: the actively dividing cell tissue taken from root tips or tips of new growths or floral shoots that are then removed and propagated in the laboratory

minuta: very small

monopodial: literally, one foot habit; a single vegetative shoot that grows continually upward, as opposed to sympodial growth, such as the growth habit of Vandaceous and Angraecoid orchids

multifloral: having more than one flower per inflorescence

mycorrhizal: having symbiotic fungi associated with roots

natural hybrid: a hybrid that occurs naturally in the wild where related species grow together and bloom times overlap

navicular: boat-shaped

nidifica: like a nest

node: a swelling or joint on an inflorescence, stem, or pseudobulb from which a flower stem, adventitous plantlet, or roots can emerge

nomenclature: a system of naming

nonresupinate: plants whose flower lips are positioned uppermost relative to the inflorescence axis; an orchid flower that does not twist the usual 180 degrees (or twists 360 degrees) before opening; see also resupinate

oblong: longer than broad, with parallel sides; width about one-third the length

obovate: egg-shaped; widest between the base and the middle

obtuse: sides meeting at an angle greater than 90 degrees

obverse: the front side, opposite of reverse

oscillate: to move in various directions

ovary: the part of the flower that develops into the fruit; where the seeds develop

ovate: shaped like the outline of an egg

pandurate: violin-shaped, narrowest near the middle

panicle: an inflorescence in which flowers are loosely arranged on a branching stem and open from the lowest or inner branches to the top

papillose: covered with small, nipplelike protuberances

pedicel: the stalk of an individual flower

peduncle: the stalk of an inflorescence that bears the pedicels and flowers

peloric: a mutation in which the petals are similar to the lip

pendent: hanging or drooping

petal: one of the three inner segments of the flower positioned between the three sepals; one petal is modified into a lip in the orchid family

petiole: the stalk by which a leaf is attached to a stem

phylad: a branch or limb of a family tree

pleurothallid: any member of the Pleurothallidinae, which includes *Masdevallia*, *Dracula*, *Trisetella*, and *Porroglossum*

plicate: folded like a fan, or pleated

pod: seed pod or capsule

pollinarium: the inclusive term for the pollination unit of most orchids

pollinator: in nature, the insect, bird, or other vector by which flowers are pollinated

pollinium, pollinia (plural): waxy pollen clumps or grains usually found in the anthers of most orchids; often yellow, distinct, and found under the pollen cap of the column

polyploid: having more than two chromosome sets in each somatic cell

pouch: the slipperlike lip on some orchids; sometimes the synsepal

primary hybrid: a cross made between two species

pseudobulb: the thickened stem of a sympodial orchid arising from a rhizome that has evolved to store water

pseudobulbless: having no pseudobulbs

pubescent: covered with hairs

pygmaea: dwarf

raceme: a simple type of flower inflorescence that looks like a long stem with flowers arising along it

rachis: the axis or stem of the inflorescence beyond the peduncle

ramicaul: a leaf-bearing stem

recurved: bent down or back

reflexed: abruptly recurved

repent: creeping, as applied to an elongated rhizome

resupinate: orchids whose labella are positioned lowermost relative to the inflorescence axis due to the bud twisting 180 degrees before opening

revolute: rolled downward or backward

rhizome: a root-bearing stem that is prostrate, on, or underground; sometimes scandent; climbing gradually or even vertically in some epiphytes, the apex (tip) of which progressively sends up leafy shoots

RHS: Royal Horticultural Society

ribbed: with longitudinal costae or ridges; costate

rostellum: a small beaklike process of the stigma that produces a viscous substance used in pollination

rugose: wrinkled

saccate: sacklike or deeply concave

scabrous: having short, stiff hairs, making the surface rough; filelike

scandent: a plant that slowly or gradually climbs upward

scape: a simple flower inflorescence that is topped by a solitary flower

secund: of a raceme; flowers occurring on one side of a raceme

seed pod: the capsule bearing the seeds of an orchid, the mature ovary

seedling: an unbloomed young orchid

segment: a part of the perianth, as the petal, sepal, or lip; any division or part of a cleft or divided region

semiterrestrial: plants that grow near or on the ground in extremely loose, open substrate

sepal: one of the three outer parts of an orchid flower; usually the topmost dorsal and the two lower lateral segments

sepaline: resembling a sepal in structure and function

sequentially: one at a time, in sequence

serrate: with saw-toothed margins

sessile: attached directly at the base, without a stalk

setaceous: bristly

sheath: a protective growth that envelops the stem

sib cross, sibling cross: a cross-pollination of siblings, in which pollen of one orchid is placed on the stigma of another that was originated from in the same seed pod as the first orchid

sibling: an orchid related to another orchid by virtue of having been produced from the same seed pod

species: the scientific category of taxonomic classification that describes a group of organisms that have in common one or more characteristics that definitely separate it from any other group; a further division of a genus

specimen plant: an orchid allowed to grow to great size and floriferousness instead of being divided

spike: a type of inflorescence with sessile flowers, or short-stalked flowers borne on an upright, unbranched flower stem

stamen: the male reproductive organ of a flower, consisting of a stalk (filament) bearing an anther in which pollen is produced

stigma: the terminal part of the ovary where deposited pollen enters the gynoecium

stipe: the stalklike support of a pollinium

subacute: the angle of the apex only slightly less than 90 degrees

subtend: immediately below or behind

sympodial: a form of growth in which each new shoot, originating from a bud of the rhizome, is complete in itself and terminates in a potential inflorescence; literally, together foot

synsepal: a feature common to many pleurothallids in which the two ventral sepals are united for most or all of their length, appearing as one segment

terete: cylindrical in cross section

terrestrial: growing in the ground, supported by the soil

tessellated: arranged in a checkered or mosaic pattern

tetraploid: genetic aberration wherein the plant has twice as many chromosome sets as normal, often resulting in very vigorous, larger plants and flowers than the normal diploid plants; also known as 4N; in breeding, a colchicine treatment can be used to induce a tetraploid

throat: the inner part of a tubular sepaline tube

tissue culture: artificial propagation of plants in a laboratory by mericloning; also known as meristemming

tribe: a primary taxonomic category of related genera

trichome: glandular hair

triquetrous: triangular in cross section

truncate: as though cut off transversely at the apex

tubercle: a small tuber or tuberlike body

type: usually the herbarium specimen upon which the published description is based

undulate: with a wavy edge or surface

unifoliate: bearing one leaf per growth

variegated: irregularly colored in patches; blotched

variety: a subdivision of a species that groups plants with a distinct form that is passed along to the progeny, which occurs within a natural population—for example, albino (var. *alba*) or dwarf (var. *minor*)

vegetative propagation: the creation of plants through division, encouragement of keiki formation, or via several meristematic techniques, but not from seed

velamen: the thick layer of cells covering the roots of epiphytic orchids; aids in the rapid absorption and assimilation of water and mineral nutrients

ventral: underside

verrucose: warty, bumpy

verruculose: covered with or having small warts

viscidum: the sticky base of the stipe or caudicle that affixes the pollinarium to the pollinator

warm temperature: for orchids, a minimum winter nighttime temperature of 16°C (60°F), with daytime temperatures of 20 to 27°C (68 to 80°F)

winged: of the ovary, with tall, longitudinal keels; column wings

zygomorphic: capable of being divided into symmetric halves in one plane as opposed to actinomorphic; also known as bilateral symmetry

SOURCES

Nurseries and Flasking Services

Note that most orchid nurseries require that you call ahead and make an appointment if you would like to visit their greenhouse(s). In addition, many nurseries have Web sites with online purchasing, photographs, and culture information. Contact the nursery for the required shipping information and certification if required.

AUSTRALIA
Hills District Orchids
(David Banks)
Northmead, New South Wales
Australia
Tel: 02 9674-4720
dpbanks@ozemail.com.au

Mount Beenak Orchids
(Clive Halls)
Three Bridges, Victoria
Australia
Tel: 03 5966-7253
mtbeenak@valylink.net.au

Orchid Species Plus
(Bill & Jan Miles)
Kingston, Victoria
Australia
Tel: 03 5345-6387
miles@netconnect.com.au

Royale Orchids
(Kevin Hipkins)
1360 Brieses Road
Peats Ridge, NSW 2250
Australia
Tel: 02 4375-1199
royaleorchids@bigpond.com
www.royaleorchids.com

Tinonee Orchids
(Ray Clement)
Tinonee, New South Wales
Australia
Tel: 02 6553-1012
clement@tpg.com.au
www.tinoneeorchids.com

BELGIUM
Akerne Orchids
Larrsebeekdreef 4, B-2900
Schoten
Belgium
Tel: 32-03-651-40-36
info@Aakerne-orchids.com

CANADA
Beaver Valley Orchids
RR#3
Princeville, ON N0C 1K0
Canada
Tel: 416-994-3248
bvo@rogers.com
www.beavervalleyorchids.com

Charles Island Orchids
Box 91471
West Vancouver, BC V7V 3P2
Canada
Tel: 604-921-7383
jwthomas@unixbc.ubc.ca

Orchids in Our Tropics
P.O. Box 394
Gormley, ON L0H 1G0
Canada
Tel: 905-727-3319
ourtropics@ica.net
www.orchidsinourtropics.com

Somerville Orchids
5138 Somerville Street
Vancouver, BC V5W 3H4
Canada
Tel: 604-327-4248
sville@shaw.ca

COLOMBIA
Orquideas del Valle
Calle 10N#9-31 Juanambú
Cali, Colombia
Tel: 572 6674943
orqvalle@andinet.com
www.orquivalle.com

COSTA RICA
Orquideas del Bosque
Del final del Boulevard Rohrmoser
3 Cuadras al Norte y 75 al Este
Costa Rica
Tel: 506 232 1466
info@costaricanorchids.com

DENMARK
Christiansen Orchidegartneriet
Hillerodvei 3480, Fredensborg
Denmark

KJ Orchids
Lykkegårdsvej 365 - 8472, Sporup
Denmark
Tel: 86 96 86 00
Fax: 86 28 66 87
kj@kj-orchids.com
www.kj-orchids.com

ECUADOR
Ecuagenera Cia Ltda.
P.O. Box 01.01.1110
Cuenca, Ecuador
Tel: 593 7 2255-237
Fax: 1-801-697-5930
ecuagene@ecua.net.ec
www.ecuagenera.com

FRANCE
Le Canopeé Orchideés
Colette et Dominique
Barthelemy
Penn an Neach Rozegad
29470 Plougastel
France
Tel: 02.98.04.27.86
d.barthelemy@wanadoo.fr
www.lacanopee.com

GERMANY
M&M Orchideen
M. Wolff
Kaeppelesweg 11
97539 Wonfurt-Steinsfeld
Germany
Tel: 49 9521 / 94890
Fax: 49 9521 / 948910
www.m-m-orchid.com/

N. Popow Orchideen
Sandkämperstr. 1
38442 Wolfsburg
Germany
Tel: 05362 / 3314
Fax: 05362 / 639 72
bpopow@t-online.de

Orchideen-Garten Joachim Karge
Bahnhofstrasse 24
21368 Dahlenburg
Germany
Tel: 05851 / 266
Fax: 05851 / 264
www.karge-orchideen.de

Orchideen Kopf
Hindenburgstrasse 15
94469 Deggendorf
Germany
Tel: 0991 / 37 15 10
www.orchideen-kopf.de

Orchideen Seidel GbR
Hauptstrasse 119a
08115 Lichtentanne
Germany
Tel: 0375 / 7929542
Fax: 0375 / 5977300
www.orchideen-seidel.de

Röllke Orchideenzucht
Flössweg 11
33758 Schloss Holte-Stukenbrock
Germany
Tel: 05207 / 920 539
Fax: 05207 / 920 540
www.roellke-orchideen.de

Wilhelm Hennis Orchideen
Grosse Venedig 4
31134 Hildesheim
Germany
Tel: 05121 / 356 77
Fax: 05121 / 383 20
www.hennis-orchideen.de

Wössner Orchideen
Franz Glanz
Hauptstr. 28
83246 Unterwössen
Germany
Tel: Franz Glanz: 0175 / 598 96 48
Tel: Maria Glanz: 0170 / 553 77 19
Fax: 08641/8627
www.woessnerorchideen.de

THE NETHERLANDS
Botanische Orchideeën
Herman ter Borch
Coendersberglaan 46
5709 MA Helmond
The Netherlands
Tel: +31-492 592271
Fax: +31-848 330915
www.botorch.com

Orchideeën Wubben
Tolakkerweg 162
3739 JT Hollandsche Rading
The Netherlands
Tel: +31-35 5771 222
Fax: +31-35 5772 103
www.orchidwubben.com

Reinhart Orchideeën
Westerveen 16
9751 HW Haren
The Netherlands
Tel: +31-050 4062455

NEW ZEALAND
L & R Orchids
(Russell Hutton)
Tuakau (North Island)
New Zealand
Tel: 64 9 236-8392
lrorchids@xtra.co.nz
www.lrorchids.co.nz

Paradise Orchids
P.O. Box 16006
Bethlehem, Tauranga
New Zealand
Tel: 64 7 552-5570
www.enternet.co.nz/users/
    pondeeza

SWITZERLAND
RA Orchid
Roland and Esther Amsler
Untermattstrasse 27 / Auen
8370 Sirnach TG
Switzerland
Tel: 0041 / 071 960 02 92

UNITED KINGDOM
A. J. Keeling & Sons
Grange Nurseries
North View Road, Westgate Hill
Bradford, W. Yorks BO4 6NS
U.K.
Tel: 01274 682120

Mansel and Hatcher Ltd.
Cragg Wood Nurseries
Woodlands Drive
Rawdon, Leeds LS19 6LQ
U.K.
Tel: 01132 502016

Plested Orchids
38 Florence Road
College Town, Sandhurst
Berks. GU47 0QD
U.K.
Tel: 01276 32947
plestedorchids@aol.com
www.plestedorchids.com

Royden Orchids
Perks Lane
Prestwood, Bucks HP16 OJD
U.K.
Tel: 0194 863224
orchids@royden99.freeserve.co.uk

UNITED STATES
California
Andy's Orchids
734 Oceanview Ave.
Encinitas, CA 92024
U.S.A.
Tel: 888-514-2639
info@andysorchids.com
www.andysorchids.com

Golden Gate Orchids
Tom Perlite
225 Velasco Ave.
San Francisco, CA 94314
U.S.A.
Tel: 415-467-3737

Hanging Gardens
Dan Newman
210 27th Avenue #5
San Francisco, CA 94121
U.S.A.
Tel: 415-305-8355
hgardens@earthlink.net

Monterey Orchids
P.O. Box 2286
Monterey, CA 93942-2286
U.S.A.
Tel: 206-600-6273
www.montereyorchids.com/

Petite Plaisance
P.O. Box 386
Valley Ford, CA 94972
U.S.A.
Tel: 707-876-3496
www.sonic.net/orchids/

Seal Rock Orchids
1825 Brindle Lane
Eureka, CA 95501
U.S.A.
Tel: 707-845-6858
www.sealrockorchids.com

SLO Orchids
965 Branch Mill Rd
Arroyo Grande, CA 93434
U.S.A.
Tel: 805-489-3319
www.slogardens.com

Sunset Orchids
Steve Gettel
49 D Street
Colma, CA 94014
U.S.A.
Tel: 650-994-9049
stevegettel@juno.com

The Orchid Bench
32531 Rhoda Lane
Ft. Bragg, CA 95437-8736
U.S.A.
Tel: 707-964-0183
paphlady@aol.com
www.orchids.org/donors/donors/
    53.htm

Connecticut
J & L Orchids
20 Sherwood Road
Easton, CT 06612
U.S.A.
Tel: 203-261-3772
jlorchid@snet.net
www.jlorchids.com

Hawaii
I. N. Komoda Orchids
P.O. Box 576
Makawao, HI 96768
U.S.A.
Tel: 808-572-0756
orchidhi@maui.net
www.orchidmall.com/komoda/

Tropical Orchid Farm
P.O. Box 170
Haiku, HI 96708
U.S.A.
Tel: 888-572-8569
www.tropicalorchidfarm.com

Illinois
Natt's Orchids
24645 Q 103rd Street
Naperville, IL 60564
U.S.A.
nattsorchids@nattsorchids.com
www.nattsorchids.com

Sapphire Orchids
770 S. Oakland Ave.
Villa Park, IL 60181
U.S.A.
Tel: 630-832-9775

Windsong Orchids
14N456 Factly Road
Sycamore, IL 60178
U.S.A.
Tel: 847-683-2178
grower@windsongorchids.com
www.windsongorchids.com

Indiana
Hoosier Orchid Company
8440 West 82nd Street
Indianapolis, IN 46278
U.S.A.
Tel: 317-291-6269
orchids@hoosierorchid.com
www.hoosierorchid.com

Michigan
Green Acres Orchids
1776 Glass Drive
Charlotte, MI 48813
U.S.A.
Tel: 517-543-5670
www.greenacresorchids.com

Lynn O'Shaughnessy
Howell, MI 48843
U.S.A.
Tel: 517-546-8303
Fax: 517-540-0982
freespirit@pleurothallids.com
www.pleurothallids.com

New Jersey
Chesterfield Orchid Company
P.O. Box 241
Crosswicks, NJ 08515
U.S.A.
info@orchidco.com
www.orchidco.com

Ohio
Cat Orchids
4553 Hayes Rd.
Ravenna, OH 44266
U.S.A.
beth@catorchids.com
www.catorchids.com

Oregon
Hillsview Garden Orchids
13720 S. Mulino Road
Mulino, OR 97042
U.S.A.
Tel: 503-658-5296
orchids@hillsviewgardens.com
www.hillsviewgardens.com

Vermont
Mountain Orchids
1658 Rt. 100 N.
Ludlow, VT 05149
U.S.A.
Tel: 802-228-8506
www.mountainorchids.com

MASDEVALLIA HYBRIDS BY THE FLASK
Green Vista Orchids
(David Butler)
Hornsby, New South Wales
Australia
Tel: 02 9489-5818
ejbutler@ozemail.com.au
Flasks only

Peninsula Hybrids
Gerardus B. Staal Ph.D.
635 Marion Avenue
Palo Alto, CA 94301
U.S.A.
Tel: 650-328-2404
penhybstaal@earthlink.net
www.orchidmall.com/peninsula

SUPPLIES AND SERVICES
Australia
Berleigh Park Orchids
54 Hammond Way
Thuringowa, Townsville
Queensland, Australia
Tel: 61 07 47 740 008
ian@speciesorchids.com
www.speciesorchids.com

United Kingdom
Tissue Quick Plant Laboratories
Brookside Southern Lane
New Milton, Hampshire
BH2575E
U.K.
Tel: 44 01425 616 608
tqpl@tissuequickplantlabs.com
www.tissuequickplantlabs.com

United States
G & B Orchids
2426 Cherimoya Dr.
Vista, CA 92084
U.S.A.
orchidsourceone@aol.com
www.orchidsource.com

Ja-Ro-Ca Enterprises
P.O. Box 90064
City of Industry, CA 91715
U.S.A.
Tel: 626-336-3641
cabinets@jaroca.com
www.jaroca.com

Kelsey Creek Laboratories
P.O. Box 2396
Issaquah, WA 98027
U.S.A.
Tel: 425-369-8688
kelseycreek@comcast.net
www.kelseycreeklabs.com

Phytotechnology Laboratory
P.O. Box 13461
Shawnee Mission, KS 66282
U.S.A.
Tel: 888-749-8682
info@phytotechlab.com
www.phytotechlab.com

REFERENCES

❖ ❖ ❖

Further Reading

American Orchid Society. 1974. *An Orchidist's Glossary*. Delray Beach, Florida: American Orchid Society.

Arditti, J. 1984. *Orchid Biology: Reviews and Perspectives*: III. Ithaca, New York: Comstock Publishing Associates.

Baker, G. 1989. *Masdevallia veitchiana* as a parent. *The Pleurothallid Alliance News* 1: 1, 4–5.

Barnes, H. 1991. Barnes HIDI #2: Deflasking and growing *Masdevallia* seedlings. *The Pleurothallid Alliance News* 3: 10–13.

Braern, G. 2001. Bibliographical notes on the publication of Woolward's monograph on the genus *Masdevallia* (Orchidaceae). *SIDA* 19: 633–637.

Darwin, Charles. 1862. *On the Various Contrivances by Which British and Foreign Orchids Are Fertilized by Insects, and on the Good Effects of Intercrossing*. London: John Murray.

Coats, A. 1969. *The Quest for Plants: A History of the Horticultural Explorers*. London: Studio Vista, Ltd.

Dreise, E. 1994. Seed propagation of the genus *Masdevallia*: Species and Hybrids. *The Pleurothallid Alliance News* 6: 1, 4–5.

Dunsterville, G., and E. Dunsterville. 1988. *Orchid hunting in the lost world (and elsewhere in Venezuela)*. West Palm Beach, Florida: American Orchid Society, Inc.

Escobar, R. 1991. *Native Colombian Orchids*: vol. 2. Medellín, Colombia: Compania Litografica Nacional S.A.

Ferusi, M. 1997. *Masdevallia decumana*: To infinity and beyond. *The Pleurothallid Alliance News* 4: 25, 32–33.

Fuller, G. 1993. Visual diagnosis of virus in Pleurothallidinae. *The Pleurothallid Alliance News* 5: 57–59.

Hawkes, A. 1965. *Encyclopedia of Cultivated Orchids*. Faber and Faber.

Hemsley, A. 1887. *Biologia Centrali-Americana; or, contributions to the knowledge of the fauna and flora of Mexico and Central America*: vol. IV. London: R. H. Porter and Dulau & Co.

Hirtz, A. 1990. Remarkable Ecuador. *The Pleurothallid Alliance News* 2: 1–3.

——. 1991. Remarkable Ecuador Part II. *The Pleurothallid Alliance News* 3: 16–19.

Jenny, R. 1991. History of Pleurothallids: *Masdevallia uniflora* Ruiz & Pavón. *The Pleurothallid Alliance News* 3: 27, 31–32.

——. 1997. *Masdevallia* History. *Masd. erinacea* and *Masd. platyglossa. Orchid Digest* 61: 87–90.

——. 1998. History of Pleurothallids XVII: Anne-Marie Trechslin and the *Thesaurus Masdevalliarum. The Pleurothallid Alliance News* 10: 11, 13–15.

Kelleher, J. 1984. *Intriguing masdevallias.* Wokingham: HGH Publications.

Königer, W. 1988a. *Liste Aller Gultigen Masdevallien.* Munich: W. Königer.

——. 1988b. *Liste Aller Masdevallianamen.* Munich: W. Königer.

Kränzlin, Fritz W. L. 1925. Monographie der Gattungen *Masdevallia,* Lothiana, Scaphosepalum, Cryptophoranthus and Pseudoctomeria. *Repert. Spec. Nov. Regni. Veg. Beih* 34: 1–240.

Kronenberg, H. 1993. Flowering in *Masdevallia* Ruiz and Pavón. *The Pleurothallid Alliance News* 5: 8–9.

Luer, C. A. 1986. *Icones Pleurothallidinarum II. Systematics of Masdevallia*: vol. 16. St. Louis: Missouri Botanical Garden.

——. 1989a. The differences between *Masdevallia amabilis* and *Masdevallia barleana. The Pleurothallid Alliance News* 1: 1, 6.

——. 1989b. *Masdevallia instar* versus *Masdevallia triangularis. The Pleurothallid Alliance News* 1: 4–5.

——. 1994. "The Chief" *Masdevallia princeps. The Pleurothallid Alliance News* 6: 13, 23–24.

——. 1997–. *A Treasure of Masdevallia: A Monograph of the Genus Masdevallia*: vols. 21–26. St. Louis: Missouri Botanical Garden.

——. 2000a. *Icones Pleurothallidinarum XIX. Systematics of Masdevallia: Part One.* St. Louis: Missouri Botanical Garden.

——. 2000b. *Icones Pleurothallidinarum XX. Systematics of Jostia, Andinia, Barbosella, Barbrodia and Pleurothallis subgen. Antilla, subgen. Effusia, Subgen. Restrepodia.* St. Louis: Missouri Botanical Garden.

——. 2000c. *Icones Pleurothallidinarum XXI. Systematics of Masdevallia: Part Two.* St. Louis: Missouri Botanical Garden.

——. 2001. *Icones Pleurothallidinarum XXII. Systematics of Masdevallia: Part Three.* St. Louis: Missouri Botanical Garden.

——. 2002. *Icones Pleurothallidinarum XXIII. Systematics of Masdevallia: Part Four.* St. Louis: Missouri Botanical Garden.

——. 2003. *Icones Pleurothallidinarum XXV. Systematics of Masdevallia: Part Five.* St. Louis: - Missouri Botanical Garden.

Luer, C. A., and W. Königer. 1983–1992. *Thesaurus Masdevalliarum: A Monograph of the Genus Masdevallia*: vol. 1–20a. Munich: Verlag Helga Königer.

Manning, S. 1997. Florence H. Woolward 1854–1936 Artist? Botanist? *The Pleurothallid Alliance News* 9: 25–31.

Martinez, M. L., B. C. Meza, and C. H. Karajcar. 2000. Waqanku. Variation in the color and form of *Masdevallia amabilis. Orchids* 69: 116–125.

Northen, R. T. 1980. *Miniature Orchids and How to Grow Them.* New York: Dover Publications, Inc.

Ortiz, V. P. 2000. *Las Orquideas del Genero Masdevallia en Colombia*. Bogotá, Colombia: Asociación Bogotana de Orquideologia.

Pfitzer, E. 1888. *Orchidaceae in Engler & Prantl, Die Naturlichen Pflanzenfamilien*.

Pridgeon, A., and M. Chase. 2001a. Diodonopsis. *Lindleyana* 16: 252.

Pridgeon, A., R. Solano, and M. Chase. 2001b. Phylogenetic relationships in Pleurothallidinae (Orchidaceaea): combined evidence from nuclear and plastic DNA sequences. *American Journal of Botany* 88: 2286–2308.

Reichenbach, H. G. 1861. Walpers Annales. *Ann. Bot. Syst.* 6: 188–195.

Reinikka, M. A. 1995. *A History of the Orchid*. Portland, Oregon: Timber Press.

Rhodehamel. 1988. *A Masdevallia Cultural Guide*. Indianapolis: William Ames Rhodehamel.

Rolando, I. 1996. Three thousand years of *Masdevallia*. *Orchid Digest* 60: 137–139.

Schudel. 1992. Notes on the habitat of *Masdevallia floribunda*. *The Pleurothallid Alliance News* 4: 17.

Schultes, R., and M. von Thenen de Jaramillo-Arango. 1998. *The Journals of Hipólito Ruiz, Spanish Botanist in Peru and Chile, 1777–1788*. Portland, Oregon: Timber Press.

Skittrell, S. 1991. Growing *Masdevallia caesia*. *The Pleurothallid Alliance News* 3: 23–24.

———. 1995. *Masdevallia* profiles. *The Pleurothallid Alliance News* 7: 27–28.

Staal, G. B. 1991. *Masdevallia* Hybrids I: The *M. veitchiana* line. *The Pleurothallid Alliance News* 3: 44–45.

———. 1993. The deflasking of pleurothallid seedlings. *The Pleurothallid Alliance News* 5: 33–34.

Taylor, P. 1974. An Account of the Life of the Celebrated Collector F. C. Lehmann. *Orchid Digest* (Sept/Oct.): 175–176.

Tomson, R. 1990. Marvelous Masdevallias: The Hybrids. *The Pleurothallid Alliance News* 2: 5–6.

Veitch, J. 1889. *A Manual of Orchidaceous Plants*: vol. 5. Chelsea, London: James Veitch and Sons.

Webb, M. 1990. Intermediate-growing Masdevallias-1. The species. *American Orchid Society Bulletin* 59: 1108–1115.

Werner, P. 1993. The Nicaraguan pleurothallids. *The Pleurothallid Alliance News* 5: 35–37.

Wing, Y. 1999. Orchid flowers and their pollinators. *Orchids* 68: 463–470.

Woolward, F. 1896. *The Genus Masdevallia*. London: R. H. Porter

INDEX
❖ ❖ ❖